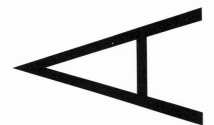

BLACK

 W. W. Norton & Company   New York | London

GENIUS

African American Solutions

to African American Problems

edited by Walter Mosley, Manthia Diawara,

Clyde Taylor, and Regina Austin

and with an introduction by Walter Mosley

Copyright © 1999 by Walter Mosley, Manthia Diawara, and Clyde Taylor

All rights reserved
Printed in the United States of America
First Edition

Grateful acknowledgment is made to Random House, Inc. for permission to reprint
"The Reach of the Oklahoma Kid" from *Always in Pursuit* by Stanley Crouch
copyright © 1998 by Stanley Crouch.

For information about permission to reproduce selections from this book, write to
Permissions, W. W. Norton & Company, Inc., 500 Fifth Avenue, NY 10110.

The text of this book is composed in Adobe Garamond
with the display set in Letter Gothic Bold
Composition by Gina Webster
Manufacturing by Quebecor Printing Book Group
Book design by Chris Welch

Library of Congress Cataloging-in-Publication Data

Black genius : African American solutions to African American problems / edited
by Walter Mosley . . . [et al.]; and with an introduction by Walter Mosley.
p.   cm.
ISBN 0-393-04701-6
1. Afro-Americans—Conduct of life. 2. Afro-Americans—Social conditions—1975– .
3. Afro-Americans—Intellectual life. I. Mosley, Walter.
E185.86.B52556   1999
305.896'073—dc21   98-39663
                    CIP

W. W. Norton & Company Inc., 500 Fifth Avenue, New York, N.Y. 10110
http://www.wwnorton.com

W. W. Norton & Company Ltd., 10 Coptic Street, London WC1A 1PU

1 2 3 4 5 6 7 8 9 0

CONTENTS

INTRODUCTION

Living within the myth of the American political system, one can easily believe that freedom is defined by the self, that is, by the limitations and potentials offered up by our individuality. *I can be whatever I want to be, according to my mental and physical abilities and the application of my will.* This, in its simplest articulation, is democracy and freedom as it is presented to Americans from all backgrounds.

All people are created equal, that's what they say. (Well, really what they say is that all men are created equal, but that phrase, no matter how much it wants to jump out of your mouth, is an anachronism.) We are brought up believing in equality, and to some degree that belief is valid. There are no legal caste systems or class barriers in America. Each man and woman has an equal vote in our political system. Wealth has no legitimate claim to privilege. Race cannot limit potential in the eyes of the law.

Therefore each and every one of us is, theoretically, competing on a level playing field. The only thing that separates us is natural ability. And even in the realm of talent every *normal* person has the chance to make a good living and a good life. All you have to do is apply yourself and everything will be all right. There are some who have exceptional bodies or minds who may do better than the average Jane or Joe, but that, we are told, is the beauty of the American way. With the brass ring of wealth and success hovering before us, everyone works to the utmost of her ability, and therefore our society, above all others, exploits the full potential of its people.

It's up to you to make a success of your own life. That is the American myth.

Why myth? Because the promise does not necessarily lead to reality. The promise is only a possibility. It is just as possible to try and to fail in America.

You could have bad luck. A poor investment, an ill-considered love affair, an untimely disease. Maybe a decision based upon knowledge passed on to you which is untrue or maybe becomes untrue over time.

Many women raised in the fifties were told by loving parents that education for them was unnecessary, because they would find a man to take care of them while they maintained his household. Forty-some years later many of these women find themselves single and virtually unemployable. They may be intelligent. They may have been strong at one time. But now the weight of the world bears down on them and they wonder about the promises their parents made.

And now their parents are old. How can age compete with the

ability of youth? How could you have saved enough money in your productive years to pay for thirty or more years of aging and infirmity in an inflationary world? What is equality in poverty? Where is dignity and nationalism when the requisite self-reliance includes how well you can manage a wheelchair or a walker?

There is a natural erosion of strength in life. And as the individual weakens, the competition that makes America strong is likely to grind a good part of its citizens into the machine they thought was their home.

Your labor builds America but America incurs no debt. You can pursue happiness, but when your legs fail there is no legal recourse except to quit the race. Many sink into poverty, and poverty, in the richest nation in the world, is a sin.

These words will mean little to young men and women who feel that the world is a feast spread upon their table. With a good education, a good job, and health, it's hard to understand what mistakes another generation (or another part of town) might have made. Experience is the great educator, but experience always comes after the fact.

It takes many years and much experience to find out what a hard place a rich country like America can be. Youth loves to rely upon its strength and individuality. The promise of success based on your truth and your beauty is almost irresistible. And when the dreams of youth are finally broken, the festering disillusionment is a breeding ground for cynicism and bigotry.

The America I'm talking about is privileged America: middle-class, white, male America. These Americans identify themselves with founding fathers and foreign policy and two hundred years of freedom. For these people America is still the promised land. And even these favored citizens may have a hard row to hoe when the machinery of capital goes into high gear.

And if the promise can be broken for even the promised ones, imagine what is in store for those who were married to, indentured to, enslaved to—the promise. If wealth creates poverty even for the preferred classes, then the poor have a destiny that can only be couched in a lie.

The idea of the Black Genius project was to address these issues in light of the black experience in America. We realized that the hope many Americans have for living the good life is not necessarily based upon fact. At the same time the cynicism that many black Americans have might also be less than well-founded.

This is a tricky issue to address because you don't have a simple equation of positive and negative at work here. Many Americans, mostly white, believe in their hopes not because of race but because of their natural ability, their citizenship, their nationality, and maybe their God. These hopefuls identify with the heart and soul of their nation. They are their nation. Their expectations of equality and fair play come from a deep notion of belonging. And though race may play some part in this notion, it is really a negligible factor.

Other Americans, mostly nonwhite, see color as the major element affecting what they can have and expect. Race becomes an equal of nationality. And race is not necessariy a gentle region. Often race is experienced as absence. Politicians, scientists, movie stars, models, and even the police are often seen for their lack of color. Prisons, welfare rolls, AIDS wards, and ghettos are thought of as regions of color. Black success is measured by the rule of white success. Wealth, employment, intelligence, and even sexuality are also measured against a white yardstick.

There is a kind of off-center balance here. On one side you have a group of people feeling, or wishing to feel, that everything is based upon the level playing field of democracy (soaked in the dangerous fuel of capitalism). On the other side you have people peering through the tinted visor of race at others who seem to have it all.

And there you have the lie.

Really it's two lies. One is held by those who believe in the smooth marriage of nationality and economics, of wealth and fairness. The other lie resides in the minds of those who believe what the tinted visor of race reveals.

The intent of Black Genius was to assemble a group of black intellectuals, artists, political activists, and economists who have broken the visor and seen beyond the fallacies of race and nationalism. Our concern was to provide a presence where absence had been, to short-circuit the illusion of race and the promise of America. We wanted to present the stories of women and men who had made it in spite of the system, those who had transcended the limitations of blind faith while at the same time refusing to accept the cynicism of race.

The thinkers you will encounter in these pages have exceeded those intentions. From Wall Street to Paris, from South Africa to Haiti, from credit card to the screen—you will experience the cold logic and passionate rage of men and women who will not fit into molds or believe what their eyes and hearts know to be lies.

The hard-earned lessons of these pages can be a blueprint for anyone seeking to circumvent the maze laid out upon the American landscape. Certainly black people, anywhere in the world, will see themselves and celebrate their victories here.

One final note about the title of this text. The decision to use the term "genius" was not to isolate our thinkers. Many of our contributors are, I believe, brilliant and unique, but the term "genius" here has an older meaning than IQ scores or accomplishment in physics. We understand genius to be that quality which crystallizes the hopes and talents and character of a people. This kind of genius is something that we all share. It is a presence where absence once reigned. It is the possibility for a people to look into their hearts and to see a life worth living.

BLACK
GENIUS

Spike Lee

A dozen years ago, the independent black film movement was locked in the uphill battle that has been its lot since the beginning, making a few courageous films—arguably the most articulate films about African American people—that very few people got a chance to see. An unvoiced question in that small community was, Who was going to be the filmmaker who would break out of the pack and extend the independent vision of black cinema beyond the college auditorium, the museum cinematheque, or the church basement and into the mainstream of popular consciousness? And how was he or she going to do it?

That question was stunningly answered for many of us one night ten years ago at the Third Cinema Conference at the Edinburgh Film Festival. (Third Cinema basically means alternative cinema.) She's Gotta Have It was brought in at the last minute, after midnight, and added to a long day's list of films to watch. Before we got out of our seats, most of us knew that black cinema would never be the same. Whatever our assumptions about the future, they had to be revised. In mid-sentence, the history of black cinema was jolted into a sudden detour.

If Spike Lee was an unlikely candidate for this role of pathbreaker, maybe it was because he was by no means the loudest, most attention-grabbing personality on the scene. But anyone who doubted his fitness for this role now has to dine on crow in the face of his follow-through, which includes eleven feature films in so many years—an incredible productivity—not to mention three dozen MTV videos, as many commercials, six books, and numerous other productions.

The films made by Spike have caused some of us to revise the notion that films speaking with integrity to the political and cultural crises of black people could be made only outside of the major industry networks. In fact, more potent film material seems to be emerging from those quarters than from those fictional films strictly defined as independent cinema.

But it is Spike Lee as cultural crystallizer who also demands recognition. It is the Spike who has produced three movies made by other young black directors and inspired a dozen more. It is the Spike who, more than any other director in history, has insisted on the introduction of dozens of talented black people into the business of making movies, on both sides of the screen. How many of the leading players in the new wave of black American cinema got either their start or a vital boost from work in a Spike Lee "joint"? We can recall pivotal roles for Wesley Snipes, Sam Jackson, Jasmine Guy, Trisha Campbell, Ernest Dickerson, Delroy Lindo, and Laurence Fishburne, among many others.

Spike Lee has opened doors, sometimes with such intelligence, wit, mellow arrogance, and fire that we little notice that no one has yet been able to follow him through some of them. He has, for instance, demonstrated a brilliant capacity to maneuver his vision to the screen by grasping resources both inside the massive communications industry and in the black community that must finally authenticate his films.

Spike, then, has been at the center of a process that beautifully illustrates black genius. By now it should be clear that by "black genius" we do not mean some egoistic solo trip. He did not do it alone. But we also have to give him credit for genius creativity, even in the sense that Hollywood uses the term. He did something unique, something large and history making. He may make it look easy, but ask yourself, Who else could have done it? He is the John Coltrane of American cinema.

CLYDE TAYLOR

DEALING TO DO
DOABLE FILMS

Life as a Very Independent *Independent Filmmaker*

I went to New York University's graduate film school. I was there between 1979 and 1982. That's where I met Ernest Dickerson. Ernest and I, I think, were two of four African American students who entered the program that year. We had a good class. Ang Lee (*The Wedding Banquet*) was in our class. Jim Jarmusch (*Night on the Town*) was two years ahead of me. Jarmusch was very instrumental to my being a filmmaker because I could pick up a newspaper and see his name in there. I worked in the equipment room, and he was someone I checked equipment out to. To see his name in the paper and to know that he had a film in theaters was a great moment for me because I knew then that being a filmmaker was doable. Here was somebody who went to the same classes I went to, who went to the same school, whom I saw every day, and he had a film in the movie theaters! I said it can really be done then.

Unlike most filmmakers, I did not decide at a young age that I wanted to make films. I made the decision very late in college, in fact. I went to Morehouse College, in Atlanta, Georgia, and I didn't know what I wanted to do. I had taken all the electives I could take and had to choose a major, so I chose mass communications. Morehouse does not have that major, but I went across the street to Clark College and was able to get into its program. "Mass comm" was TV, print journalism, radio, and film. I had my own radio show on WCLK 91.2; it was a jazz station, but they let me play disco for an hour once a week. This was back between 1975 and 1979.

Upon graduation, I still did not have the necessary tools to be a filmmaker, so I applied to the three best film schools in these United States of America: NYU, USC, and UCLA. To get into USC and UCLA, an applicant needed to get an astronomical score on the GRE (Graduate Record Examination), and I didn't get it. I still feel that a lot of those tests are culturally biased, but luckily I did not have to take the GRE for NYU. All I had to do was submit a creative portfolio. I submitted some of the writing I had done in college and some of my photography, and I got in.

Thus, I was able to come back home to New York and go to film school. It was very important that I came home because film school cost a lot of money. I would not have been able to pay rent, pay tuition, and then pay for my films too. I was also able to rely on my friends for locations, resources, and stuff like that. Now, historically at NYU, you are on trial during your first year of film school. They get rid of half the class. However, before the year-end evaluations were made, I was awarded a teaching assistantship (TAship), which I needed because I didn't have the money. My grandmother had put me through Morehouse, and she was really paying for me to go to NYU as well. I didn't want to be a burden on her anymore. Luckily I got a TAship in the equipment room a week before the faculty viewed our films. In film school, the students are not graded on their tests; they are graded on their films. The film that I got graded on was called *The Answer*. It was about a black screenwriter who is hired to write and direct a $15 million remake of *The Birth of a Nation*. In my film, we used a lot of clips from D. W. Griffith's classic. For whatever reason, the faculty hated the film. They wanted to kick me out of the school, but since they had made me a TA they couldn't do it. That's how I survived and made the cut.

The only way to become a filmmaker is by making films. It was at NYU that I really became a filmmaker. What was key for me was that I met Ernest Dickerson there. Ernest and I hooked up right away, both of us being products of predominantly black colleges. Ernest graduated from Howard University, where he was an architecture major. He worked for three years after graduation as a medical photographer at Howard's medical school. Ernest shot all of my films at NYU. He was the best cinematographer in the school, but he didn't come to the school to be a director of photography. He came to be a director, and kind of got sidetracked. He no longer shoots films. Ernest has since gone on to direct *Juice*, *Surviving the Game*, *Bulletproof*, and *Tales from the Crypt: Demon Night*.

Ernest and I really were determined that we were going to make it. We knew we had to be ten times better than our fellow white film students. This is no revelation; any successful black person knows that she or he has got to be ten times better. We knew that things weren't going to be fair, but we weren't going to let that keep us down. Years ago, I saw the films of Haile Gerima (*Bush Mama*, *Sankofa*), Charles Burnett (*Killer of Sheep*), Larry Clark (*Passing Through*), and other black filmmakers like that, and liked them very much. Yet, at the same time, I did not want to be in the position they were in. They worked four years raising money for a film, eked out one print, and then spent two years traveling around the world with this one print under their arms, going to black film festivals, screenings on university campuses, and stuff like that. I said there has got to be a different way. There has got to be a way we can make the films that we want to make, and still get distribution. Since I wanted people to see my work, that is what Ernest and I set out to do.

My thesis film was *Joe's Bed-Stuy Barbershop: We Cut Heads*. It won the Student Academy Award in the summer of 1982. I graduated that May. With that award, I was able to get an agent. He said, "Well, we're on our way." I was on *Entertainment Tonight*. There were a couple of articles about me in the *Village Voice*, and in the *New York Times*. Because of the award I had on my mantel, I thought that the studios were going to start calling. I was young, I was talented, and I was a good filmmaker. My agent said, "Just leave it up to me and we'll go places." So I waited by the phone and waited by the phone. My agent would say, "I've been in this industry, son, many a year and you have to be patient." I saw that a number of my classmates who I felt had less talent than I had were getting jobs doing music videos and ABC Afterschool Specials, but I couldn't get anything. So I waited by the phone and waited by the phone. Then Ma Bell turned the phone off, and Con Ed and Brooklyn Union Gas quickly followed with their cutoffs.

I realized that if I was going to do what I wanted to do, I could not really rely on any agent or anybody else. Since I did not want to write a script, go out to Hollywood, and try to hawk it there, I decided to write a script and raise the money independently. The first project I tried was a film called *Messenger*. I got involved with a bogus film producer who never delivered the money he was supposed to raise. That was the summer of 1984. I was in preproduction for this film for six weeks. The film was fully cast. The crew included many of my classmates from NYU who had put aside their entire summer to work on a film that never materialized. It was a fiasco; it was terrible. People were mad at me, and rightfully so, because they lost a lot of money and weren't going to get paid for the time they wasted either.

This was really a critical moment. I remember going back to my little studio apartment, running the water in the bathtub, sitting in it, and crying until the water drained out and I was as wrinkled as a prune. I said to myself let me try one more time. I wasn't going to try to analyze where I went wrong. I had committed the mistakes that all overzealous, young filmmakers make. You try to do too much; you try to do stuff that's beyond your means. It is analogous to a guy who can only hit singles going up to the plate and trying to hit one out of the park. If that's not in your game, you shouldn't do that. As for all that stuff I tried to do that I didn't have either the money or the necessary skills to do, I said that I was not going to go down that road again. This time I would write a script for two or three people in a room, and that would be it. Black-and-white, cheap, quick, "let's shoot it!" That film was *She's Gotta Have It*.

We shot *She's Gotta Have It* in the summer of 1985 in twelve days. The total budget was $175,000. We never had that amount of money in one lump sum. When we began, we had only $10,000. I had gotten a grant from the Jerome Foundation. In fact, the American Film Institute had given me $25,000 to help me make *Messenger*. When *Messenger* went down the tubes, I thought I could move that money to *She's Gotta Have It*, but the institute said hell, no; we gave you the money for *Messenger*. So they took the money back.

By hook or by crook though, we got the film made. Monty Ross, who was my partner at the time, and I wrote everybody we knew and asked them for contributions. Later on, we formed a limited partnership. While we were shooting for those twelve days, we kept every empty soda can and bottle and with the nickels we accumulated we were able to buy another roll of film.

I always try to tell this story about our humble origins, of how we got started, because a lot of the time when successful people talk, they never really tell you about the nights they had to go without food in their stomachs, and what else they had to do without. You just hear about their success, and therefore you think that these people got to where they are overnight, which is not the case. I did not just roll out of bed and start doing Nike commercials with Michael Jordan, or directing a film like *Malcolm X* that cost $35 million. We started by saving our empty soda cans and bottles, and the nickels added up to the cost of another roll of film.

I think that what we did is really representative of what African Americans as a people have been able to do in this country. We have always had to make do with what we've got. It would have been nice to have had a lot more money, but that wasn't the case. When audiences come to see a film or a play or listen to a recording, they do not want to know that you didn't have any money, or that you were going through a divorce while you were engaged in this artistic endeavor, or that your mother died, or that your children drowned in the ocean. They don't want to hear that. All that matters is what's on the screen, on the stage, or on that CD or cassette. So we didn't want to use our budget as an excuse.

When we finally made *She's Gotta Have It*, we were able to sell it to Island Pictures for $475,000, and with that advance we paid the lab costs and the people who worked on deferred salaries. *She's Gotta Have It* went on to make $8.5 million on an original budget of $175,000. With its success, we were really able to do what we wanted to do for the most part. Because *She's Gotta Have It* was financed independently, I was able to exert creative control. Since the day I started working, I have always had final cut on my films.

August 6, 1996 marked the tenth anniversary of *She's Gotta Have It*, and I have been very fortunate to make, on average, a film a year. In 1996 we made two films. Since then we have made our first full-length documentary, *Four Little Girls*, for HBO. It tells the story of the four little girls that were murdered in the bombing of the Sixteenth Street Baptist Church in Birmingham, Alabama, back on September 15, 1963. Our latest feature film, *He Got Game*, a basketball movie starring Denzel Washington, was released in May of 1998.

I am very happy about our productivity because I think the only true way to intelligently evaluate an artist is by looking at an entire body of work. So often today, somebody does one movie,

one album, one play, or one book, and she or he is then pro-
claimed a genius. It doesn't work like that. You have to be consistent; you have to put together a body of work. That's how you
evaluate artists. I mean, if somebody comes into the NBA and
has a good year, they say this guy is the next Michael Jordan.
That is bullshit. If he can do what Michael Jordan has done for
ten years—be at the top of his game every year—then he can be
compared to Jordan. If, on the other hand, he's been in the league
only one year, how could we make that comparison? You just
can't do it.

We've tried to vary the way we get money for our films. You
have to be able to adapt. In a lot of ways we came full circle with
Get on the Bus. We financed this film a lot like the way we
financed *She's Gotta Have It* ten years before. *Get on the Bus* is
about a diverse group of African American men who leave South
Central Los Angeles and travel across these United States of
America to Washington, D.C., for the Million Man March. The
film was the idea of two producers, Bill Borden and Barry Rosen-
bush. They were sitting home one night and saw this segment on
the local LA news about a group of men who had returned from
the march. They had gone to DC as strangers, but came back
lifelong friends. Bill and Barry had the foresight to see a movie in
that story. Now, I was unable to attend the march because the
patella tendon had been removed from my left knee three days
before. I had to watch it on CNN, and I must admit that I did
not know there was a film there. I felt that the march was a good
subject for a documentary, but I didn't see a feature movie. About
a month and a half later, Bill and Barry called me up along with
Reuben Cannon. Barry and Bill are white, and they knew it

would have been problematic for them to make that film themselves without having some brothers up in there. So they called Reuben, and Reuben called me. They said they wanted to fly to New York to see if I would be interested in the project. I agreed to do the film.

Bill Borden, who has a relationship at Columbia Pictures, said that Columbia had already said it would finance the film. The budget, however, was only $2.4 million. I was not ecstatic that Columbia Pictures would finance a film at that low level. Columbia wasn't doing me or us a favor. It was getting me (and usually I get $5 million a picture) *and* an entire movie on top of that for $2.4 million. This was John's Bargain Store here.

I told Reuben that we shouldn't take the money from Columbia. If we really wanted to stay true to the spirit of the march, which I feel was about self-determination and self-reliance, we should try to raise the money ourselves. Then once we'd made the film, we could go back to Columbia and let it distribute the film in a negative pickup deal. Reuben agreed. We knew plenty of Negroes running around with plenty of money. So we made up our list and just started calling people. Since the budget was $2.4 million, we decided that anyone who wanted to buy into this film could invest either $100,000 or $200,000. We ultimately got fifteen people to invest. Some of the people who came together to finance the film were Will Smith, Danny Glover, Wesley Snipes, Johnnie Cochran, Bob Johnson, Aulden Lee, Robert Guillaume, Gerald Busby, Calvin Grisby, Larkin Arnold, Charles Smith, Reggie Blyth, Reuben Cannon, and myself.

African Americans spend roughly $416 billion in this country. That's not million; that's $416 *billion*. Negroes are the biggest consumers on this earth. We buy more alcohol, more cigarettes, more beer, more hair care products. We spend more money on leisure entertainment than anybody in the world, but we own very little and very little of the $416 billion that we spend ever comes back into our community. It think it was just great that that was one of the main messages of the Million Man March. That is why we chose to finance *Get on the Bus* in the way that we did.

Now, $2.4 million is not a lot of money when you consider that the average cost of a Hollywood film is, I think, somewhere between $35 million and $38 million, not including what is spent on marketing, prints, and advertisement. You know, $2.4 million is really pennies; that's nothing; that's like "poop-butt" money. Yet, we still had a hard time raising that much. The deal was this: we told potential investors that if they invested in this film, we would give them back their money with interest before the movie even opened. Indeed, before the movie opened, we had a lunch at which every investor got a check for his investment plus interest. We were able to do this because, while the film cost $2.4 million to make, we sold it to Columbia for $3.6 million. That's right!

That's how we did it, but there were still black men who, when asked to back the film, said no. I think a lot of their reluctance can be attributed to a slave mentality, a basic straight-up "house nigger" mentality. We all know about Willie Lynch, the Jamaican slave master who reportedly told Virginia slave owners in 1712 of a foolproof method of controlling slaves: divide and conquer. Lynch is quoted as having said, "Distrust is stronger than trust, and envy is stronger than adulation, respect, or admiration."[1] We've been tricked into thinking that we cannot trust our fellow African American brothers and sisters. We're brothers, all right, but don't let niggers mess up your money, excuse my language. A lot of these guys had white managers, agents, and financial advisers who told them not to invest in the film. They tried to block African American men, strong brothers who are giants in the fields of business, sports, and entertainment, from coming together. If Steven Spielberg, David Geffen, and Jerry Katzenberg can put aside their differences to create a company that is bigger than the sum of them, then why can't we do that? We just have too many different camps out there, with somebody over here, over here, over there, over there. There are far too many black people, with a whole lot of money and a whole lot of clout, who are not in the fold.

We hope that the way we financed *Get on the Bus* will serve as a model not just for financing films but for financing anything. I'm glad to see how the entire Black Genius project was financed by using the advance for this book. This is the way we have to do it. As we go toward the twenty-first century, it is all going to be about ownership. The people who do not own stuff are going to be the ones up the creek. That is why we have always, right from the beginning, tried to have a self-reliant attitude.

We had some of the same problems with *Malcolm X*. We never really had the money that we needed to make that film, and Warner Brothers knew it. Once we ran out of money, Warner Brothers let the bond company take over and fire all the editors while we were in postproduction. Warner Brothers, which thought the film was too long, wanted it to be two hours, while we felt that there was no way we could do justice to the life of Malcolm X at that length. Warner Brothers could have helped us, but chose to let the bond company come in and take over. We wanted to continue to work on the film, but we didn't have the money and didn't want to knuckle under.

Among the things Malcolm talked about were self-determination and self-reliance. That's what it took to finish *Malcolm X.* I made up a list of people whom I could call on to bail us out. Those were the hardest calls I ever had to make. The people on the list could not be investors in the film, and according to the tax laws could not treat their contributions as write-offs. It just really had to be an act, a gift, of love. The first person I called was Mr. Bill Cosby. I tracked him down. I asked him how the family was, told him that he and Camille looked good in that *Jet* "Photo of the Week." He then said, Spike how much do you need? Since Bill was the first on a long list, I decided to give him the low number. I told him the amount. He said, Come to my accountant's office tomorrow morning. I took the subway in from Brooklyn and arrived there before the office opened. A check was waiting for me, and I ran back home and deposited it. Then I went to the next person on the list, Ms. Oprah Winfrey in Chicago. I called her up and told her that I was very happy about the success of her show and the high Nielsen ratings, that she and Stedman looked very good in that *Jet* "Photo of the Week," and that she had been looking very slim and trim recently, too. Then I told her the predicament we were in, and she said, How much do you need? I gave her the high number. She asked for the address so she could send the check out via FedEx, and, just like FedEx says, it was there, guaranteed. Then I went to Prince and Janet Jackson. I called Magic Johnson and Tracy Chapman. Then came the big call to Michael Jordan. There's one thing about Michael Jordan; he's very competitive. He is one of those dudes who doesn't like to lose on the basketball court, or at golf, poker, tiddledywinks, or Ping-pong. So I made a note to tell Michael how much Magic gave. "Money" wrote a check for the money. Because of the individuals who gave the money, we were able to keep working on *Malcolm X*. Warner Brothers had no idea where the funds were coming from. We decided to make an announcement on Malcolm's birthday at the New York Public Library's Schomburg Center in Harlem and to talk about the prominent African Americans who came together to help finance the film so that we could get it into the theaters the way we wanted it to be. Not by coincidence, on the next day we got a check from Warner Brothers, and we were back on the payroll.

Those are some of the struggles we have had to overcome. We did a film for $175,000 that was shot in twelve days, and ten years later we did a film for $2.4 million that was shot in eighteen days. You just have to adapt. You've just gotta try to make it work. There really is no better time than now to be a young film-maker. There are so many opportunities, not just for African American filmmakers, but for filmmakers in general. The field is wide open. If you can write a good script, it is guaranteed that the film is going to get made. It might not be right away, but it will get made. We're happy that in our first ten years or so we've been able to start to create a body of work, and we're looking forward to the next decade.

Notes

1. William Lynch's statement was included in a tract entitled "Let's Make a Slave Kit," which circulated at the Million Man March in Washington, D.C. Louis Farrakhan referred to Lynch in his Million Man March speech, and Lynch's notoriety has since grown. It seems more likely that Lynch is a folklore figure, the subject of an urban legend, rather than an authentic historical actor.

Walter Mosley

Black genius comes in many guises and manifests itself in myriad ways. This is evident in the writing of Walter Mosley.

Walter is the author of five critically acclaimed mystery novels featuring the character Easy Rawlins: Devil in a Blue Dress *(1990),* A Red Death *(1991),* White Butterfly *(1992),* Black Betty *(1994), and* A Little Yellow Dog *(1996).* Devil in a Blue Dress *was made into a motion picture directed by Carl Franklin and starring Denzel Washington and Don Cheadle.*

In Easy Rawlins, Walter Mosley has created someone seldom seen—the black male working-class fictional hero. We identify with Easy because of his typicality: a World War II veteran, part of the wave of migrants from Texas to California who came seeking opportunity and a black American dream of stable employment and found both less and more. No stranger to violence, though he does not go looking for it, Easy operates in a phantasmagoria of Los Angeles, an

LA noire, *made memorable by tough lawbreakers, jazz clubs, and marginal mortals trying to stay alive on a diet of the blues and the glories of days past. If we seem to have always known Easy, it is because he is our fathers, our uncles, typical Americans, human beings* tout court, *black men who seem not to exist anymore because so few of us are willing to assume responsibility for what happens in our communities and so many of us have chosen to forget the class from which we came.*

It is no simple task to create a character like Easy. Writers who succeed in engendering such great figures (like Twain's Huck Finn, Dostoevski's Karamazov brothers, or Balzac's Goriot) are remembered by them. Walter's literary genius is also apparent in his dialogue. It is so simple and so natural, yet so colored by the local culture of black Los Angeles, that it appears artless. The reader can see and hear Walter's characters so loudly that their reality invades any illusion of fiction.

Walter made publishing history by giving the prequel to the Easy Rawlins series, Gone Fishin', *to Black Classic Press of Baltimore, Maryland, a small independent publishing house, which brought it out in 1997. Walter placed the novel with Black Classic Press as a way of showing other writers that a book could be successfully published by other than a mainstream press. The gesture proved to be a political and financial success.*

Always writing, always creating new characters, Walter has also published RL's Dream *(1995) and* Always Outnumbered, Always Outgunned: The Socrates Fortlow Stories *(1997), which was the basis for the HBO film of the same title, starring Laurence Fishburne. He is currently working on more Socrates Fortlow stories. His science fiction novel* Blue Light *was published in October 1998.*

Walter has been an extraordinary literary citizen in many ways. He founded PEN American Center's Open Book Committee. He serves on the board of directors of the National Book Awards, the Poetry Society of America, and the Manhattan Theater Club and is a past president of the Mystery Writers of America. In 1996, he was named the first artist-in-residence of the Africana Studies Program of New York University.

The Black Genius series would not have existed without Walter Mosley. His energy, boldness, and excellent sense of timing made believers out of everyone who worked on this project. He did not hesitate to exploit his many connections in the publishing industry or his rapport with many of the essayists included in this book in order to make our dream real. It is a measure of Walter's genius that he can create magical things where other people only have abstract ideas.

MANTHIA DIAWARA

GIVING BACK

1

The national deficit is nothing new to black Americans. Debt is in our blood. The debt of the sharecropper to the plantation store. Dues to the white union rep. There's the debt to America and the debt to society. Many a black soldier has marched over to Europe and Asia and Saudi Arabia to pay our debts there.

We pay in body fluids. Sweat when we're lucky, blood when we're not; sexual juices when solace is sought; tears as we give our children away to so-called schools and streets and prisons.

We've been paying for a long time. Paying for what? Paying for the greatest of all American commodities—freedom.

We were paying back when America was fat and happy; when its captains of capital reaped profits from every bank, brothel, and fruit stand in the world. If a banana was sold in Brazil, America got its share. If the Chinese needed rice or some Middle Eastern despot needed muscle—America made out.

America did, but black America did not.

We were yet another economic colony. We could produce, borrow, and buy, but we could not own. Millions of black Americans couldn't vote until the 1960s. And then, just as the doors of political and economic power began to open for us, America's international economic hegemony began to fade. Ever so slowly the walls got higher. Even white Americans began to see that the freedom America offers is not a promise of security.

Freedom doesn't guarantee a place to live or food to eat. Freedom has nothing to do with paying doctor bills or keeping a job. Freedom doesn't concern itself with love or death or life or happiness.

Freedom is somehow, almost abstractly, connected with the right to vote. This vote is another kind of currency. But, like the American dollar, it loses value every day. You spend it, but the return doesn't seem to be worth the price you pay.

This is a new lesson for white America. For decades that portion of our nation believed in the courts and the Congress—and the great corporate benefactors. If you were an American, you had to be glad. In years gone by, this segment of the American political landscape was known, in part, as the silent majority.

Now that silence has become a wail.

So these people, who at one time ignored the protests of disadvantaged blacks, are now deafened by their own cries of despair. Their jobs are on the line. Their children are the victims of encroaching poverty, ignorance, and senseless violence.

"How can we help you?" the white working class asks. "When the good life wanes even for us?"

This too is nothing new. The only help most black Americans

know comes from outsiders helping themselves to our labor and our culture. From the cotton fields to rock and roll, we've been plundered.

You work a whole lifetime, and your entire estate is a pair of diamond chip cuff links and a sorely worn Bible that never gave up its secrets. But you don't hear many people complain. Why bother?

It's a lesson that every black child learns: "You might as well stop your cryin' 'cause they ain't nobody to heed them tears."

Nobody except those who know what it's like to live the blues.

The blues are the breath of our tragedy. The blues live in shanty homes and condemned men's cells. The blues hold a grim knowledge of women and men who survive when any sane human being would just lie down and die.

The blues are the black man's culture, the black woman's race. They are our identity and why we recognize each other in all of our hues and features, religions and origins. The high yellow socialite from a well-respected Atlanta clan knows the pain and emptiness of the coal-colored cowboy riding the lonely north Texas range. She knows because their lot is the same. Their ancestors all experienced slavery and the aftermath of slavery; what America told us was freedom. They both see a world that is invisible to most of white America. To them the beating of Rodney King wasn't a crime; it was the picture of a common history that started centuries ago. They saw, consciously or not, tens of millions of Rodney Kings and hundreds of millions of white men with sticks.

This yellow woman and that coal-colored man are driven toward a common awareness by the blows rained down on us by a shared history. Black history, not white.

And on some overcast June when the yellow woman and coal-colored man pass each other on a lonely street, there is a flash of recognition, shared self-knowledge.

"I know you," they both think. "I might not like you. But you are one of mine. I wish you would act differently. I wish you would speak like a normal human being. But I understand you anyway. I hear the echoes that follow you down."

They are family in the best, and worst, sense; family because they feel each other's pain. This feeling is our common identity and our begrudging compassion. It isolates us and makes us who we are.

And who are we? Black people, African Americans, brothers and sisters, soul, blood. A family that has had to endure separation, isolation, and the jeers of demented hatred. Our common history and culture is mainly one of loss: loss of our African heritage and culture, loss of the ownership of our bodies, loss of our children.

The poetry of the blues tells us all of this. It often sings in a voice of despair. But it's the hope and courage of the blues that make us listen and understand.

We know that our survival is in our hands. No school system, no political boss, no union is going to deliver us. A poor black man has to divvy up his one pork chop among his buddies and go to bed unsatisfied because it's better to go hungry than to see your friends starve.

The place of our imprisonment was the South, the rural South. During the aftermath of slavery we took on many of the traits of rural people. The hard work, the hard life. We did what you do to survive when life is a struggle. If a child was in the road, hungry and orphaned, someone took him in. If an old woman could no longer work the land, she found her way to some cousin's kitchen to help with the biscuits and to share her hard-earned wisdom.

We helped one another. That's what poor people do. Not a smiling, singing kind of help; not the banking of good deeds in hope of a better life after this one. We helped each other because the blues cannot be denied. The chorus of our communal discontent cried out for help. All through the dark century after the Civil War, there were callused black hands reaching out to protect and serve our race.

2

What can I do for my people?

This question is asked by African Americans in every walk of life. Young gang members looking to watch a brother's back. An eighty-year-old domestic folding that hard-earned twenty-dollar bill into an envelope destined for faraway grandchildren, and great grandchildren, caught in a web of welfare and poverty. The successful entertainers who give away millions to ensure that black youths have opportunity. Even the daydreaming, would-be Lotto winner imagines *giving back* to those, like her, who never had a chance.

In colleges black students and professors strive to redefine the canon of literature, the pages of history, the definition of art. Why? To give back. To reopen roads to self-respect and self-knowledge closed centuries ago by slavery. These students often go out into the community to help by teaching and showing other, less fortunate young people that there is a way out of violence, poverty, and despair.

Everywhere dreams of success, or survival, include an element of helping, improving, defending the race. This desire to help, I feel, was developed in those dark years when all we had was our fair share of little to nothing. In that world everything passed between us—our clothes, our old books, our food. If there was a party, and food left over, everyone went home with a heaping paper plate for tomorrow when hunger returned.

What I'm talking about is not unusual among poor people in America, or poor people anywhere. What is unusual is that it was never white people helping us, or rarely was it so. White people cheated, robbed, and killed us—it still happens today.

Even when we were helped by whites, it was usually an act of charity, not a sharing between equals.

If you wanted help, and self-respect, you looked to black folk. You don't have to bow your head to a brother. He helps you because it's right. He helps you because he understands what you need, and he knows that he's only a slender breath away from the same need. He knows that he may have to come calling for help before long.

I heard one of our premier entertainers (a millionaire many times over) saying that he still kept his old apartment back in the 'hood because he knew there was a good chance he'd have to go back there one day. I laughed. Many black people across America got a good chuckle out of that declaration because we recognized the slender breath. This brilliantly successful black man could still smell the collard greens simmering in his mother's kitchen. He could still hear the exhaustion in his father's sigh. He's closer to poverty than many middle-class white bureaucrats because he hears the same blues we do.

But there's something different.

This man can't send out plates of food or pass down his grown children's clothes to his neighbors. He can't put up fifty thousand poor grandmothers in his kitchen. He can't do these things and he knows it. So he gives his time, his money, and his intelligence. His heart is with us. And we've taken his aid; we've expected it. Expected it because our expectations ride on our skins. A black man in a big house is me in a big house. A black man with a million dollars is my dream.

And so we enter a new phase in our history, here across the sea of time. After years of fighting for our place in this land, we find the body of our people beleaguered. The scars are deep on our communities. The burned-out buildings and boarded-up stores. Our young men have been idled by unemployment and jailed for the privilege. Our young women carry on the battle with one arm while cradling their children (our future) with the other.

Still, we've made great advances. Our entertainers and sports heroes, our CEOs and literati. We've taken back the music, conquered the world with jazz, rock, and rap. While the Congress and the police wage war on our black communities, we have sent our pioneers out into the world of capital and culture. These women and men are the hopes and dreams of the main body of our race.

This same philanthropist, the one who keeps his apartment in the 'hood and gives away millions, was the topic of a discussion I had a few years ago. A man told me that he was mad at the philanthropist (we'll call him Phil) because Phil wouldn't give his cultural organization $200,000 to help them achieve their goals.

I said that Phil had already given away $40 million that I was aware of. This seemed to me enough for a lifetime. The man I was talking to didn't agree. His group had demonstrated that they had good intentions. The fact that Phil wouldn't meet their demands proved that he was unworthy of our common background. Not only did Phil owe his success to our race; he owed it specifically to this organization. Why? Because they had done their part. They had demonstrated the need. And, because Phil had the resources, he owed them the help.

I told the man that if Phil gave money to every single worthy cause he would soon be broke. This argument made no headway. I realized that this man had the same expectations that Phil expressed on that late-night TV show. They both seemed to be saying that poverty is waiting for all of us; we're all in the same sinking boat.

A lifelong friend of Joe Louis once told the champ that he should be putting money away. Louis told him that he could still go back to his old job, unloading trucks. Neither Louis nor Phil, nor the men asking them for their money, seem to expect much. After all it's a white man's world.

Or is it?

Maybe there's a new world out there waiting to unfold. Maybe it's no longer a dream but a reality awaiting us. A part of this world belongs to us now. Our history is open to us through small black presses and a growing number of African American bookstores. We have a toehold in the television industry and a small interest in the movie-making market. An educated, hardworking, computer literate member of the work force can land a job in spite of her race, religion, or sex.

Maybe survival isn't our only goal anymore. Maybe we can aim at success.

3

But if we are to aspire to success in current-day America we must, to some degree, play by the rules of the house. I don't pretend to have an exhaustive definition of the rules. They change rapidly and often according to the whim of the head god in America's true pantheon. This god's name is Profit. Profit throws the dice every week or so at the stock exchange, at the box office, at corporate headquarters in New York, Tokyo, Saigon, and Johannesburg. He (I suspect that Profit is a male god) changes the rules with a shrug of apology. He's sorry that you've lost your job, your house, your lung. He offers you guns and drugs and TV fantasies as possible wild cards in the desperate game of American Chicken.

Profit wants us to play his game. Without our active involvement he could not survive. But he's not worried. There aren't two people out of a hundred thousand who could even imagine a world without him.

So, while we're working for a better world and a kinder deity, we must try to understand the rules according to our needs and our placement in the American, and the international, hierarchy of Profit.

One good thing about the deification of economics is that race, religion, gender, nationality, and even species have less and less to do with stakes in the game.

We care about our race, but Profit doesn't. Therefore we have to play a double game. We have to build ourselves in this amoral environment while helping to build a foundation for the deliverance of our people. We have to do both at once in order to have even a chance at success.

To begin the process of understanding this complex maneuver, I have tried to come up with five basic rules that always seem to be effective in Profit's game. They are, I believe, as follows:

1. Value is measured by the possibility of future returns.
2. Power is a question of placement and influence.
3. Sadly, yesterday is gone.
4. Working harder and working together are the challenger's best chances to make it in hostile territory.
5. Finally, love, real love, is often the most painful touch that a modern-day human being can feel.

I haven't forgotten the title of this essay. Every one of these points is about us, black people, giving back to ourselves, restoring what was lost and making up for what has been stolen. But what we give must reflect and exploit the quixotic rules of the game.

We're not simply struggling to survive in a white man's world any longer. Now we're involved in a great international economic battle where we must see ourselves as ascendant and possible heirs to the fortune.

And so the rules.

Any gift given or resource shared must contain the value of future returns. Knowledge holds the greatest value. Yet anything that allows others to build is what we should strive for. Patronizing businesses that are good for the community or that are owned by our own people is a top priority. If you've gone out into the wider world and found successes, you might try to find some way to allow the people in our community to share in that success. This might include black stars seeking talented black directors for a movie project now and then; successful black writers bringing a book to a black publisher once in a while; black investment analysts spending a few hours each month counseling community clubs or churches.

You may note that I'm not suggesting that anyone devote all of her or his work or time to giving back. The world is too large for anyone to be able to turn her or his back on it. We need to be involved with every aspect of the international economy. We also need to bring our family along with us.

If you have influence, use it to open doors. Accept positions on cultural and planning boards. Don't shrink from participating in organizations that have no other people of color involved. They should have us there. We belong in every aspect of American decision-making life. Once you're in the seat don't be quiet or too understanding. If we write the books, we can edit them. If we see the movies, we can make them. If we bleed for America, then America can bleed for us.

The saddest of the rules has to do with what has gone before. Our history, our memories, our contributions to society—all gone. Not gone from our minds and hearts. Not gone from our culture either. We have helped to build this country; nothing can change that. This world of Profit, however, does not hold still for fond memories and truth. What matters is what you've got in your pocket and how much that can affect tomorrow.

This is true not only for us. Ask any ten children of any race to name the first three presidents, the dates of World War II, or when women took the right to vote. The fact that most teenagers, and their parents, cannot answer these questions isn't the problem. The problem is that they aren't embarrassed by their ignorance. This history, they believe, is not vital. It doesn't play a role in everyday life. Everyday life is on the job or on the TV. In short the lives that most of us live are the lives we are forced to live by immediate needs, influences, and pressures.

Little importance is attributed to history. Even less value is placed on our children and their minds.

Yesterday is gone, but we must hold on to it anyway. Its meaning is the sense of our lives. We must be careful not to fictionalize and romanticize our stories. We must look at the beauty and the failures of our history with equal love and understanding.

Probably the hardest thing for black Americans to learn is how to work together. We already know that the promise of freedom is at best an illusion. We already know that white society isn't going to pull us out of the hole it dropped us into. Follow every rule you can, and you have a less than equal chance of attaining the American Dream. Especially if you're poor, extra especially if you're poor and not white.

We all know that one man or woman working for minimum wage can't pay the rent, put food on the table, and money in the bank. That's just not possible. And so there has to be an alternative. *Our* alternative, not the government's welfare, not some foundation's grant. One man can't pay the rent, but maybe eight men can. Cooking for twelve is just as easy as cooking for two.

We need to work together and we need innovation.

Dormitories, maybe, run by a church or the NAACP.

Expenses could be lowered and self-esteem could rise.

Investment funds could be begun so that these young people would have a place to put their money that is secure. Who knows? Maybe living and working together could start people talking. Maybe we'd sow the seed of partnership and trust.

If we don't do this on our own, it won't get done. If we don't build our own lives, we won't have life at all. Let's put the power in the hands of our youth. Let our young men and women feel the strength of their labor.

The last rule is only tangentially connected to Profit's domain. It is my claim that real love, the love of others and love of self, is often painful and sometimes seems harsh.

If we do love each other and we love our race, then we have to be critical of ourselves and honest. We don't need charity or self-pity or defense. We can't expect our brothers and sisters to crucify themselves for us. We can't reach out to someone who is not putting out his hand.

Love is an act of recognition, empathy, and sharing. Love is not the act of giving, but is, in itself, a gift.

We can't go to Africa with empty suitcases hoping to load up on a culture that we left behind four centuries ago. We must go with full hearts hoping to share what we've learned, which is quite a bit, with what our ancestors have become.

We can't expect our children to have pride in themselves if we can't give them a stake in building their own lives.

We can't support the men and women who say that the white man is too much for them. We have to say, "No, sister. No, brother. You're wrong about that. You've got the power in your hands." There's love in that phrase, but many people will be angry when you say it. Angry because we have lived through many generations in which white America has done its best to disable our love for ourselves. The expectations of love are too much for many of us. It's easier to share the feeling of defeat; the false blues.

To love someone is to believe in her or him. To believe in someone is to expect the highest standard of her or his humanity. If we can achieve this kind of love, we can do anything.

My goal here has not been to lecture. I don't believe I have many, if any, answers to our monumental problems. I just want to open up the discussion a little bit. I want to throw out some possibilities that we might discuss in the weeks and years ahead of us.

I wanted to say that I feel positive about myself and my people. We have the heart, and we have the ways. I believe that we can love each other without pulling ourselves down. I believe that we can love each other without feeling sorry or sad.

Haki Madhubuti

Like a half moon, the image of Haki Madhubuti is radiantly sharp and clear among those of us who share a history that goes back a few decades, but remote and obscure to the rest of the wider public. In other words, his contributions are far less widely known and recognized than they would be if the creativity of black people in the interest of black people were generally understood as a central part of the human story.

Let me insist for one minute on looking at the example of Haki Madhubuti through a lens that recognizes both sides of the picture, both the keen appreciation and the obfuscation of his career. If Haki Madhubuti is less well known than he might be, there is an ironic twist to that neglect. Turning from the blindness of our century toward the light, we see not obscurity but brilliant successes following the paths that Haki Madhubuti has chosen. He has been one of the most popular, best-selling poets and writers in the nation. Breaking onto the black literary scene in the 1960s, his first book of poems, Don't Cry, Scream, *sold over 200,000 copies by the 1970s.*

If we watch more closely the silent orbit of his career, we will notice that Haki Madhubuti keeps on growing, following one major effort with another. His success as an essayist has been phenomenal. His book Black Men: Obsolete, Single, Dangerous? *has sold 750,000 copies, a lot more copies, I suspect, than some of the black public intellectuals who are the chosen darlings of the media ever sell of their books.*

The publishing industry has cast a pall over black book publishing through the false notion that black people don't buy or read books. Behind that screen of negation, Haki Madhubuti has fashioned other triumphs. He founded Third World Press and has spearheaded a black-to-black publishing industry that continues to show very solid growth outside the notice and the bean counting of the major publishing houses. While publishing twenty-one books of his own, as well as dozens by other writers, he has also managed to build an educational institution for black youth in Chicago, the Institute for Positive Education / New Concept School.

By now you get my drift. The illumination of an extraordinary life's work sits in its light beside the inability to appreciate or even tolerate such work when it does not worship the icons of the mass media or the values of a racialized marketplace. Such a paradox highlights a dilemma of the public sphere that remains a challenge for the next century.

In the coming years, may the half-hidden orb of careers such as Haki Madhubuti's come fully into the light within a new, less blind concept of the mission of humanity.

CLYDE TAYLOR

"AS SERIOUS AS
FIRST LOVE"

Building Black Independent Institutions

I want to share with you in this essay sketches of a life, my life, which has been dedicated to the development and liberation of black people. Liberation is a 1960s term, but I believe in it. This has never been a small commitment to me. I am as serious about this as first love. For the last thirty-six years, the single most compelling question that has invigorated and energized me is this: How do I, how do we, how do all of us take ownership of our lives?

In order to maintain my poet's license, I thought that I should start off with a poem. The poem is significant because it deals with my transformation from Don L. Lee to Haki Madhubuti. The "L." stands for Luther, my former middle name. The poem is titled "What Ever Happened to Luther?"[1]

he was strange weather, this luther. he read books, mainly poetry and sometimes long books about people in foreign places. for a young man he was too serious, he never did smile, and the family still don't know if he had good teeth. he liked music too, even tried to play the trumpet until he heard the young miles davis. He then said that he'd try writing. the family didn't believe him because there ain't never been no writers in this family, and everybody knows that whatever you end up doing, it's gotta be in your blood. It's like loving women, it's in the blood, arteries and brains. this family don't even write letters, they call everybody. thats why the phone is off 6 months out of a year. Then again, his brother willie T. used to write long, long letters from prison about the books he was reading by malcolm x, frantz fanon, george jackson, richard wright and others. luther, unlike his brother, didn't smoke or drink and he'd always be doing odd jobs to get money. even his closest friends clyde and t. bone didn't fully understand him. while they be partying all weekend, luther would be traveling. he would take his little money with a bag full of food, mainly fruit, and a change of underwear and get on the greyhound bus and go. he said he be visiting cities. yet, the real funny thing about luther was his ideas. he was always talking about afrika and black people. he was into that black stuff and he was as light skin as a piece of golden corn on the cob. he'd be calling himself black and afrikan and upsetting everybody, especially white people. they be calling him crazy but not to his face. anyway the family, mainly the educated side, just left him alone. they would just be polite to him, and every child of god knows that when family members act polite, that means that they don't want to be around you. It didn't matter much because after his mother died he left the city and went into the army. the last time we heard from him was 1963. he got put out the army for rioting. he disappeared somewhere between mississippi and chicago. a third cousin, who family was also polite to, appeared one day and said that luther had grown a beard, changed his name and stopped eating meat. she said that he had been to afrika and now lived in chicago doing what he wanted to do, writing books, she also said that he smiles a lot and kinda got good teeth.

The Context of My Life

I consider myself primarily a poet; a poet in the African griot tradition; a keeper of the culture's secrets, history, and short tales; kind of a rememberer. As a black poet, I have a certain sense for language—both its beneficial and destructive powers. As a writer who is well aware of his own cultural heritage, I am extremely affected by anything that alters that heritage. In America, not only has my African heritage been altered, to put it politely, but also African American people have been mentally, and in many cases physically, disfigured.

We are not who we used to be. I am keenly aware that all people change. However, we have been transfixed, made motionless by others. We have been transformed into people who are altered, who are unrecognizable from our original African selves. We are people who, by and large, have been taught to deny reality as we hurriedly try to fit into somebody else's world view.

It seems to me that the larger question at all times in the psyche of the best poets, writers, critics, artists, scholars, and teachers is, How do we arrive at the truth? In finding the truth, how do we translate truth so that it informs and creates the possibilities for a better life for the majority of those people of this complex nation? How do we translate truth so that it makes better people and empowers them to do good work so as to impact positively on public and private policy and on the structures that influence and direct our lives?

The task of finding a common truth is a difficult one. Those thinkers blessed with the talent, skills, cultural insights and urgencies, resources, and time to engage in this important pursuit approach it in their own individual ways. Each discipline may seek the same end: truth. However, our understandings of truth in a multicultural world are often intellectually and pragmatically at odds. Due to our varying cultural orientations, educations, and commitments, good people with a common aim often arrive at the same corner, in the same city, with different expectations, concerns, and conclusions.

There is this grand tradition in this country of a free informed press. Well, you know the saying "The press is free as long as you own it." Nonetheless, this is no small right. The ability of a great many people to argue, debate, publish, and thereby capture the essence of our best minds in print, allowing the reading public the time to study the core of their thinking, represents the cornerstone of a democratic society, and I do believe in democracy. That is partially why I write and why I publish.

What I do as a publisher, as a writer, as a teacher, and as probably one of the freest black men you will ever meet, I can do only in a few places on this planet. I realize and understand that. Yet, I am deeply concerned about the corruption, cynicism, dishonesty, abuses of power, sexism, and incompetence in our own ranks. I am concerned about our leaders' looking evil in the eye and smiling with their palms up. I am concerned about our tendency to tap-dance, rather than to take moral and ethical positions because it means that we must act morally and ethically. I am concerned about African American people who control large urban school systems who have proven beyond a doubt that things can get worse. I am concerned about African American people who have serious personal assets, serious personal wealth, and do not share their resources or their knowledge with the less fortunate of our people. I am frightened by the deals and the treaties that are made in the name of "The People" with the enemies of the world, as we lie to our children about possibilities and the future.

What is missing in much of our leadership and community is a moral rebuilding consciousness. We need a home-based regeneration. This re-creation must come from home-based activity in all walks of life. It will not be an easy task, but it is one that demands the absolute best from all of us. John W. Gardner, in his important book entitled *Morale*, states, "What makes a collection of people a society is the cohesiveness that stems out of shared values, purposes, and belief systems. When the inner cohesion dissolves, nothing remains." I would contend that our inner cohesion, or what I would call "our inner spirit," has eroded with the acceptance of integration, with the acceptance of a national welfare system and a Euro-American world view of success and possibilities. I think that many of our people have lost their way, but regaining the incentive is not impossible.

We need direction and a redefined purpose to focus our lives upon shared values, common needs, individual commitment, an understanding of the future, and a willingness to accept light rather than weakening darkness. We need family. We need leadership. We need institutions, badly. Black people in the Western Hemisphere are the real miracles in this landscape. We need only to recapture our original music to survive this war. However, as we enter the twenty-first century, survival clearly is not enough.

We have survived since we have been here in the West. The crucial need today is for measured progress and development for the majority of our people, not just for the talented few. We need a new leadership that truly believes in our community and is willing to invest its time, resources, and spirit in that rebuilding. Again quoting Gardner, "There is risk for those who take the lead in rebuilding. People who act and initiate make mistakes. People seeking the path to the future often wind up in blind alleys. Those who have the confidence to act creatively to regenerate the society must also have the humility to know the danger of overestimating what they can accomplish" (p. 26).

History, accurately understood, is very important in our struggle. As former chattel people, slaves in this country, we would be absolutely foolish and stupid to turn to former slave traders, not masters but former slave traders, for answers, serious aid, or empathy in our struggle against them. That is not intelligent. Albert Coombs says that there are just two types of intelligence—intelligent intelligence and stupid intelligence. The black struggle has been like trying to hold on to a slippery bottle of clear, life-saving water. One may steal a drink or two, but in America, the real requirement for liberation is a remaking of the mold in which the bottle was cast. Such a challenge, it seems, would take a lifetime and then some to complete, but that does not mean we should all go into debt, give up, and join the killers of the world.

One of the great tragedies of modern education is that most people are not taught to think critically. The majority of the world's people, those of the West included, are taught to believe rather than to think. It is much easier to believe than to think. People seldom think seriously about that which they are taught to believe, because we are all creatures of imitation and habit. If something was good enough for our parents, we generally accept it as good enough for us, whether it is religion, history, politics, sex roles, or television sitcoms. Ignorance is visited upon the African American community daily in the form of smiling politicians, culturally insensitive merchants, greedy landlords, teachers with babysitter mentalities, and rapping young brothers working in the underground economy who have absolutely no understanding of their importance to the black community. It is not unusual for ignorant people to talk about how ignorant other people are. We are taught to memorize uninteresting and often unimportant facts and theories, rather than given insight into how to cope with and overcome the difficult personal and public obstacles confronting us. As a result of this grim situation, most people's thinking does not lead to long-term solutions. More often than not, especially for the poor, this lack of critical thinking leads to the creation of more problems. Therefore, if one does not have the "correct education" to act, attack, and eradicate problems emanating from this racist, service-orientated, information-gathering, corporate economy and technologically oppressive society, all one is left with is one's own "practical experience and home-based knowledge." And that is not enough.

Often this home-based education equips one only to survive

in one's limited community, at a subsistence level. African Americans who do not have access to the latest information or the functional knowledge needed to participate in a market economy are generally rendered powerless in their own communities and are insignificant at the city, state, national, or international levels. Such a condition of powerlessness stems from their not comprehending current racial, political, and economic realities. It is also the product of accepting incorrect or bad ideas. Most black people have been swimming between bad, marginal, and worthless misinformation since our forced migration to this land. Ideas and their creators run the world. Christianity is an idea. Islam is an idea. Buddhism and Hinduism are ideas. Politics, science, and technology are the results of ideas. Capitalism and socialism were ideas before they became reality. Mathematics and physics grew from the imaginations of creative people. One's place in the world is due partially to the ideas that a culture has forced on one and/or the ideas that a person "freely" accepts and uses.

Concepts of manhood and womanhood are genetically and biologically determined in addition to being the result of acculturation. Most cultures in the world are dominated by the male imperative. That is, most nation-states revolve around and are fueled by the ideas of men, and this speaks in part to why the world is in such a wretched state. Men and women are socialized and nurtured differently. Generally, men are taught or educated to run the world or run things in the world. Women, on the downside, are taught or trained to do the work and do the bidding of men in the world. Obviously, there are women who run things. However, they are in the acute minority, and the things that they are in charge of are not defined as critical or important to the state's existence in most cases. Most people, men and women, as the result of the universal patriarchal culture believe without question that this is normal and therefore right. Why? Because we have always done it that way.

Racism has been described as the American metaphor. In fact, racism in America is not only alive and well; it is a growth industry. As we make our way into the new millennium, we are no closer to solving this international problem than we were when W. E. B. Du Bois gave us his insights on it in the early part of the century. My generation grew up in the fire of clear definitions. Racism—that is, white world supremacy as now understood by many people of color worldwide as a European aberration—has wreaked havoc on many cultures. A misinterpretation of the enemy's motives and actions can lead to intellectual fuzziness and historical whiteout. Historical memory is necessary for any people. However, to a people who are trapped in the historical paradigms of its conqueror, such memory is absolutely essential. We live in difficult and dangerous times, and, if nothing else, accurate history is a major element in psychological protection. History can also provide insightful direction because the past often reveals secrets of the future. For example, if all black children were introduced to the history of the culture of our people, beyond an enslaved context, maybe their view of themselves would rise above the limited expectations of others and themselves. By no means is this an idle assumption. Historical memory that stresses creativity and building values, economic productivity, ownership, and winning rather than dependency and childish consumption has bred a good number of American whites to come out winners even when the win is questionable and of little historical significance, such as Operation Desert Storm or the Gulf War. This kind of nurturing can mean the big difference in the psychological feelings and development of a people. That the homecoming parade that followed Desert Storm was longer than the war itself is a serious comment on the historical context and nature of American political and military realities.

I am trying to put my life and our lives into context. Why else would I do what I do? Why spend thirty years building a publishing company? Why spend twenty-six years building a school for children? When you look at communities that are self-empowered, you find men and women who have devoted their lives to building institutions that further develop their concept of themselves. These self-empowered people do not have to go out into never-never land and try to find something that they can identify with, that is given to them by people who do not even like them. I am not even getting into racism. I am saying they just do not like you. One of the tragedies of black life in America, and even in the diaspora, is that too many people of African ancestry never acquire insight into their own existence. They just do not know who they are, and this confusion about identity and source is at the core of our ignorance.

Thus, the question of education has always been very important to me because the education I received in the black community was entirely different in content and context from that of whites. Not only was my training not a challenge; it was discouraging. The major pieces of information I absorbed after twelve years of education were that I was a problem, that I was inferior, that I was ineducable, and—guess what?—that I was a victim. I began to see the world through the eyes of a victim. If you are a victim, you can never be a winner because you wallow in victimology.

Flying Lessons

I will never forget how hard my mother worked to make ends meet for my sister and me. Our material lives were impoverished. I grew up around pimps and whores slammin' Cadillac doors. We did not have a television or a record player, a car or a telephone; nor did we have too much food. We were lucky when the lights and the gas were on at the same time. We acquired much of our clothing from secondhand stores, and I learned to work the streets very early.

But my life began to change when I was introduced to other worlds. One year, on my birthday, my mother took me to a five-and-dime store to buy me a gift. She bought me a blue plastic airplane with blue wheels, a blue propeller, and a blue string on the front of the plane so that I could take it home and roll it on the linoleum floor. I was happy to get that airplane, boy. Then the following week she took me and my sister to Dearborn, Michigan, where she occasionally did domestic day work. This was back when our mothers cleaned up white folks' homes. Dearborn was where the men who ran the automobile industry lived. I quickly noticed that they lived differently. There were no five-and-dime stores in Dearborn at that time. There were *craft shops*. There were *hobby shops* where white mothers and fathers brought their children airplanes in boxes. In the boxes were wooden parts and directions for assembling and gluing small airplanes. It might take a day or two or a week or so for the son generally, but sometimes the daughter, to assemble a plane. If he could not do it by himself, he would ask his mother or father to sit down and help him put it together. And guess what? After the plane was put together, the little boy did not roll it on the floor. He took it outside and it flew.

Do you see my point? What is happening here? In this small slice of life, you see two different types of consciousness being developed. In my case and that of other poor youth, we would buy the plane already assembled, take it home, and hope that it rolled on the floor like a car or a truck. But it was an airplane! In Dearborn, the family would invest in a learning toy that the child would put it together, and through this process learn work ethics, science, and math principles. As a result of all that, the plane would fly. I was learning to be a consumer who depended upon others to build the plane for me. The child in Dearborn worked on his plane, made an investment, and through this labor and brain power produced a plane that flew. Translating that into the larger world, I was being taught to buy things and to use my body from the neck down, while the white upper-class boy was being taught very early to prepare himself to build things, to run things, and to use his body from the neck up. Two different worlds. My world depended upon others and on working for others. His world consisted of controlling, running, making things, and having other people work for him.

It is so un-American. People of African ancestry are caught between a hurricane and a volcano when it comes to the acquisition of life-giving and life-sustaining knowledge. Too many of our children are trapped in urban school systems which have been programmed for failure. And all too often the answers to what must be done to correct this injustice are left in the hands of those most responsible for creating the problem. If your child, your sister, or your brother is sleeping and a rat starts to bite at her or his head, you do not ask the rat to please stop biting at the child's brain. If you are sane, if you are normal, if you are a loving parent or sibling, you go on the attack. You try your damnedest to kill the rat. Now, can I get an amen on that? So our kids are coming up among rats, and I see that we are not moving.

Discovering Black Boy

When Clyde Taylor first called me about participating in this series, I told him that I was afraid of the term "black genius" because I was like everybody else. "There's nothing special about me. I am very serious about that."

When I was thirteen, and I will never forget this, my mother asked me to go to the Detroit Public Library to check out *Black Boy*, by Richard Wright, and I refused to go. I had bought into the concept that black is bad. I didn't want to deal with nothing that was black. The self-hatred that occupied my mind, my body, and my soul simply prohibited me from going to a white library in 1955 to request from a white librarian a book by a black author, especially one with "black" in the title. That is rough, but I and millions of other young blacks at the time were products of a white educational system that, at best, taught us to read and respect the literary, creative, scientific, technological, and commercial achievements of others. No one actually told me, "You should hate yourself." However, the images, symbols, products, creations, promotions, and authorities of white America all very subtly and often quite openly taught me white supremacy, that is, taught me to hate myself. The white supremacist philosophy of life was unconsciously reinforced in black homes, in black churches, clubs, schools, and communities throughout the nation. Therefore, my refusal to check out *Black Boy* was in keeping with the culture that twenty-four hours a day not only denied me and my people the fundamental rights and privileges of citizens but also refused to admit that we were even human beings. Few articulated it in popular culture at the time. We lived in apartheid USA. But *Black Boy* somehow attached itself to my mother's mind and would not let go. Finally, I went to the library, found the book on the shelf, clutched it to my chest, walked to an unpopulated spot in the library, sat down, and began to read the book that would profoundly change my life.

For the first time in my life, I was reading words developed into ideas that were not insulting to my own personhood. Richard Wright's experiences were mine, even though we were separated by geography. I read close to half the book before the library closed. I checked *Black Boy* out, hurried home, went into the room that I shared with my sister, and read for the rest of the night. Upon completing *Black Boy* the next morning, I was somehow a different type of questioner in school and at home. I had not changed totally, but the foundation had been planted deeply. I became more concerned about the shape of things around me. I also read Wright's *Native Son*, *Uncle Tom's Children*, and *Twelve Million Black Voices*. Wright painted pictures with words that connected me to the real me. I could relate to Bigger Thomas because his fears doused an internal rage for the same things that I had experienced. Layers of ignorance were removed just by my mind being opened to a world that included me as a whole person. Wright entered my life at the right time.

Lessons from "Boot" Camp

After my mother's death I took the Greyhound bus to Chicago, where I stayed with an aunt for a while. Then I rented a room at the YMCA. I completed high school in Chicago and ended up in Saint Louis, Missouri, in the U.S. Army, at seventeen years old. The military was a poor boy's answer to unemployment. The army changed my life, and this change brought me where I am today.

On the way to Fort Linwood, Missouri, for basic training, I was reading Paul Robeson's *Here I Stand*. We arrived at boot camp, and the white, middle thirtyish drill sergeant ordered us off the bus. We were about 200 men, 3 blacks including myself and 197 whites. The black men had all joined voluntarily, but most of the white men had been drafted. This was 1960 and the army was practicing integration. As I stepped off the bus, the white drill sergeant spotted Paul Robeson's face on my book. He snatched the book from my hands and barked into my face, "What's your Negro mind doing reading that black Communist?" Of course, mean thoughts ran through my mind; it was the first time I had heard a double negative used so creatively. The drill sergeant ordered, "All of you women up against the bus."

There weren't any women there. The whole deprogramming had started. We jumped up against the bus. He held my book, Paul Robeson's book, over his head and commenced to tear the pages out and give one to each of the recruits to be used, according to his orders, for toilet paper.

By this time, I was questioning my own sanity for having joined the military and examining my options. Luckily, I was reading John Oliver Killens's *And Then We Heard the Thunder*, a powerful and telling book about black men and the Europeans' second war on the world, commonly referred to as World War II. I learned from Killens the importance of using one's time wisely and of never speaking from the top of one's head in anger when one is outnumbered. As I stood, lips closed, cold and shaking with fear, anger, and loneliness while the drill sergeant destroyed my copy of Robeson's work, I decided upon four propositions that will stay with me for the rest of my life. And that is why I am here tonight.

One: I would never, never again apologize for being black. I am who I am, and I realized then that if black literature had taught me anything, it clarified for me that I was a man of African ancestry in America serving time in the U.S. Army, rather than the U.S. prison system. Two: I would never again put myself in a cultural or intellectual setting where people outside of my culture were raised to know more about me than I knew about myself. This meant that I had to go on the offensive and put myself on a reeducation program to prepare myself internally and intellectually as an African in America, as a black man. That is how I got into publishing. There weren't any books, and those that existed were going out of print. I will come back to that.

Three: I was in the U.S. Army because I was black, poor, and ignorant of the forces that controlled my life and the lives of other men, black and white, with whom I was to train. These forces were social, economic, and political, and I needed accurate information on all of them. So while many of the other brothers in my platoon searched for fun, I visited libraries. They could not understand why I chose to be alone with books. The reason was that I found a new set of friends, uncritical friends, in literature. I was like a sponge. Reading became as important as water, food, and even sometimes sisters. Four: This is critical. If ideas were that powerful, able to cause such a reaction, then I decided, at seventeen, that I was going into the idea business. That's where I was going. For that drill sergeant to act so violently against a book that contained ideas he probably did not even understand was frightening. He was reacting to the image and the idea of Paul Robeson that had been created by white monied, political, and mass media power brokers. You ask the average young person out there today who Paul Robeson was, and she or he will look at you like you are crazy. One of our great, great heroes! From that day on, I have been on a mission to understand the world and to be among the progressive women or men who want to change it for the benefit of the majority who occupy it.

Coming of Age in the Black Movements of the Sixties

My two years and ten months in the military were essentially my undergraduate education. Concentrating on history, political science, black literature, and, of course, black poetry (the written and oral music of our people), I read close to a book a day. I read and reread, and studied the history and culture of black people and extended my studies to areas of political economy. One of the most influential writers to impact on my thinking was W. E. B. Du Bois. Du Bois had already articulated the problems of the twentieth century. As I studied his work, I began to see possibilities for myself for two reasons. Du Bois, who devoted his life to the uncompromising development and liberation of black people, was the same color I am. If you do not think that this is significant, you do not know anything about black folks. There is a real color problem in our communities. In addition, Du Bois's writing represents liberating medicine for our minds. All of his work, whether in sociology, politics, fiction, or poetry (he was a poet too), led to the reconstruction of the black mind.

I came out of the military in August of 1963 with the plan to go to the university in September under the GI Bill. Something happened in September that changed my life. Four little girls, four daughters, were murdered in the bombing of a church in Birmingham. For a young man like me who had been trained to be a killer, the question was "What do you do?" Do you join these crazy people who are killing our children, or do you begin to move in a direction of liberation? That is where I went, and I think that is where I am still today. And that is where I will be until I die. It is as simple as that.

Black literature informed my life as I came through the sixties. You see, brothers and sisters, the revisionist history of the 1960s is really not correct. The sixties changed America for the best. I entered adulthood in the sixties via the U.S. Army into the streets of Chicago to be absorbed by the black arts, the civil rights, and the Black Power movements. These movements not only saved my life but also gave it greater meaning and a greater cultural purpose. I had been subtly taught to hate myself, as I said earlier. In the military, I had also been taught to kill people who looked like me. The movements which encompassed all the 1960s and part of the 1970s cannot be dismissed by a draft-dodging vice president and self-righteous politicians born with the silver spoons of privilege in their oatmeal.

Scores of contemporary revisionist historians and political scientists are now trying to paint the movements of the sixties as destructive forces in American life. This may indeed be a serious concern from their point of view. However, most participants in these movements felt that the struggle to share local, state, and federal power; the opening up of public facilities to all on an equal basis; the empowerment of the disenfranchised with the vote; the recapturing and redefining of the black African image in the African world mind; the equal participation in the educational process by the underserved; the enlargement of living and working space for people of color; the redefinition of what it means to be a woman in a male-dominated society; and the open and raw disclosures of the worldwide destructive powers of racism, white world supremacy, and the maintenance of Nazi-like regimes from South Africa to South Carolina, was what the black movements of the sixties and early seventies were about. It seems to me that was rather sane.

However, the main point is that the black movements afforded young African Americans of that period a context for discovering identity and purpose. They also supplied them with serious proposals for the future. The movements prevented many young women and men from being swallowed by the ever-present lowest common denominator, street culture. The movements existed as an extended family creating a culture that would provide for those who were productive and caring. They gave young people something to care about that was not insulting to their own personhood. They defined relationships and challenged us to defend and to define our own limited resources. Finally, one of their major contributions was in the arena of ideas.

There were no black or African American studies programs. There may have been one or two African studies programs at major universities. It was very clear that if we wanted to move toward consciousness, we had to buy whatever books there were to buy, carry them in our back pockets or knapsacks, and swap, exchange, or share them with each other. That is how we got this knowledge. There was no course on African American literature or on black writers. We got it from the streets. For the first time in the lives of many of us, we were confronted with ethical, moral, spiritual, political, historical, and economic questions and dilemmas. Through our day-to-day activities, we were forced to think at another level about the United States and the world. Often our lives depended upon the quality of our thinking and our decisions. Such critical thinking at such a young age matured many of us, and we began to see that our struggles were deeply attached to international realities and liberation struggles in other parts of the world. We were reading on our own the works of Carter G. Woodson, Frantz Fanon, Amílcar Cabral, E. Franklin Frazier, Gwendolyn Brooks, Margaret Walker, Richard Wright, John Oliver Killens, Kwame Nkrumah, Julius Nyerere, and Marcus Garvey. One could go on and on. It was great. We loved and cared for each other. The black movements that existed then do not exist today. This is not to suggest that there are no movements today. The profound difference is that there is now no national black political movement of any consequence.

Filling the Void: Free World Press and the New Concept School

Even during the 1960s and 1970s, there were many streams, but there was only one river. There existed a national consensus on broadly defined goals and objectives. Whether one worked for the NAACP, CORE, SNCC, SCLC, the Urban League, the Nation of Islam, the Panther Party, Us, or the Congress of African People, one had a connection, a force, a greater purpose and definition that was beyond one's personal geography.

Today, however, what is on the horizon for most young people is street culture. Street culture is a culture of containment. Most young people do not realize that it all too often leads to a dead end. "Street culture," as I am using the term, is a counterforce to movement culture. Street culture in contemporary urban reality is synonymous with survival at all costs. This world view is mostly negative, because it demands constant adjustment to circumstances that are often far beyond young people's control or understanding, such as economics, education, housing, employment, nutrition, law, and so forth. In urban America, traveling to and from school, church, work, welfare offices, or recreation can often involve life-and-death choices for young people, especially young males. There is no national or local black cultural movement to direct or protect our youth today.

In response to this void, a group of us came together. All of us came out of the fire of the sixties, and we began to ask, "What can we do?" I decided that I was going to be a writer. I didn't care if anybody published me. I was going to write. I said that once I sold my first book or made any money, I was going to do what the man who published me did. I was going to start a publishing company.

With my first $400, I started Third World Press in a basement apartment, about the size of a table, that I shared with other animals and a mimeograph machine. It is a business. It became very clear to me at the outset that if we were going to make this business work, it had to be run in accord with business principles, but not cut-throat business principles. We had to develop a humane way of dealing with business, while at the same time getting out here and competing.

When I started Third World Press in 1967, some thirty years ago, there were only about three or four black publishing companies in the entire country. Today there are about seventy. When I started Third World Press, there were only about ten black book stores in the entire country. Today there are about 250. When viewed through a wide lens, black publishing has indeed made progress.

Then, in 1969, a group of us, including my wife, came together, and agreed to start a school. We all came out of the Chicago public school system not knowing much about ourselves and our people, so we were sure that we could do at least as well as, if not better than, some public schools. We started the New Concept School in a storefront. Then we moved to two storefronts, and after that we bought a building about ten blocks from where we had started. We stayed there for about twenty years, and about seven years ago we bought a half a block in Chicago. Why? Because we are as serious about our school and ourselves as first love.

It has not been easy. Neither the Press nor the school has ever missed a payroll, and we do not have big benefactors. We do not have large pockets. We do have people like Walter Mosley, Wesley Snipes, Ossie Davis, and Ruby Dee donating money to us. We do have a community out there helping us because our tuition is so low that it does not cover the cost of running a school. And we are not on the periphery, out in the suburbs. We are in the middle of the black community in Chicago.

My advice to young people is essentially "You have got to start now." You have got to start thinking about building black independent institutions now, and stop thinking about what Fortune 500 company you are going to work for. You may indeed have to go there to get some experience, and to learn some of the secrets, but what about our communities? What about our communities? When we examine well-defined communities, we see that they and the people who control them have institutions that reflect their ideas and their values. When we look at black communities and their major institutions, all we see is the church. Once we move beyond the churches, we find very little. There are bars, taverns, and liquor stores all over the place. There are beauty shops and barbershops, which we need. But quiet as it's kept, the major economic institution in the black community is the church. It is a billion-dollar institution, and the great majority of the churches do not even bank at black banks. So it seems to me that if we are seriously considering our liberation, we must begin to think about developing institutions that not only reflect us and serve us but also give us at some point some leadership in terms of where we are going as we move into the new millennium.

I and the people I work with began working in two areas, education and communications, because we were political people who came of age in the politically dominated era of the sixties. We just moved right in and said, "Okay! Boom! Let's try to do this with our lives." These were not people who couldn't do anything else. These were men and women who were at the top of the line. My wife received her undergraduate degree from the University of Illinois at nineteen. She had a master's degree from the University of Chicago before she was twenty years old. At twenty-one, she was chairing a department at one of the community colleges in Chicago. She left there to come teach in our school at a salary of $400 a month because she believed in it. (And I wasn't thinking about marrying her then.) The point I am just trying to make is that, at some point, we as young people have to dream. We have to think the impossible.

The school started with two or three staff members on Saturdays and evenings. Then it expanded to thirty students, five days a week, and from there to one hundred students. Now we have a half-a-block campus and close to three hundred students. The reason the New Concept School succeeded is that we do not hide that we are African. We have one of the best academic programs anyplace in this country. We will stand with anybody. Being African centered is critically important. Memory is very instructive here. African people did not swim, motorboat, or frequently fly to America. The real horrible connection between Africans and Europeans must not be forgotten, negated, or minimized. The African holocaust is seldom explored or taught in our schools. I know that people want to forget it, but this relationship between white slave trader and enslaved Africans has been the glue connecting us for over a millennium.

Brothers and sisters, there are over 100 million people of African ancestry in the Western Hemisphere, all facing similar problems. Whether we are in Canada, South America, the Caribbean, or the United States, we all have the same problems. The fight for self-definition and self-reliance is like using a shovel to dig a hole in steel-reinforced concrete. There are over 69 million people of African ancestry in Brazil who speak Portuguese. There are over 35 million people of African descent in the United States who speak English. We do not even talk to each other. I maintain that this lack of communication is a learned activity, and acutely cultural. Over 100 million people moving and working for the same goals in the same hemisphere pose a threat to anybody's rule. Our codes, our names, our street addresses, our employment, and our articulations in their languages may be different, but the basic relationship has remained the same. Black folks are still dependent upon white folks in America. To Africanize or to liberate this system from its exclusive Euro-American model is indeed a progressive and often revolutionary act.

An African-Centered Education

Another memory: I will never forget taking a trip to Tanzania in the 1970s. I went there actually for the "Six-pac," the Sixth Pan

African Congress. After the day's work, I walked alone and as the sun set and the streetlights illuminated the city of Dar es Salaam, I noticed three children about a block away huddled close together under a lamppost. As I approached these kids, I noticed that my presence was not important to them. I smiled at the reason why. The three of them, two boys and a girl, were deeply engrossed in reading and discussing a book. I walked on without disturbing them in their obvious joy. These were poor African children using the only light available. At one time, that kind of enthusiasm for learning was the reality for the great majority of our people. What happened? The history of the fight to educate Africans in America is one that is rarely told in this age of integration. In fact, if the truth were ever unshackled, it would reveal that students in black schools, along with black church members, led the fight for modern full education and political equality in the United States.

This fight was never a battle to sit next to white children in the classroom. It was and still is a struggle for an equal and level playing field in all areas of human endeavor, whether it is finance, law, politics, the military, commerce, sports, entertainment, science, technology, or education. Many believe that if we have first-rate facilities, buildings, supplies, environment, teachers, and support personnel, the quality of education will follow. This is obviously not true. We now understand that there is a profound difference between going to school and being educated. Close to half a million children frequent the Chicago public school system each day, and less than 20 percent are truly receiving a first-class education that is remotely close to that offered by the best private schools.

For the last twenty-five years, I have been involved in the independent black school movement, which grew out of the black empowerment struggle and initiatives of the 1960s and has developed African-centered schools around the country. It also has established a national professional organization, the Council of Independent Black Institutions. The great majority of persons involved in the first generation of this movement were the products of public school systems who knew firsthand the type of schools we did not want. From the beginning and continuing thereafter, we were cultural workers who had been tremendously influenced by our major thinkers: Du Bois, Woodson, Fanon, Garvey, Harold Cruz, Chancellor Williams, E. Franklin Frazier, Mary McLeod Bethune, even Paulo Freire, and others. The critical examination of schools and education always has been central in our analysis.

The development of our school in Chicago, the New Concept School, had indeed been a labor of love, and I can assure you there has been a love of that type of labor. If the love had not been there, we would not have a school. The twenty-six-year development of the New Concept School has been extremely difficult; it has taxed all of us physically, emotionally, and financially.

There is no question of our students' becoming educated fools. The fear that book learning will disconnect one from the community has a long tradition in the black community. In fact, in our communities, a distinction has always been made between schools and education. Since we had to fight so hard just to get a foot in the schoolhouse door, most Africans in America understood that a quality education would not necessarily be the result of such an endeavor. James D. Anderson in his very powerful and brilliant book *The Education of Blacks in the South, 1860–1935* makes it clear that Africans in America viewed education as a birthright, in the same light as freedom. The first two types of institutions that Africans built from the ground up with their own hands and resources were schools and churches. Therefore, our continued inquiry into the state of black education must be insightful and informed. Among the major questions that we all must ask ourselves are these: What is more important than the enlightened education of our children? Should one's children have any obligation to their own people and culture? Who is ultimately responsible for providing education: the family, the state, or others? These have become very important questions.

As we move on toward what we think is an African-centered education, we must never lose sight of the fact that black people in America must function and excel in the cultures in which they live. But if you are black and graduate from an institution like New York University with the perspective and understanding of your culture that other cultures inculcate in their children, you can go into a Fortune 500 company or any other company outside of your culture as a guerrilla warrior. Now, a guerrilla warrior may go "tied down"—you know, suit, tie, hair slicked down—but she or he knows why she or he is there. The blood, however, goes in saying, "I'm the only one. My real job is to keep all y'all out, 'cause otherwise I won't be the only one anymore." We must tackle, absorb, decipher, reject, and appreciate European American culture, in all of its racism, complexity, contributions, liberating ideas, and models. However, if one is to become and remain a culturally whole African or black person, one must be first and foremost concerned about the culture of one's own people.

I can walk into your home and tell you exactly where you are at by what is on your wall, what kind of books you read and what is in your video library; but to really tell where a family is, walk into the children's rooms. Darth Vadar, Mickey Mouse, Donald Duck. And you wonder why the children are literally climbing the walls. An African-centered, multicultural education is driven by truth, a respect for knowledge, a desire to learn, and a passion for excellence.

The logic behind this African-centered education is that, in most cases, a person's contribution to society is closely related to his or her understanding and perception of himself or herself in relation to the culture in which he or she functions and lives. Such a culture can be either one that enslaves and shortens life or one that liberates and gives life. The best protection for any people can be found in a culture that is intellectually and psychologically liberating. We should be about the development of whole persons and should begin that wholeness with an active understanding and assessment of our own involvement in our communities at the local, city, state, and national levels.

Think about the normalization of Malcolm X. It occurred psychologically and intellectually when he was a young man locked up in prison. I say that Malcolm X was "normalized," rather than "radicalized," because he was introduced to ideas that challenged and liberated his mind and put his people closer to the center of civilization. He saw in the teachings of Elijah Muhammad and others a self-protective shield, as well as the core of wisdom for the making of a new black person in America. From that point on, Malcolm X prepared himself to go on the offense, to be

proactive and combative in a self-reliant and self-protective man-
ner. Any person from any culture that is functioning sanely
would have acted the same way. That is not radical; that is normal.

How do you normalize children from birth? My children came
into a cultural home. I was with my wife in the bed when my
children came out of her womb. I cut the umbilical cord. We
held our children together. We took the umbilical cord and
buried it in our backyard, and our children grew up in a home
surrounded by themselves. There is no doubt that they know
who they are. We take that same kind of philosophy and put it
into the schools that we have been involved in for the last twenty-
six or so years. They have produced two or three generations of
students who can say, "I'm ready. I can go anywhere in the world
and don't have to apologize to anybody, because I know that the
culture I come from can stand beside any culture in the world."
That is what these independent black institutions accomplish.

Children educated in these African-centered, multicultural
schools grow up normal. When they get black, it is not radical; it
is not something unusual; that is where they are supposed to be.
All education must lead to deep understanding and mastery. Of
what? The forms of knowledge that generate self-reliance and a
deep reflection on the state of one's self and one's people in the
highly charged, competitive, and often oppressive world.

One must be anchored in one's self, one's people, one's history—in effect in one's culture—before one can truly be a whole
participant in world culture or multiculturalism. Do you understand my point? Imagine a big table. Let us call it the table of
multiculturalism. On one side, there are Asians coming to the

table of multiculturalism. They are coming strong. The Koreans, the Japanese, the Chinese, the Indians are coming. They are all coming to the table of multiculturalism with thousands of years of serious culture, ready to do battle. On another side of the table, the Europeans are coming. There are Slavs, Nordics, the French, the Irish, the English, the Germans, all coming ready to do battle at the table of multiculturalism. From down south, the Brazilians are coming. The Mexicans are coming. Folks from all over the Southern Hemisphere are coming to do serious battle. Then here, you have got the Negroes. We are coming to the table, after having been taught by everybody else, having absorbed everybody else's culture, and having been denied our own. We come to the table, and guess what we do? We argue *their* points.

Do not misunderstand me. I am not saying that everything black is right. What has happened in Rwanda, Burundi, and Zaire sickens my heart. I do not care what anybody says; you cannot blame that on white people. Talk about the legacy of colonialism all you want, but you do not kill babies. Some of us do have evil in our hearts, but the best of our culture raps at evil and pulls it out. Love of each other must be central to all of this. Regardless of the ethnic group you are from, there has got to be this love.

African-centered cultural studies must lead, encourage, and direct African American students into the technologies of the future. This is how the new statements about power, control, and wealth are being made in the world today. Black students must have a deep understanding of the political, racial, economic, scientific, and technological realities that threaten the very survival of African people locally, nationally, and internationally. They must be grounded in a world view that promotes cross-cultural communications, understanding, and sharing. Yet they must be self-protective enough to realize that the world is not fair and that one's own interests often come into conflict with the interests of others, especially when race is involved.

Therefore, if we want our children to achieve significantly, they must achieve and adhere to the following principles, which we teach at our school. One: Possess a deep understanding of the world in which you will have to function. However, the foundation of that knowledge must be anchored in positive self-concepts and taught in an environment that encourages growth. If one is secure in oneself, what others project will be less appealing, confusing, and threatening. If you are grounded in yourself, you can go to India and not become an Indian. You can deal with Europeans all over the world and not become European. Two: Realize that all education is foundational. The values we practice are introduced early in school and nonschool settings such as the family, the media, church, entertainment, sports, and so on. Three: Understand that successful development is difficult even *with* a quality education. Many people have serious academic degrees but cannot find a job, and sadly their degrees are so limited that they cannot even think about how to create a job for themselves. Furthermore, education can be fun, but it is often hard and boring work that requires a commitment far beyond picking up a basketball, or learning a new dance or handshake. It demands quiet time. And finally, four: Understand that multiculturalism, if it is to mean anything, must exist among enlightened cultures that bring their best to the table for discussion.

In Conclusion: A Prose Poem

Let me conclude here. We cannot minimize culture. We cannot minimize vision. We cannot minimize the internal struggle within all of us to make our mark, to say something that is meaningful, important, and critical. We must be skilled doers in this world, walking and working with a humility that is focused on wellness. Research shows that people who are driven by ambition, goals, and achievement only are more prone to illness than those who place more stock in harmonious relationships.

Second, we must take responsibility for the wellness of ourselves and our people. We must free ourselves from sickening doctor-patient relationships. Be careful about looking to others, to so-called experts, to make us well. We must become more adult-like and responsible in attacking that which is not right in our communities and in our lives. Stand up; speak truth to power.

Third, we must—and this may hurt—eat correctly. We must take responsibility for everything that goes into our bodies and our children's bodies, as well as make sure that our families and our extended families and friends are aware of life and life-giving alternatives. The diet that I have chosen as appropriate for myself is based upon the correct use of fruits, vegetables, whole grains, beans, sea vegetables, and clean water. I know it is a bit much for most people, but you should try to come close to it. To that I add daily study, yoga, and meditation to connect myself to a higher inner self and exercise the inner and outer body with the mind. Also advisable is a program of good physical exercise. I suggest walking, cycling, and swimming.

It is clear also that we must have an unwavering faith in our-selves, in our people, and in the possibility for a great future. We cannot take the victim approach. Our faith cannot be a blind one, but must be based upon adherence to study and creative produc-tion. It can happen by developing support networks that include, but go beyond, the extended family, networks of sisterhood and brotherhood and relationships connected with child care centers, schools, political organizations, food co-ops, businesses, and boys' and girls' clubs. These relationships must be commitments for life. We should act as if we are never really going to retire. If each rela-tionship is to function in our best interest, it will foster optimism and optimal benefits for its members.

Finally, brothers and sisters, it is beauty, security, health, love, enlightenment, and happiness we seek. We can find such music only in a functioning social family-hood whose members are aware of its source, soil, and soul, and who come as studious searchers for spiritual strength to a space that is devoid of stress, staleness, and the sameness that produces silliness without stop-time. Our laughter should be smiles promoting a healing sim-plicity, rich in silence, rich in stillness, solitude, and silver, that encourages sharing, saving, service, support, and intellectual spe-cialness. All subtly stimulating a shining sure sameness that makes sense for our struggle.

Notes

1. *Killing Memory, Seeking Ancestors* (Detroit: Lotus Press, 1987), pp. 43–44.

George Curry

George Curry is editor in chief of Emerge *magazine and a regular panelist on Black Entertainment Television's* Lead Story. *Before taking over as the editor of* Emerge, *the nation's premier African American news magazine, in 1993, George served as the New York bureau chief and as Washington correspondent for the* Chicago Tribune. *Prior to joining the* Tribune *in 1983, he worked for eleven years as a reporter in St. Louis.*

As the editor of Emerge, *Curry has not shied away from controversy. Those of you who are regular* Emerge *readers, as I am, may recall some of the cover stories, like the one that asked, "Is Jesus Black?" Or the two-part series entitled "Farrakhan, Jesse and Jews, Can They All Get Along?" I particularly remembered the story "Kemba's Nightmare," which looked at a twenty-four-year-old woman who is serving a twenty-four-year sentence for her minor role in a Virginia drug ring. In two of his boldest moves, he commis-*

sioned a 1993 cover story that depicted U.S. Supreme Court Justice Clarence Thomas with an "Aunt Jemima" kerchief on his head, and in November of 1996 he ran an illustration of Thomas as a lawn jockey.

Under Curry's leadership, Emerge *has won fifteen prestigious journalism awards. The* Detroit News *describes the magazine as the most important African American publication in the nation. I would call it one of the most important* publications *in the nation. The* Philadelphia Daily News *says that* Emerge *is a "feisty slam-em-to-the-wall publication for African Americans that's quickly gaining a reputation for taking no prisoners in its search for truth." In 1995, the Washington Association of Black Journalists named Curry its journalist of the year for reshaping* Emerge. *Finally, in 1996, Curry also won two first-place awards from the National Association of Black Journalists.*

DAVID DENT

GET ON-LINE!

The most difficult part of the assignment I have been given is the requirement that I talk to the man or woman who woke up this morning with only five dollars and no job about what he or she can do that will help him or herself and other members of the race. That is a serious challenge, and I will try to work within its constraints.

What I do here is out of character for me in the sense that I am not going to attack anybody. I will not even talk about Clarence Thomas. Instead, I will discuss something that is really, really important to us, and that is the information superhighway. As our society moves from an industrial to an information-based global economy, we have a unique opportunity and challenge at this critical time in history. So much is at stake.

For the first time, African Americans can enter an arena and not have to play four hundred years of catch-up. Dr. Martin

Luther King, and later President Lyndon Johnson, liked to use the metaphor of a track meet to describe the status of African Americans relative to that of whites in America. Dr. King said it was akin to letting one group, whites, run for four hundred years, while the other group, African Americans, remained confined at the starting block. Then, with the passage of civil rights legislation years later, African Americans were suddenly free to enter the footrace of life. No matter how fast blacks can run, they will never be able to catch up with the group that has been running for four hundred years. Therefore, he argued, we need measures that will, in some sense, attempt to equalize the race before either group crosses life's finish line. The good thing about the information revolution we are undergoing is that African Americans now have the ability to start out at the gate along with everyone else. The downside, of course, is that if we do not, there will be an even greater gap between the haves and the have-nots, the rich and the poor, and blacks and whites.

Statistics on African Americans' computer ownership and Internet usage vary, and the reality is constantly changing. A recent study by researchers at Vanderbilt University, using data collected in late 1996 and early 1997, found that 29 percent of black households owned home computers, compared with 44 percent of white households. Black households with incomes in excess of $40,000 had ownership rates higher than comparable white households (65.4 percent to 61.2 percent); the reverse was true for black households earning less than $40,000 (27.3 percent to 13.3 percent). Only 31.9 percent of black college and high school students had access to a home computer, compared with 73 percent of whites, although black students were more likely to express an intent to buy a computer in the next six months. Blacks in general are slightly less likely to have ever used the Internet than whites (22 percent to 26 percent). Internet usage in the six months prior to the survey was slightly higher among blacks with incomes over $40,000 than among comparable whites (38.8 percent to 36.7 percent); among those with incomes under $40,000, whites were more than twice as likely to have used the Internet than blacks (10.4 percent to 4.7 percent). As for students, blacks were significantly less likely to have used the Internet in the six months prior to the survey than whites (31.1 percent to 58.9 percent), although usage by black students who have home computers is nearly identical to that of similarly situated whites (63.8 percent to 66.7 percent).

There are not as many good excuses for the low rates of computer ownership and Internet usage by African Americans as one might imagine. The data I have seen indicate that the lack of computer ownership by African American households is not confined to the "underclass," whoever that is. The study just cited suggests that racial disparities in student access to home computers cannot be explained by household income; differences in ownership persist when the data is adjusted for students' reported household income. It is in the middle brackets, where people have discretion with regard to purchasing a computer or something else, that African Americans should not be lagging behind whites. As for affordability, the cost of computers has gone down tremendously. They can be had for less than $1,000. If you cannot buy one new, buy one used. There are places that specialize in used computers. Finally, most black folk have telephones. They are almost as common as toilets. Because people have telephones, we should not act like we do not have them. If you have a telephone, you can hook up your computer to the Internet with a modem.

We are not totally out of the game. However, the potential exists for the gap between blacks and whites and the rich and the poor to widen. We must focus a great deal more attention on this issue, particularly as it relates to kids, and prepare for the next round. The day is fast approaching when the world will be divided into people who have had access to computers at home and at school their entire lives and people who have not.

To demonstrate how technology has altered our lives, we need only look back at the past two decades. In just twenty years, we have moved from mainframe computers to PCs (personal computers). Twenty years ago, we did not have "Call Waiting," "*69," or "Caller ID" features on telephone lines. We did not carry around cell phones, nor did we have CDs or CD-ROMS. We would not have thought of making a direct deposit to our checking accounts, and heaven help the poor critter who suggested an automated teller machine (ATM) or, even worse, banking on-line! All of this came about within the last twenty years. Television was once dominated by the Big Three networks: CBS, ABC, and NBC. There was no CNN, BET, MTV, CNBC, Court TV, MSNBC, or Fox Network News. They all came into existence within the last twenty years.

Nonetheless, if you think that we experienced tremendous growth during the past twenty years, I would say that, compared with what we are about to undergo, that was a slow period. Experts estimate that the sum total of human information doubled between 1750 and 1900. It doubled again between 1900 and 1950, again between 1950 and 1960, and again between 1960 and 1965. By the year 2000, information is projected to double every seventy-three days. That is absolutely astounding! How are we going to tap into this tremendous explosion of information? Well, it will not be by going to the local public library or to the library on campus and checking out a book you have looked up using the Dewey decimal system. That day is over. This vast array of information will be conveyed largely through computers or, more accurately, through the interconnected computers that make up what we call the Internet.

The amount of information available to us now was unimaginable just five or ten years ago. Much of this is made possible because of the Internet, which did not come into existence, believe it or not, until 1969. At that time, the Defense Department developed a way to link computers so that researchers could share information. Now the whole world is sharing information, and anyone can use the Internet to receive or send information all over the world in a fraction of a second. According to the Internet Society, the companies providing information to the Internet increased from 100,000 in 1989, to 1 million in 1992, and close to 10 million at the end of 1995. By the turn of the century, just two years from now, that 10 million will have become 100 million. Conservative estimates are that in 1993 there were 10 million users of the Internet; in 1995, there were nearly 50 million; and by the end of this decade there will be over 1 billion users. So if we are not on the Internet, or on the Net or the Web (short for World Wide Web), as they say, then we will simply be left back in the starting block while the rest of the world passes us by.

Of course, the most popular service on the Internet and on the on-line services is E-mail. Think about my earlier reference to things that came into existence within the past twenty years and include in that category the fax machine. We went from the post office to overnight delivery companies, like Federal Express. They were too slow, so we resorted to the fax machine. What we once thought was a fast mode of communication, the fax machine, is now being overshadowed by E-mail, which we use at home or at work. Instead of spending so much time on the telephone and playing phone tag, we now simply exchange E-mail messages at a time that is convenient to us.

The beauty of the Internet is that you can do what you want to do on it. You are your own entity. So if you were interested in business and do not want to deal with race issues, you can set up your own business. You can sell around the world without leaving your home. There are people making money on the Internet simply because they are faceless. No one sees your black face. You can make money all over the world if you have a product. You will not get "redlined," because no one need know what color you are. If you are interested in issues dealing with the African American community, you can do that as well. This thing is so important. There was a headline in the *African Sun Times* that read "Bill Gates Moves on Africa." Do you think that he does not see dollar signs there? He is going to supply the wiring and everything else. He is not crazy; he is going to make money. He has gone global by making moves into China and all these big markets. We had better be aware.

This is just the beginning. In the future we can expect what are called smart houses, which will keep track of the items in your refrigerator that you run out of and remind you to pick up replacements at the store. Engineers have already designed smart cars that will map directions and replay them via global positioning satellites, so men will no longer have an excuse for not asking for directions. There will be smart roads with sensing devices that will alert drivers when they are following others too closely or swerving out of control. Smart TVs will be interactive with radios and computers that will allow you to shop from home. In his book *Being Digital,* Nicholas Negroponte says that today "the thermostat is reporting the temperature of the wall, not whether you feel hot or cold. Future rooms will know that you just sat down to eat, that you have gone to sleep, just stepped into the shower, took the dog for a walk. A phone would never ring. If you are not there, it won't ring because you are not there. If you are there and your digital butler decides to connect you, the nearest doorknob may say, 'Excuse me, Madam,' and make the connection." And that is not all. "If your early morning flight to Dallas is delayed, your alarm clock can ring a bit later and the car service [that is supposed to take you to the airport] automatically notified in accordance with the traffic predictions" (p. 212).

Not that long from now, everything is going to be voice activated. You will be able to enter your home or car without a key; they will recognize your voice. ATMs will instantly cash your checks because your voice matches a voiceprint on file. This technology will wipe out all kinds of jobs in the banking industry. I already have on-line banking; I do not have to deal with anyone as it is. We are going to lose many sectors of the job market because of this and similar advances. And, yes, we will be seeing more companies moving outside the country and more companies facing foreign competition as well.

Technology has already changed our lives. Look around you. It has invaded our offices, homes, cars, airplane seats, and hotel rooms. The impact of this new technology poses some serious challenges arising from its impact on our families and our communities. Will we still gather around the television as we once did? Or will each family member seek his or her own link to cyberspace? When I presented these ideas at NYU, someone in the audience remarked that when you go on-line you are sitting at a terminal by yourself in your own seat. The Internet can in effect bring people together, but it seems that a good deal of the communication is occurring between the user and the computer and not with other people. How, then, can the Internet create and sustain black communities when it involves isolated individuals looking at a computer screen, not even aware of the people around them? Perhaps every family will have two, three, maybe four phone lines so that everyone can be on-line at the same time. Individuals will probably do fewer things with their families because they are dealing with communities in cyberspace. But the isolating tendencies of the Net does not prevent us from using it as a vehicle for coming together for the Million Man March or any other kind of march we want to have. We have to be aware of the limitations and find ways to make this technology serve our needs.

The Internet has other potential downsides or drawbacks. How can we prevent our children from being exposed to on-line pornography? Hate groups? Child molesters? In the workplace, technology will provide us more flexibility to telecommute from home, which means that we can spend more time with our families. Or for recovering workaholics like me, it will mean a further blurring of the lines between work and play.

Blacks especially have reason to be concerned about how the First Amendment plays out in this new electronic environment. Will we see a further erosion of privacy and increased surveillance of blacks much like that experienced during the high point of the civil rights and Black Power movements? These concerns are well based. Just because you are paranoid does not mean no one is following you. They used to say if you want to hide something from a black person put it in a book. Now they are saying if you want to hide something put it on the Internet. The surveillance, the following, the invasions of privacy, that is already here. There are some devices you can sign onto that will prevent people from trailing you on the Internet. Let us not kid ourselves; the Internet is not really there to help produce a more informed society. It was originally used by the Defense Department so that scientists and researchers could share the same computers and the same information. The chief concern right now is not how best to provide information on the Internet, but how to sell advertising. Despite this, it is still such a potent tool that I think we cannot afford not to use it. Whether on the Internet or in just plain everyday life, you basically do not have much privacy. People can get on the Internet and find your E-mail address, your home address, even your Social Security and unlisted phone numbers. That is a reality; it is already happening. But anywhere you go, marketers will find you and send you junk mail. Let's be honest; some people see a conspiracy if it rains outside. We've got to get beyond our fears and realize that we cannot afford not to be in this game.

Now, what does this social transformation mean to African Americans overall? In a word, everything. Writing in the *Atlantic Monthly*, Peter Drucker noted that the economic position of African Americans improved faster than that of any other group in American society in the fifty years since the Second World War and, indeed, in the entire social history of our country. Three-fifths of America's blacks rose to middle-class incomes; before the Second World War the figure was only one out of twenty. But half of that group rose to middle-class incomes and not to middle-class jobs. Since the Second World War, more and more blacks have moved into blue-collar and middle-class wages in jobs requiring neither education nor skills. These, however, are precisely the jobs that are disappearing fastest. In other words, the decline in industrial work has hit African Americans disproportionately hard.

The ability to communicate by computer has led to the creation of what Drucker called "the knowledge workers." In this new world order, the emphasis will be on brain, not brawn. Workers will need an above-average education and a different mind-set. Knowing where to find information, rather than being able to regurgitate it, becomes increasingly relevant. We must adapt if we are going to remain valuable assets during this social transformation. There will have to be a quest for continuous learning. It follows that we will have to change the old ways of doing things. In biology classes, it will no longer be necessary to learn about a frog by dissecting one. With the technology that we have now, a student can design his or her own frog, give it frog-like behavior, and then stimulate its muscles. Through playing with this information, this frog, the materials that students absorb will have more meaning.

Now, what can we do about all of this? What can we do so that we do not find ourselves on the exit ramp of the information superhighway? The first thing you should do is to read as many books as you can on the subject. Bill Gates's book *The Road Ahead* is really good. There is Nicholas Negroponte's *Being Digital*, which I have mentioned. *The Digital Economy: Promise and Peril in the Age of Networked Intelligence*, by Don Tapscott, is yet another possibility. There are many others.

The second thing I would suggest is that adults get on-line. Don't just leave it to the kids. We need to acknowledge that children are not afraid of this technology. That is why the average age of users of the Internet is twenty-one and steadily declining. Adults, on the other hand, seem frightened by it. Under the circumstances, it is perhaps best to let the kids serve as the teachers and for us adults to play the role of the pupils. If we do not master the Internet, we will be left behind. Allan Cahill, a former fellow at Apple Computer, recalled how his daughter told him, "I don't understand why you adults make such a big deal about technology. Kids just use computers to do stuff. They don't think of it as technology. Like a fridge does stuff, it's not technology. When I go to the fridge I want food that's cold. I don't think about the technology that makes food cold." So simple but so true. Adults should think of computers not as technology but as a place, as the kid said, "to do stuff." This new place will alter the way we do stuff at work, or in business and in our personal lives.

America Online, Compuserve, and MSN are all surprisingly easy to master. In addition to gaining access to the Internet, you can read the latest news, send and receive E-mail, check out the latest sports scores, join on-line discussions, find the cheapest airline ticket and book the seat, track down long-lost friends, look at want ads from another city, and get information on what car dealers actually pay for cars and then negotiate a deal. All of this can be done on-line for about twenty dollars a month, which is less than a dollar a day.

To return to the challenge posed by Walter Mosley and company, if you have only five dollars, then go to the public library; many of them have computers. Or find someone who has a computer. It is possible that neighbors, friends, or a local high school or college teacher will let you have the experience of using a computer. The Urban League has job-training centers that give you access to computers. We are not limited. We can go as far as our imaginations take us. We mentioned a place in *Emerge* that makes mailboxes available to homeless persons. Even if you are homeless, you can get an E-mail address. I am suggesting that we have to find creative ways to use this system and that even if you do not have five dollars, there are ways in which you can benefit from it.

Now, if you have more than five dollars, but less than enough to purchase a new computer, buy a used one. There are a number of stores like Second Byte Sales and Service of Pikesville, Maryland, which specialize in selling used computers. As someone told one of our writers at *Emerge*, "Just because you can't buy a Lexus doesn't mean you can't buy a car." Of course, I prefer the Lexus, but that is another story. When you buy a computer, purchase a modem; it allows the computer to communicate with the outside world.

Once we have done our reading and purchased our own computers with modems, the next thing we do is take care of our families. Purchase computers for your brothers and sisters, nephews and nieces, starting them off as young as possible. We cannot start them too soon. As a community, I feel, we must make sure that the have-nots have access to computers in this digital information age. Studies indicate that white kids who lack a computer at home are substantially more likely than black kids to use the Internet at places other than school or work, like the homes of friends and relatives, libraries, and community centers. Every church—and I do mean *every* church—should have a computer lab for kids whose families cannot afford them. That means black sororities and fraternities should perhaps skip a step show or a party and spend some money on kids who do not have access to computers. That means that our social organizations should make sure that there are computers in the housing projects. We cannot afford not to do this. As a person who grew up in public housing, I understand what it means not to have any money. That is why I am emphasizing that we should have computers in the housing projects.

Of course, we should continue to put pressure on the government at every level to make computers available in the schools and public libraries, especially those in communities where our least-well-off citizens reside. We have to politicize the issue of computer and Internet access, mobilize around it, and insist that there be public outlets in the schools and libraries, at the same time that we make a community-based effort to ensure access in churches and community centers. This is not an either/or proposition. The bottom line, however, is that this is something we are going to have to do for ourselves. As with everything else, some of us are waiting for somebody else to give us a computer and liberate us. Yet, we as a group exercise $400 billion a year in spending power. We can accept responsibility for this.

In our workplaces, we can urge our employers to join us in this effort. Instead of just giving a computer away to anybody, see that the gift goes to our youth. Use the computer to start a Saturday school to help kids with their homework and train them in the use of computers.

Parents, I do not care what your kids say. If you can afford to buy some little "Air Jordan" gym shoes for more than $100 a pair (and I know how much they cost because I buy them for my own son), then you can almost afford to buy a computer. Just skip a couple of pairs of tennis shoes or something else your kids do not have, but think they must have. Skip some of these Nintendo or Sega games the kids are glued to and buy them a computer.

You have to reach people where they are. Say a kid is obsessed with sports. Get a laptop and show her or him how she or he can check the stats or calculate the league standings. My son loves sports. He knows everybody's stats. He and I had a big argument about Shawn Kemp versus Michael Jordan. My son is independent; he goes with Shawn Kemp. He does not follow the crowd. So if a kid is interested in a subject or topic, then teach her or him about it using a computer. The same holds true with regard to teaching people to read. Teach them using whatever area they are interested in. If it is music, go the music route and bring them along that way.

Do not expect to get any support from most African American athletes for any of these efforts, because most of them have set themselves apart from our communities. You have not seen me defend O. J. Simpson, and you never will. Nor any of the others. It almost seems as if they are required to divorce themselves from our communities if they want to make it. So I do not look to them for anything. I think it is important that we try to give our kids some perspective and tell them—and I agree with what Charles Barkley said—these people are not role models. Try to get your kids interested in computers and do some dunk shots on them. They have a better chance of getting hit by a meteorite than of becoming a professional athlete. More than a million people play football every year at the high school level. Of that million, 30,000 make it to college. Of that 30,000, some 1,600 make it into the NFL. Yet we allow our kids to suffer from an overemphasis on sports. I do not have anything against these athletes. I was a quarterback on my college's football team, but I was also an honor student. We have to redirect some of these kids so they will not grow up to be like some of these athletes, but in terms of expecting anything from them, I would not hold my breath on that.

Our kids have a right to have access to a computer. This should be very high on our civil rights agenda because without access to this technology, without mastery of the computer skills that will allow us to acquire and change jobs in an information-based society that is global and growing more global every day, we will be left behind. At one point in this country's history, farmers made up 90 percent of the population; now they are down to about 3 percent. We cannot be left behind with the 3 percent when it comes to the information superhighway, with 90 percent of the world passing us by. This is a challenge we all must face. Unfortunately, it is one we do not think a whole lot about; those of us who have computers use them without giving access issues a second thought. But the world is undergoing a techno-logical and information explosion and is changing every day. If we do not accept the challenge, we will be left back in the starting block.

Internet access should be one of the highest priorities of our civil rights organizations. The Internet could be our "talking drum." Think back to the Million Man March. We were there. If we had to rely on the mainstream media for information about the Million Man March, we probably would not have been there. (I do not like the term "mainstream," because the white-controlled media cannot be main and a stream at the same time; it would be more appropriate to call it "mainriver" or something like that.) The march was promoted strictly by the black media, particularly black radio. *Emerge* devoted an entire special issue to the march before it took place. The "mainstream press" became involved only right before the march, when it realized how many people were coming. Even then it focused, totally obsessed, on Farrakhan. (They would not call him "Farrakhan"; rather, they pronounced his name "Farrakawn.") If we really had an active community on the Net, we would not need them. That is the magic of the Internet. We can bypass the mainstream and have an alternative form of communication without all the distribution costs.

I have tried not to be overly technical; I really could not be even if I wanted to. My goal has been to stimulate thought; to give you some idea of where we as a society are going and how important an issue computer access is to our community. The discussion cannot end here. We each must study the issues further ourselves, pass the word around, and get more of our people involved. Do not worry about what we cannot do. When we start worrying about what we cannot do, we get into trouble.

I spoke at a Unity Day service at a church in Miami at the request of my former assistant football coach. The church did not have Men's Day or Women's Day; it had a Unity Day. I told my coach that I would pay for my own ticket and that they could skip the honorarium too because they could not afford it. When I gave my speech, however, I said that I wanted the congregation to do just one thing: create a computer lab for the kids who do not have computers at home. When I said that, a member of the church got up and said, "I'm a computer programmer and I'll run it." When we start looking within our own communities, we can come up with the resources. We can do it. We have the ingenuity; we have the intellect. It is just a matter of committing ourselves to doing it, because we cannot afford not to do it.

Melvin Van Peebles

Melvin Van Peebles is a man of destiny. He seemed destined to become a legendary figure in his times, and whenever opportunity knocked, he was ready with an answer. And opportunity knocked on several occasions. His ability to seize or manufacture several careers explains why he has often been likened to Brer Rabbit, the mythical trickster figure who has inspired many an African American seeker after success and fortune through his wiliness, determination, and flexibility.

Any one of Van Peebles's careers would be enough to satisfy seekers in those fields. He has had major success as a film director and play-wright, and significant achievements as a novelist, songwriter, screen-writer, and actor. We may learn something by seeing how these careers developed, narratively. Born in Chicago, Van Peebles got a degree from Ohio Wesleyan University. In the Air Force, he was trained as a bombardier-navigator, and through this experience *became interested in astronomy. But before he could follow this inter-est, he worked as a cable car operator in San Francisco. He wrote an essay about operating the cable cars and, on the basis of its success, developed the essay into a book. Then he turned this project into a film. After these adventures, he went to Holland with the intention of studying astronomy. While there, however, he learned that the short films he had made caused him to be invited to a prestigious film festival in Paris. He followed his films to Paris, with the deter-mination to make more movies. The obstacles to his filmmaking ambitions caused a slight detour; he made a precarious living as a crime reporter for a magazine called* Hara Kiri. *In order to overcome licensing restrictions against directing films in France, he wrote five novels in French in order to qualify for a chance to become a director. Finally, he was able to direct and complete his first feature film,* The Story of a Three-Day Pass.*

When this film was invited for showing at the San Francisco Film Festival, the film community there was surprised to learn that the director of the film La Permission *from France was a black Ameri-can. As a result, doors opened in Hollywood that had been firmly shut before. With* Watermelon Man, *Van Peebles became one of the first black directors to complete a film in Hollywood.*

He turned down a three-picture deal to make Sweetback's Baadasss Song. *This ground-breaking movie had a crucial develop-mental influence on the wave of black exploitation movies that imi-tated it badly, as well as on the black independent film movement that saw other, liberationist ideas in the film. Moving on, he wrote and directed the innovative musical* Ain't Supposed to Die a Nat-ural Death *and put out eight musical albums in which he pioneered a combination of rap and singing and storytelling. His careers as actor, playwright, director, cabaret artist, and screenwriter* (Panther) *have all kept very much on track.*

But somewhere along the line Van Peebles found time and talent to establish another surprising career by becoming one of the first African Americans to occupy a seat on the New York Stock Exchange as a financier. Asked to write a book about this experience—which is a long way from the cable car operator experience—he wrote and published Bold Money. *It is out of this unusual background that he was asked by the Black Genius forum to address the subject that he faces here.*

CLYDE TAYLOR

BLOOD MONEY OR
MONEY AND BLOODS

Well, today in the business world, Alan Greenspan, the Federal Reserve chairman, urged the House Banking Committee to appoint a commission to come up with a better estimate of increases in the cost of living than the consumer price index, which most economists believe overstates inflation. Moreover, Greenspan denied that he intended to talk the market down by warnings. Okay, well, let's start a little further back then. I was just kidding folks, just kidding.

Money. I'm always astounded that minorities, especially the African American minority, have this ambivalence about money. I have really, really tried to understand the genesis of our economic plight. Part of that genesis, I believe, is justice. People want to believe in justice, or people want justice. This creates an oxymoron: justice, capitalism, and colored folks.

The situation is as follows. Now, let me step deep, deep, deep down into your psyche, and into my psyche, too, at one stage in the game. You're faced with a dilemma: you want to succeed. The truth is that success is possible in America. There's success for African Americans in America, but it is not a just system. Therefore, you are haunted by the thought, If I succeed, am I overcoming discrimination, or simply dampening its effect? Look, now a minority person from another situation, not an American situation, knows that when he comes here, he's on a humble, that is, he must be deferential and submissive in order to succeed. Our problem is we're told we're not on a humble, but we know we *are* on a humble. If you succeed, someone will tell you, "See I told you, you weren't on no humble." So you have an ambivalent feeling, not about success, but about a success where you had to work five to eight zillion times harder than the white man. The anger at that success causes us, many times, and in many cases, subconsciously to cut off our noses to spite our faces. I mean people say, "Oh, Mel, you made it." Yeah, I made it. Okay, but I made it working eighty-five times harder than the cat standing next to me ever could.

Now the dilemma is this: Do I go that extra zillion yards and have to hear this shit, or do I cut off my nose to spite my face? I say that we must go that extra zillion yards, but we don't have to forget it. You can't help anybody lying on your back. In Paris, as some of the people who know me from there are aware, I used to eat out of garbage cans. But that made it possible for me to do some of the things that we're now seeing come to fruition. If *Sweetback* spawned the blaxploitation era, it spawned it for only one reason. It made money. The Golden Rule is "He who has the gold, makes the rules."

This brings us right back to Greenspan in a whole 'nother way. What Alan is saying is, well, money is not being spent fast enough by the people who are making the money, and therefore we're heating up the inflation rate, and therefore I will make a move which will take the bond yields up, etc. Don't worry about all the gobbledygook. Don't worry about the gross national product, bond yields, and this, that, and the other. All it means is that capitalism is trying to keep itself afloat.

The business of America is business. You got to be in it to win it. You got to be in it to win it! Don't let anybody say different. Now, that's the trick, because they get us from a very early age, and they tell us two messages. One message is "It's all a level playing field." Now, you know it ain't a level playing field, but if you win, they say, "See, I told you it was a level playing field." That tends to slow us down. That tends to prevent us from going at 100 percent. If you got everybody else out there pushing at 110 percent, you can't half-step at 85 percent and make it. In any situation, if you're 5 percent, just 5 percent, not in accord with what you're trying to do, you're operating at only 90 percent because you need another 5 percent to neutralize the ambivalent 5 percent so that leaves you at only 90 percent. Suppose you're 25 percent ambivalent; then you're operating at only 50 percent. You need to neutralize the ambivalent feeling, and that neutralization slows you down.

This is why we have not been able, as individuals, to take charge of our destiny to the fullest extent. We can't take charge of our destiny, because implicit in its fullest extent is an equal extent. And we know it's not an equal extent. That's a heartbreaking thing when everything you see, everything you hear is telling you, "Hey, you got it even." You don't have it even. Our greatest stumbling block is the dichotomy posed by the dilemma of success in a racist society.

I look at things from a completely different perspective. American culture is so sure that it has a headlock on the black mind-set that it is given the liberty to do what it wants. Have you ever seen what a certificate looks like when you buy this, that, and the other stock? Very weird thing about that. It doesn't say anything about your race, age, or creed. You are in complete anonymity. All the broker wants to know is how many dead presidents you've got to cough up. That's all he or she wants to know. The stock market is the one place you are free. It is not like when you go out there to catch a cab, and they go past you when you're trying to go out with your old lady. It is not like trying to buy a house. You don't have to try to do anything, because the stock market is the one place you're not asked any questions. Now, you would think that the door of pure money would be closed to us, but it's not closed, because they figure they got a lock on your mind. The man has an Achilles pocketbook, I'm telling you. He has an Achilles pocketbook, and that's where the deal is.

Now, let's talk about Thoreau, Henry David Thoreau, of Walden Pond. Thoreau says that there are two ways of being rich. You can either have a lot or not need a lot. I suggest that you learn to not need a lot, at least for openers. Once you've got a grubstake, you can make that grubstake grow. Very little, by very little, by very little. You know what a trillion dollars is? It's just a whole pile of pennies, y'all. That's all it is. It's just a pile of pennies.

Personally, I was able to do it because I didn't spend my lunch money. I just finished shooting a movie. I made a lot of money. They paid me my salary, but then they also gave me what they call a per diem (a daily allowance). Everybody else was at the bar. Shucks, I took my bottle, went on up there with it, and saved all that money. I brought all my per diem back. Do it every time. All that money's just sitting there. All those possibilities are just sitting there.

So you're not in that big per diem class. Great, there are still other ways. You don't need all those things. If I want to watch the New York Knicks play basketball, I go home at three o'clock so I can turn on my television and get it warm. I'm gonna tape it because the show is at six o'clock; that's the kinda television I got. Doesn't matter, I still get to see it, in black-and-white. It's black and white anyhow, ain't it? But you are told and you are made to believe that you have to have this and that. And you know all the man is doing is taking away the next rung of the ladder out of your pocket so that you can never get that grubstake. Once you got the grubstake, "Please, Miss Thang." Once you've got the grubstake, two snaps. Am I right? Unless you act the fool and turn it into a BMW, just keep on going. Just keep on going. That's the way you do it.

We sniff at many immigrants we see. We say, well, they work twenty-four hours a day, and the whole family gets together and pools their money. Next thing we know, they're rich. But what offends us—and what should offend us—is that it's not just. We helped build this country; not just helped, we did all the damn work. We're still being treated in the same way. Okay. That and a buck fifty will get you a subway token. Don't cry about it. Never confuse winning with an acceptance of racism. You win by not allowing your mind to be turned into "I got to have, I got to have." You *don't* have to have. As good-looking as you all are, the chicks are gonna like you anyhow, and the guys are gonna think you are fly. That is not where it's at; it's got to be inside. Remember, a courageous person is never without arms.

And that is what Brother Greenspan is talking about. Let me break down what he's saying. On Wall Street, the market is going bananas. Right now, it's a bull market and it's making a lot of money. But investors are not buying a whole lot of luxury or nonluxury items, because they know the value of a dollar, like my grandmama used to say. They're saving their money, so we have to make them loosen up on it. Those larger folks are talking in trillions and zillions, and it might confuse you. But it's the same as that ol' saying: "God bless the child that's got its own." Now if a few of us get our own little by little, what you decide to do with that is your own lookout. People say, "Well man, I don't want to let the people down". If, after you've made your capitalist money, you decide you want to give it to old folks' homes, AIDS research, or Uzi's, you've got the money to do it. That is the way. I can say it here because I had nothing, did not have a thing. Had a whole lot of luck too. All that entered into it, but you gotta *not* need. Not need. See the need for what it is. It's to keep you broke, to keep draining your power. There's a difference, a major difference, between giving somebody a fish and teaching him or her how to fish.

There are three obstacles. The first is making the money. The second is keeping the money. The third is investing the money. Making the money is a major, major problem for us just because of the amount of money we have and do *not* have in our salaries.

But even with that you can save some of it. That then moves you into the next class automatically because if you save some of it and you ain't making much, that already means you got number two's ass kicked. Because you didn't let yourself *hafta*! I gotta have. I wish there was some other way I could bring you this wonderful, brillant news. I don't know another way, and I'm leery of even suggesting this because it's not just. It ain't as hard for other people. But I'm not going to let that psych me into cutting off my nose to spite my face.

I remember when I was in Paris, I was sitting on the steps of L'Opéra and a brother came past; he said, "Man you look down." I said, "Uh?" He said, "Looks like you need something. Here's a grubstake." The guy gave me five bucks. I was able to parlay that five bucks into the rest of my career because I needed five bucks so that I could go into a restaurant with someone, but if things went funky I had my share of the bill. I just made sure it never came to that, but all you need is that little grubstake to begin to build on. I bought my first apartment in Paris with a down payment of $400. I called all my friends, and we got the $400. It was just a single room with a shower and a sink; the toilet was a hole in the ground outside. People said, "Man, look, for that amount of money you can live in three rooms." I said, "Yeah, but it's rent." I used what I paid on that place as an equity down payment on the place that had the three rooms. It ain't rocket science, y'all. You say, "Oh man, I can't do it. I can't do it." That's what they want you to do. That's the deal, because then you have no economic power. I think we all agree this is a capitalist society. And what is the bullet, what is the hammer, what is everything? MONEY! MONEY! God bless the child that's got his own. It don't have to be big money. All it has to be is money. And it can grow, and you can make it grow.

I often tell the story about when I was in the air force: I'd see planes going along, and at a certain altitude, these white trails would come out from behind the plane. You ever see that? These white streaks coming from the rear of a plane? I asked, "What's that? Why do some planes do that?" A guy explained to me that the streaks were ice. Ice? Yes, there's moisture in the air, but the air is so pure up there that the moisture has nothing to form on. A combustion engine gives off tiny bits of carbon. When the carbon is released at high altitudes, water forms around it and turns to ice. So the trails we're seeing are all of these granules of ice. That's the way it is with other things; if you can get this one little particle, then the stuff begins to form around it.

I was recently looking at people who were millionaires. A lot of these people were small workers nobody knew. They had a number of traits in common. They were able to live within themselves, and they were able to acquire meticulously. They had *habits* of acquiring meticulously. Now, what's interesting about this for me is that if half of you would demonstrate these traits, and the people began to see them work, it could spread.

Immigrants, now, come from a society where they did not expect justice. They are just happy to be in America. I'm telling y'all there's money in the streets here. There's money in the streets. Now you've got to work. Yes, you do. You've got to work four times harder; if you don't want to work four times harder, you could probably get away with being just three times smarter. You don't just have to have, as we say in Yiddish, every *goyim narhus*, meaning gentile token that people rattle. You would be surprised how that adds up. If it adds up among enough people, that represents a very large sum. That's why churches do well. The parishioners all get together and put their collection in one place. At least they can see one thing that can be built. Maybe instead of a temple, they could build a factory. Or they might have invested in Intel stock at the right time; it would be a whole 'nother thing, but I ain't gonna get into that. As salaama bacon. You all do what you want to do. But that becomes financial power. And that's the only, only power anybody respects in our culture.

There's money and there's bloods. We think we're powerless, but we've got all the power in the world because the man thinks we're fools, so he leaves us the place and opportunity to make the deal. You can make the deal, and you don't have to ask anybody anything. You could buy stock in the Ku Klux Klan, if they had such a thing; they would sell it to you. Isn't that interesting?

There are a thousand places where your color is not questioned and you can make money. When I was on Wall Street on the American Stock Exchange, I was the first black trader. It was a very, very funny phenomenon. I never made a mistake on the Wall Street exchange. All the other traders, especially new traders, would make mistakes. I never made a mistake. I'd like to say I was that smart, but that wasn't the deal. Most of the traders had a black working as second-in-command who'd been there a zillion years and kept training the boys, the sons of the guy who had the seat, etc. Once the brothers realized I was down, if ever I was about to make a mistake, one of them would bump me. I had the smartest people with the most training looking out for me. I said, "Hey, hey," and often the brother would look right at me and call on someone else. I knew it meant "Melvin, you don't want this."

At certain levels, there is unity out there. There are people waiting to give you that hand. Brothers and sisters waiting in the cut. That's how I got to the San Francisco Film Festival. Yes! I had a film. I was at a party in Paris, and I met a brother, a homeboy. The guy and I began to talk, and he said, "Well, what are you doing?" I said, "I'm a writer mostly, but now I'm making a film." He said, "Oh great, what, a documentary?" I said, "No, it's got a story." He said, "Oh yeah, what do you shoot in—sixteen, thirty-five?" I said, "I'm shooting in thirty-five." He said, "How long?" I said, "It's a feature." He said, "You are making a feature?" I said, "Yeah, and what do you do?" He said, "I'm head of the San Francisco Film Festival." He may not come when you call Him, but He's always right on time. Now, the brother was smart. He had other people on the board and when he invited me to the festival, he never told anyone that I was American, let alone black. He just invited another French delegate. That's how I got to the festival. But you got to be up there. I'm telling you, there are all these little corners, man, all these little corners. There are people ready to step up and say, "Hey." There are people of good will. I know you've got your assholes, but there are people of good will out there, too.

I had made *The Story of a Three-Day Pass*, and that embarrassed Hollywood, which was my intention. I was offered a job immediately thereafter because to have the only African American participant in the festival be a French delegate, living in France, was a shameful situation. I was offered jobs. However, if I had taken the jobs immediately, then I would have been declared the African American genius, different from others, etc. I would have been lionized, and that would have been the end of that. So I refused. However, that required Hollywood to find black directors. At the time, there could only really be one successful black in each thing. Two gentlemen, quite a bit older than I, got their opportunities. Gordon Parks, who had been around, who was legendary with his photography and with his awards, and who had been trying to get into Hollywood for years, was suddenly "discovered." He made a movie called *The Learning Tree*. Moreover, Ossie Davis, who had also been around for years, and who had been trying to break into Hollywood not only as an actor but also as a director, was "discovered." He did Chester Himes's *Cotton Comes to Harlem*. Meantime, Hollywood kept after me because I was the jewel in the crown, so to speak. I agreed finally that I would make *Watermelon Man*, with the provisio that it be shot in Hollywood, since both of the other films had been shot on location because they didn't know how these spear-throwing black bucks, subject to running amok, were going to act, or how the unions, these right-wing unions, would take to blacks actually giving orders.

With a great deal of trepidation they therefore agreed to allow me to shoot *Watermelon Man* in Hollywood. So, I'm there, and I asked whether I could have some minorities, not just blacks, not just Asians and Hispanics, but also women, on my crew. It turned out that the government had looked into Hollywood, and they had preempted the government and said there's no racism here. Each union had one minority; the carpenters' union had one, etc. Every time a liberal director wanted a mixed crew, they would yank this person off whatever show he or she was on and put him or her on that show. The one minority in each union worked 365 days a year. But they only had one. So I said, look, I'd like so and so. Oh, I'm sorry our carpenter's busy. They meant our *black* carpenter. So I said, look, what about somebody else? They said, you've got to understand the rainfall of Kilimanjaro is twenty-seven inches at its peak, and also. Yeah, uh huh, I got you. So after they explained all this to me, why we couldn't have minorities on my crew because they were all busy, I said, "Okay, I agree." Now, the first rule of the block is "Don't write no check with your mouth that your ass can't cash." I understand the inherent racism, the inherent insensitivity, but I don't say nothing, 'cause I ain't got nothing in my pocket. We went on and we went on until a few days before shooting began, after they've built the set and spent a quarter of a million dollars. "Oh, hey, Mel." Everybody loves me by this time. I go out with the guys fishing. I don't know anything about fishing. But I hear them, and I start talking about bait and this, that, and the other. After three weeks they think I'm just one of the local rednecks. So then they say, "What we gonna do tomorrow, Mel?" I say, "Well, I'm leaving." They say, "What do you mean you're leaving?" I say, "I quit." "What do you mean? You can't quit. We've invested $250,000, and this set and everybody's coming in, and we've already signed the actors. If you quit, we'll sue." "Well, you know, I make fifty-nine dollars a week at the post office; you gonna have a long walk trying to collect a judgment from me." There are two ways of confronting the guy. I can confront him where he's got no back-down, or I can lead him back. He says, "Well, what's the matter?" I say, "I'm lonesome, man." Well, this equals something of Stepin Fetchit, or something in his past that he can deal with in a way. I don't care what he deals with; all

I want is to win. All I want is for my people to win. I don't care if I have to kiss ass. That's why Listerine was invented. As far as I'm concerned, if that gets that young boy and that young girl a little closer, a little closer, to being somebody, what they should be, I'll carry his weight. I'll carry it, I don't mind. So I said to the guy, "Couldn't I have some folks on the crew?" He said, "I told you we looked them up and nobody's available." Meantime, I had made a list of every qualified camera operator, dolly operator, sound engineer, and makeup artist. That's how we broke Hollywood because the man has an Achilles pocketbook. I had a $250,000 hook up his ass. If I hadn't, man, I would have been gone. Don't write no check with your mouth that your ass can't cash. When it's going to cost him he will then find folks. "Yeah Mel, we didn't know it was that serious. Sure, come on, let's get an apprentice-ship program going." I said, "Oh thank you, man, I sure was lonesome." I just let it go at that. That's how we began to get minorites in the union. That's just one answer.

You have got to know that you have overcome the essential dilemma that faces us. We do not want to downplay the difficulty of our brethren and ourselves in this racist society, but you can succeed. I've been called a lot of things, but nobody could ever call me a wimp. I succeeded, but I didn't let it change me. It does not have to change you. I took the money from *Sweetback* and did *Ain't Supposed to Die a Natural Death*. People said, "How can you do that?" I said it wasn't my money. It's the money of my people, which I had a scheme to collect so that we could do something else with it. That's the deal. After we did that, we got black shows on Broadway. Then I went the other way. I said, "Will everybody give me some bread, please?" Now we want to do this or we want to do that. Oh, man, I ain't got it. Okay, I'll work within the framework of our psyche, and that is to do things that are so delectable that we *have* to do them. Then the money I took, we used it, BAM, BAM, BAM, and that's how we did it. You may not know, but we did it. I tricked y'all. It could have been done another way, but I'm saying we're past that. That's blood money, and that's money and bloods.

bell hooks

bell hooks was born in Hopkinsville, Kentucky. She received her B.A. from Stanford University and her Ph.D. from the University of California at Santa Cruz. bell has taught at Yale University and at Oberlin College. Since 1993, she has been a Distinguished Professor of English at City College of New York. She is the author of a number of influential books, including Ain't I a Woman: Black Women and Feminism *(1981), which* Publishers Weekly *called one of the twenty most influential women's books of the last twenty years;* Feminist Theory: From Margin to Center *(1984);* Talking Back: Thinking Feminist, Thinking Black *(1989);* Yearning: Race, Gender, and Cultural Politics *(1990), which won the Before Columbus Foundation's American Book Award;* Breaking Bread: Insurgent Black Intellectual Life *(with Cornel West) (1991);* Black Looks: Race and Representation *(1992);* Sisters of the Yam: Black Women and Self-Recovery *(1993);* Teaching to Transgress: Education as the Practice of Freedom *(1994);* Outlaw Culture: Resisting Representations *(1994);* Art on My Mind: Visual Politics *(1995); and a poetry collection,* A Woman's Mourning Song *(1992). Her most recent books include* Killing Rage *(1995),* Bone Black: Memories of Childhood *(1996),* Wounds of Passion: A Writing Life *(1997), and the film book, of course,* Reel to Real: Race, Sex, and Class at the Movies *(1996).*

bell hooks (or Gloria Watkins as some of us call her) is more than the author of books. She is perhaps the most important black public intellectual and commentator who has been "elected" by the public, rather than handpicked by the mainstream establishment. How? Because we read her and respect her work. Why? Because she teaches us resistance, which makes this a better world. As a public intellectual, bell hooks is a door opener and a bridge builder for those of us in the academy. She and folks like her are forging connections between us and the community, between us and London, between us and Paris, between us and Africa.

It is bell hooks's empowering aura that places her among the rare academics whom one can say one is envious of, in public. She is almost unique in that she is a black intellectual whom students write about. I still remember the Village Voice *article in which a former student who had encountered her as an instructor at Yale said that bell hooks had empowered him to be a writer. He is not alone. bell hooks has persuaded many of us to write prolifically and for audiences we would otherwise scarcely have considered receptive to our work.*

Manthia Diawara

SIMPLE LIVING

An Antidote to Hedonistic Materialism

I want to reflect on the whole notion of black genius and relate it to what is happening now. This essay is really divided into two parts. The first part raises questions about the meaning of black genius, while the second part considers what it means to try to direct our work toward the collective well-being of black people in the diaspora, which is the goal that black genius ought to be pursuing.

The current focus on black thinkers and public intellectuals has led many folks to speculate, with much fervor, about the possibility that we are witnessing a resurgence of W. E. B. Du Bois's vision of a "Talented Tenth," by which he initially meant "leadership of the Negro race in America by a trained few." Contemporary thinkers, however, do not call attention to Du Bois's 1948 memorial address, delivered at Wilberforce State University, wherein he critiqued his earlier idea of a Talented Tenth. There, he acknowledged that when he suggested the need for a talented group that would spearhead racial uplift, he simply assumed that these individuals would be committed to the collective well-being of black people, and that they would want to use their talents on behalf of the race, indeed on behalf of everyone. He contended:

> I assumed that with knowledge, sacrifice would automatically follow. In my youth and idealism, I did not realize that selfishness is even more natural than sacrifice. . . . When I came out of college into the world of work, I realized that it was quite possible that my plan of training a talented tenth might put in control and power, a group of selfish, self-indulgent, well-to-do men [and women], whose basic interest in solving the Negro problem was personal; personal freedom and unhampered enjoyment and use of the world, without any real care, or certainly no arousing care, as to what became of the mass of American Negroes, or the mass of any people. My Talented Tenth, I could see, might result in a sort of interracial free-for-all, with the devil taking the hindmost and the foremost taking anything they could lay hands on.[1]

This powerful declaration was made by Du Bois in 1948, yet I feel that it awesomely and prophetically describes the current relationship of today's "Black Talented Tenth" to masses of black people. Indeed, one cannot simply invoke the term "black genius" and assume that there is any direct correlation between, on the one hand, black people in the diaspora who possess exceptional intellectual ability and, on the other hand, liberatory efforts to create a local or global cultural context that affirms and sustains collective black self-determination. Significantly, the word "genius" also means a person who strongly influences, *for good or ill*, the character, conduct, or destiny of a person, place, or thing.

More often than not, the black genius in the United States has had little or no contact with masses of black people. This is especially true if that genius has been nurtured in predominantly white educational institutions. Even though individuals whose talents have been nurtured in such environments can actively choose as an insurgent act of resistance to direct their work toward masses of black people, this is rarely the case, largely because the mechanisms of reward—whether recognition, status, or monetary gain—remain highest for those of us who turn their backs on the masses. By this statement I do not mean to imply that black people trained at black institutions are inherently more inclined to direct their work toward black self-determination. Irrespective of whether they are at predominantly white or predominantly black academic institutions, institutions are by nature and direction structurally conservative. Their primary function is to produce a professional managerial class that will serve the existing social and political status quo. Given that the ideologies of imperialist, white supremacist, capitalist patriarchy form the basic founding principles of culture in the United States, and the ways of thinking and being that are taught via these very educational institutions, it should be evident that the fundamental concerns of the academy in general are at odds with any effort to affirm black self-determination.

Currently, the vast majority of black academics, writers, and/or critical thinkers, whether they pitch their work to a predominantly white or black audience or to some combination of the two, do not choose to be dissident voices challenging imperialist, white supremacist, capitalist patriarchy. In those cases where an individual begins writing with the hope that her/his work will make her/him famous and/or produce huge monetary profits, this self-interested foundation will preclude, from the onset, identification with the concern for black self-determination or the well-being of masses of black people. It is more likely that her or his identification with blackness will reflect solidarity with black folks who share similar class aspirations.

Indeed, if we return to Du Bois's critique of the Black Talented Tenth, or the solidarity of black genius, it is evident that he began to see that the class aspirations of this professional, managerial group—which is to say its desire for individual upward mobility within the existing class structure of this society, especially as it pertained to profit making and status—would ultimately lead it to betray the interests of the black masses.

More than ever before in our political history, black people in the United States confuse reformist efforts aimed at securing civil rights and equity with agendas for black self-determination, decolonization, and liberation. I do not in any way want to devalue the place of civil rights reform in our lives, because we would not be where we are today if it were not for those reforms. However, while reforms are important, they do not constitute radical interventions aimed at transforming society in ways that ensure the collective well-being of masses of black people. Let me be clear, and I have said this many times before: black capitalism is not black self-determination. In the last ten years, we have witnessed an unprecedented commodification of blackness, in relation to academic and/or popular discourses about race and culture. On the academic front, where the interests of market forces converge with burgeoning mainstream cultural interests in reading about blackness, there is an ongoing infusion of works by and about black writers that is almost completely divorced from any collective effort to galvanize masses of black people.

If my tone sounds somewhat harsh, it is because Black History Month and Women's History Week have just ended as I write this, and I have been all over the country, hearing the despair that young black people feel. Clearly, there is no sense on their part that there is any collective black genius that is in any way meeting their needs, galvanizing them, and helping them to understand what they must do to make life happen in a meaningful way.

Those individual black people who have come to power, either in the academy or outside as cultural brokers of blackness, without linking their work to any efforts to enhance the well-being of masses of black people can do so precisely because there is no network of accountability[2] that critically examines the impact of their work. Often, these individuals police and actively seek to delegitimize and silence the voices of dissident black genius which both affirm black self-determination and consistently oppose imperialist, white supremacist, capitalist patriarchy.

For example, in my own experience, the people who have used the mainstream media to say that my work should not be read (such as Stanley Crouch, who referred to me as a "barking dog," Adolf Reed Jr., who described me as a "hustler," and my colleague Michelle Wallace, who gave me the most vicious trashing in the *Village Voice*) never refer to the substantive content of my work. It is not me or what I do that makes an impact; it is my work that makes an impact. People bring those battered books of mine to me and tell me that this book did this or that for them. They do not say, "bell hooks, she . . . ," because they do not know "bell hooks, she." They say, "This is what the work did for me when it entered my life." It is the work that galvanized them. The test, the proof is in what that work enables them to do in their lives. I know it is not me that does this, because sometimes they are disappointed when they actually meet me because I am not what they expected.

There can be no meaningful discussion of black genius in relation to the black masses, and to black self-determination, without a recognition of the political and social differences that place us at odds with one another and/or the way in which an ethics of competition leads us to devalue one another's work, even if we do not differ politically. We also have had a tradition of black genius not being affirmed or nurtured within the spheres of blackness, particularly if it is transgressive in any way: if it is gay, if it says anything that the world does not want said, if it departs from a certain kind of essentialist blackness. One goal of the Black Genius series is to suggest that black people can create spaces wherein we nurture one another. Part of what we lack is even a forum where we can be critical of each other, with integrity, and recognize that to criticize someone's ideas is not to invalidate them as a human being. The Black Genius series represents a moment in which we are enacting the practice of trying to say that there is not just one of us up here representing the race. A willingness to do more collaborative work with each other like this series would open up and expand the space for dialogue about differences and black pluralism.

At the same time, the patriarchal mind-set of the culture as a whole colludes with the intentional design of individual patriarchal males who seek to maintain a lineage of intellectual genius that makes it seem as if men have always been the more significant black political visionaries. Even the poster for the lecture series that gave rise to this volume excluded black female visionaries from its purview, stating that "Du Bois shall meet Garvey here" and that "Black Genius is present in the mother/child and it is in Mandela."

While the historical lineage of visible black genius in relation to radical discourses opposed to colonialism and white supremacy may have been at some point primarily, if not exclusively, male, this is certainly no longer the case. In our times, some of the most radical critiques of imperialist, white supremacist, capitalistic patriarchy are emerging from black women thinkers whose work is consistently rendered less visible and/or devalued. Examples include Lorraine Hansberry, Audre Lorde, Toni Cade Bambara. Toni Cade Bambara, who died in 1996, was the subject of a very vicious reminiscence in *Ms.* magazine. I read the piece, laid my head on my table, and wept. Toni Cade Bambara is one of the people without whose work I would not be here. This reminiscence of her did not have a paragraph that talked about her work. It said she was not a good housekeeper, she was not a good friend. I did not mind people remembering her in that way; that was not the point. All of it might have been true. We remember Toni Cade Bambara because she gave us work that uplifted her/us and inspired us. When I got a copy of *The Black Woman*, I saw that I was not the only black woman who was out here thinking about gender, struggling with Black Power, and trying to justify a position for ourselves other than prone. It was just amazing to have that book, and I wrote a letter to *Ms.* saying that Toni Cade Bambara's book was, for many of us, what the *Feminine Mystique* was to many white women in America who had not begun to think about the crisis of their lives until Betty Friedan defined it for them. Many of us needed the anthology *The Black Woman* to begin to think about our lives. That book is one of the works that inspired me to write *Ain't I a Woman: Black Women and Feminism.* That reminiscence hurt. (We have to check out what we are doing as black folks because the little negative reminiscence was written by a black woman who had ostensibly been a friend and a colleague of Toni Cade Bambara.) The most substantial piece of writing that I saw in a mainstream journal about Toni Cade Bambara did not refer to her work. It did not give her her due for what she gave to many of us.

Let me tell you this one little story about Toni Bambara which may put her "disorderliness" in context. When I went to meet her for the first time in her home, which was then in Atlanta, Toni was writing an article. The living room had a bunch of junk spread around. And I remember Sister Toni got up, got a broom, and just swept the junk away. The level of intellectual fellowship that took place that night between her, myself, and Beverly Guy-Sheftall was awesome. Here was a woman who was living in the heart of a black community in a place in which—and I ain't going to lie—I would not live. Girlfriend said, "I likes to be with my people." And that is where she was. These are the things she taught me. In Buddhism, as many of you know, we are taught that it is not always what great teachers say; sometimes it is just being in their presence. What Toni taught me in those moments is that the circumstances around us do not matter; what matters is the intellectual work we will do in our conversation here today. That is how the sister should be remembered: for the work that she did as a black-loving black woman committed to black self-determination every step of the way in her life.

Indeed, as Toni Cade Bambara's work exemplifies, the writing of visionary contemporary black women thinkers usually has a more radical edge precisely because it includes a critique of patriarchy, while simultaneously insisting on a union between theory and practice which privileges the experiential as the site where change and transformation are registered.

In keeping with the agenda of this series, I want to refer to some work I have done which I see as being most specifically directed toward advancing the collective well-being of black people. This work proposes an alternative strategy for healing the pain in our everyday life. *Sisters of the Yam: Black Women and Self-Recovery* was the first book that I specifically addressed to black women. When I tried to publish it, I was told that there was no audience for the book. We are always assaulted with the assumption that black people will not buy books. Somehow white women are interested in their self-recovery and they need lots of self-help books, but black women are supposedly uninterested in the subject. I remember sitting there with white folks from my publisher and telling them that there were enough bell hooks fans that if we do a small first printing, that first printing will sell no matter what. (Walter Mosley has pointed to the racism that is so deeply inherent in the publishing industry.) I had to convince these people, even though all my other books had been selling well, that some work directed toward black self-determination and the well-being of a more mass black female audience would sell.

I chose to do a self-help book because I could see that masses of black women were not reading my little feminist theory books. By "masses of black women," I mean a broad spectrum of black women because I have always had black women readers. As I indicated in *Breaking Bread*, I used to envy Sister Shahrazad Ali, who wrote *The Blackman's Guide to Understanding the Black-woman*. Everywhere I went, on the bus, at the barbershop, I would see black people from every walk of life cracking, opening, reading her book. I said to myself, "Hey! I'm going to learn from Sister Ali." And I did learn from her. I realized that, if I really wanted to produce work that addresses masses of black women, then I would have to write a different kind of book. And that book was, for me, *Sisters of the Yam*.

Of course, black women have bought that book. Everywhere I go black women come waving their copies of *Sisters of the Yam*. I did not get big bucks to do that book; my advance was $4,000 or $5,000. My point is that, when we decide to use our "genius" for black self-determination, we often find that we are not rewarded to the same extent or in the same ways that we would be if we were pitching ourselves to a so-called "crossover" or "mainstream," usually meaning white, audience.

I remember my first trip back home after I got my Ph.D. I was driving a used, beat-up Volkswagen, and my parents were very disappointed. They wanted our whole community to see that I was now somebody, not the domestic maid that my mother was, nor the janitor that my father was, but somebody. The way that I was going to register that "somebodyness" was not through service to my community. It was going to be registered in terms of things, like whether I would buy my parents a house, what kind of car I was driving, and what sort of clothes was I wearing. "Girl, get your hair fixed! With all that money I know you can do something with that hair."

On some level, the masses of black people have asked our talented groups to register their power through materiality. We have not demanded that they register it through service. In the days of strict racial apartheid, it was much easier to do both—that is, be of service to the community and reap a reward or status for what one did. As someone who grew up in an all-black community, it was easy for me to get my little chump change by reading; I used to go around reading to the people who could not read. They would give me a quarter, and I would buy my little outfits and stuff. It was easier to do that in a segregated black community because resources brought into that community were recirculated there. Or I could stand up in my church and be counted. In the traditional black church, the amount of money one gave was published, so one could be counted in this way. So there were numerous ways that we could mingle service to community with other kinds of reward.

With assimilation and racial integration, however, so many of our talented groups of people live outside of black communities, including myself. How do we register our service in a nonmaterial way, because we go back home so often? Those of you from Africa, those of you from the Caribbean know what I am talking about. You go home and people register your service not in terms of what you have been teaching those students at NYU. "What you got to show for it? What goods are you bringing back? What kind of car you driving?" How can we talk about the forms of service we give when we do not live amid those constituencies that we are talking about?

That brings me to a subject that I am currently working on—healing and everyday life, particularly with regard to the tremendous pain that hedonistic materialism creates in the daily lives of African Americans across classes. And if you do not know what hedonistic materialism is, it is just wanting things, all out of control. Let me use myself as an example. Six months ago, I decided that I did not have any jewelry and needed to buy myself a ring. So I bought one ring, and then I felt that I needed another ring. Before I knew it, in the space of six months, I acquired more and more and more rings. I tried to get at what had gotten into me, what the purchases symbolized. Hedonistic materialism was driving me like a maniac.

I began to look at other African Americans, cross class, and to think about how much pain I saw in their daily lives, how much stress and mental delusions are caused by constant feelings of lack. I am not talking about the basic necessities of life here. I am talking about the kind of stress we feel because we cannot have the level of material plenty that we want. Many of us are driven by unrequited yearnings stimulated by fantasies of wealth and privilege.

We share the pains of hedonistic materialism cross class. Those of us who are materially privileged are leading lives in discontent because we are perpetually spending and hoarding. We who are privileged spread the message to the less privileged that their lives have no meaning if they do not have the freedom to fulfill hedonistic desires for material goods. The black women and men I talk to who live in housing projects keep saying that they want things endlessly because they feel that things will make them somebody and give them the value they feel they do not have.

Systems of domination like white supremacist, capitalist patriarchy are among the sources of people's unhappiness. My friend Betty, a young woman now in the army, told me, "It's American to be constantly craving and to feel that you're no good without things. That's what makes you an American." Yet, many people have already made the connection that a culture of domination needs people to be in these constant states of yearning. The pain is actually caused by those systems that make you feel that you are disempowered in your life, you are not anybody, and whether or not you can read and write, you are somebody if you own the right kind of tennis shoes.

Hedonistic materialism is propelled by the necessity to sustain our culture globally. Black people who live in the United States are Western. American cultural imperialism is the same as Eurocentric cultural imperialism. Black people in America do not think about ourselves in relationship to other black people in the diaspora or to other people globally. It is important for this country to make its people so obsessed with their own liberal individualism that they do not have time to think about a world larger than the self. Everything in our culture is telling us that anything that we can do for money is okay. What is happening to black people is no different from what is happening to the culture as a whole, but I think it is more personified in our lives at times because of where we sit in the class/economic totem pole.

We live in a culture where young people in particular have trouble achieving access. When I interviewed the rapper Lil'

Kim, I was struck by the fact that we live in a culture where young people like her can do hard-core rap and make a lot of money, but cannot learn how to read and write on a level they might want to in this society. This culture will actually give them access to great wealth before it will give them access to the basic tools of survival in a literate society. This is why the craving is so intense. Girlfriend had on these big diamonds, bigger than the one on my little teeny ring. She looked at me like "What's that? Did you get it out of one of those bubble gum machines or something?" She had never heard of me. She talked about her life story, how she was kicked out of home at fourteen or fifteen, making it on the street. She can move toward money, but she cannot move toward the things that might spiritually sustain her self-esteem. The money has not enhanced her self-esteem at all. She is still feeling the tremendous pain of abuse, of being unloved, of being abandoned, and she is trying to cope with that. Some of that pain is expressed as rage and hardness. The mass media want us to feel no compassion for suffering young black people, and to see them as hard. I am not saying that the hardness is not real, particularly when it manifests itself, when one of these folks is assaulting you or doing something else to you. But I do believe that we will not counteract that rage if we do not first deal with the pain and grief of unlove, abandonment, and abuse that underlies it.

A white interviewer asked me whether I felt that Lil' Kim was empowering herself. I said that if a young woman were selling her pussy on the street for $10 and can sell it on MTV for $50,000, you might say that on a certain level she is empowering herself. But if you are talking about sexual agency, she is not empowering herself. To have your sexuality be a commodity within the system of exchange means that you have to divorce it from a certain set of spiritual and emotional fulfillments. I tried to talk with Lil' Kim on that level, about what she longs for in her life, how she might go about getting it, and what the messages are that she is sending out to other young black folks about what they might long for in their lives.

Many people feel that this relentless yearning is a new thing that has come into people's lives. Black people over the age of thirty say they did not always feel this way about their lives. If we study the lives of southern black people who lived well during the Depression, we see that they had lives of sustained well-being because they were committed to living simply: eating healthy food they grew themselves, clinging to spiritual traditions that emphasized substantive values like integrity of one's word and right action, as opposed to fantasies of hedonistic materialism.

Many black people live simply, because they have no access to material plenty; yet, rather than seeing this experience as a choice, they actually feel that there is something wrong with the way they are living. The mass media conveys the message that if your life is simple it has no meaning. If only black people could see themselves as politically engaging in a gesture of interbeing which enables them to live in greater harmony with masses of people on the planet. When we black people commit ourselves to living simply as a political action, as a way of breaking the stress caused by unrelenting hedonistic desire for material objects that are not needed for survival, or essential to well-being, we will not be talking about ebonics. We will be out in the streets demanding that the public schools have enough teachers so that all kids, cross color, can read and write in standard English and in Spanish too. We spend so much time with our yearning and fantasizing about what we are going to buy that we cannot be out in the streets arguing and calling Mr. Clinton out for taking funds from the public schools. Those of us who make political the practice of living simply and have resources that might be redistributed can engage in philanthropy that enhances the collective well-being of black people.

There are a few simple steps anyone can take to begin living simply. When I started to think about this subject, I talked to groups of individuals who felt that they were experiencing the issues associated with hedonistic materialism in their lives. They did not have a clue as to what they were doing, or how they were actually spending their money. I am a big advocate of writing down every penny that you spend during an entire month, so that you can see where your income goes. Even if your monthly income is only twenty-five dollars, look at what you are doing with that. Start telling yourself that you do not need something to be happy, and see if it does not work.

Simple living does not make you better, but it might give you greater peace in the life that you are living. Suppose you are working in a factory, and there is nothing but stress on your job all day. Then you come home to nothing but "Gi'me; gi'me; gi'me!" and "What can I get and when am I gonna get it?" That can make your life all the more miserable, certainly more miserable than if you were able to come home to an atmosphere of peace. One of the things readers liked most about *Sisters of the Yam* was that I raised the simple question of healing and how we talk to one another as black people. Do you tell your children:

"Get your black ass over here. I ain't gonna tell you again"? To what extent does that cause stress, pain, and an atmosphere that is not peaceful? I have gotten feedback from people with families who say that they never thought about the tone of voice they use with their kids. Changing such simple things can make a difference in their lives. You do not need money; you do not need to go anywhere. You just control your own way of speaking. Simple, but it may have a major impact on a kid who will remember being spoken to in caring tones, rather than in self-devaluing tones. We teach by our own embodied presence. A lot of the time, we adults say something different from what we do. The first thing we can do is embody in our habits of being and our own actions the things that we feel are healing and affirmative of blackness.

Embracing a strategy for living simply in everyday life, irrespective of one's level of material privilege, would enable masses of black people to eliminate the unnecessary suffering caused by the unrelenting desire for material excess. Were the masses of black people to embrace the philosophy of living simply as a way of countering the genocidal abuse in our lives fostered by imperialism, white supremacy, and capitalism, we would also be uniting our struggle with that of most people on the planet who are daily grievously victimized by the material excess of this society. There is a bumper sticker which reads "Live simply so that others may simply live." A political choice to embrace living simply can liberate and enhance our collective well-being, and heal and soothe some of the pain in everyday life.

Notes

1. Reprinted in *Writings by W. E. B. Du Bois in Periodicals Edited by Others*, vol. 4, *1945–1961*, ed. Herbert Aptheker (Millwood, N.Y., 1982), 78–79.

2. As Farai Chideya discusses more fully in her essay, we have agency in relationship to the mass media. Black people and the members of other groups go out and pay to see racist and degrading representations of ourselves. We have to assert more agency here. Think about *The Bell Curve*, which made arguments that allowed people to return to racist biological determinism and to say that black people are inferior. National Public Radio reported on a survey that said that most white Americans think that black people and anyone of African descent are biologically and genetically inferior. Now, think about the fact that we go to a movie like *The Long Kiss Goodnight*, in which Samuel L. Jackson plays a kind of flunky/Mammy role to a white woman. Throughout that film—and it is an entertaining film, I will give it that—he is asked almost six times, "Are you this stupid by choice or were you born that way?" The very repetitive nature of that question, always coming from the smarter white person, reinforces the very same kind of thinking that is manifested in *The Bell Curve*. Now, we know that Sam is making some money, but why is he doing that? What is his intervention? Does he have an opportunity to say as an actor, "I don't wanna say this, and these are the reasons why"?

I have discussed the need for a network of accountability for intellectuals, but where is our network of accountability when it comes to cinema and the choices people make in regard to movie making and movie viewing? We have a tendency to say, "Well, at least they're working, at least we're seeing them," but not that people can be working and still assert agency over what they do.

Julianne Malveaux

People have forgotten what genius is. Genius resides in the collective spirit, the character of a people. I think the term got highjacked maybe four hundred years ago when people noticed that some individuals embody the collective spirit of a people more than others. That remains absolutely true today, but it is nevertheless the generative possibility within a wide collective body of people that is the source of genius. Julianne Malveaux represents that duality very well.

Some years ago, June Jordan published a piece in her book of essays, Civil Wars, *that the* New York Times *rejected for its op-ed page. She was rightfully annoyed by the decision because it was a brilliant, insightful essay. Jordan pointed out that, at the time, no women of color were nationally syndicated columnists. That circumstance has changed. There are more than one now, but surely none of the women who have broken into this area has more visibility and dynamism than Julianne Malveaux. A good headline to capture her career move into syndicated column writing, television, and the other kinds of work she has done might be "Neo-African Warrior Goddess Slam-Dunks the Media Channels."*

"Neo-African warrior goddess," that's a marvelous mouthful. It is a phrase that the black independent filmmakers Julie Dash and Alilay Sharon Larkin applied to themselves. "Neo-Africans" are peo- ple of African descent who are living a more modern, Western version of the African experience. "Warrior" needs no explanation. As for "goddess," in some African religions, every individual is the child of one god or goddess or another and thereby a reflection of divine spirit. In using the term "goddess," Dash and Larkin were aligning them- selves with a long line of particularly determined, strong African and African American women who have played a crucial role in the development of black genius. We must appreciate those women who despite the resistance to women's leadership step forward, take their positions, and show us the light. Malveaux is one of those. She is fol- lowing in the tradition of Sojourner Truth and, more specifically in terms of her professional career, the tradition of Ida B. Wells.

A few background details confirm her immense energy. Julianne Malveaux is an economist, a writer, and a columnist whose weekly column, syndicated since 1990 by King Features, appears nationally in some twenty newspapers. She has written columns for Essence *and for* Emerge. *She is a regular contributor to* Ms. *magazine and* U.S.A. Today. *She is also a weekly contributor to the* San Francisco Sun Reporter, *a black newspaper in San Francisco. Until recently, she was the host and executive producer of the* Julianne Malveaux Show, *a very lively radio program. She also appears regularly as a commentator on social and political issues on* CNN & Company *and* PBS's To the Contrary. Dr. Malveaux, who holds a Ph.D. in* *economics, is president of the National Association of Negro Business and Professional Women's Clubs and vice chair of the board of the Center for Policy Alternatives. Her many publications include the co-edited book* Slipping through the Cracks: The Status of Black Women *(1986) and, more recently,* Sex, Lies and Stereotypes: Perspectives of a Mad Economist *(1994).*

CLYDE TAYLOR

WALL STREET, MAIN STREET, AND THE SIDE STREET

I am just a bit daunted by this notion of black genius because I think that it is a redundant term. To be African American and to survive, and to survive with at least a modicum of sanity, is at times intrinsically genius. So I am not sure when we talk about genius whether I ought to tell you about one of my foremothers, Dr. Sadie Tanner Mossell Alexander, the first African American woman to receive the Ph.D. in economics in this country, or about a sister who was a maid. In the room where I write, I keep a picture of my great grandmother over my computer. She was a maid in Des Moines, Iowa, and I keep her picture over my computer because she cleaned houses, so that I do not have to.

In the context of this forum, people have talked about various issues. The issue I feel most strongly about is industrial transformation—what it has meant for African Americans in terms of a class analysis, what we are missing, and what we are not dealing with. Although my topic is "Wall Street, Main Street, and the Side Street," there is a subtopic that I need to address first; it might be called "Is This as Good as It Gets?"

I am a 1960s kid. Those songs that I once slow dragged to I now use to motivate my intellectual output. Remember the song "Is This as Good as It Gets?" The question is appropriately raised in an economic context because people are really happy about what is happening in the economy. For six years, we have essentially seen annual economic growth that has averaged about 2.6 percent. It has ranged from a low of about 1 percent to a high of about 4.5 percent. It looks great. It looks wonderful. All of the economic indicators are in line. Why would anybody be disturbed to live in America right now? Is this as good as it gets?

Inflation is containable and, if it is not, Federal Reserve Chief Alan Greenspan will show up at the Senate Banking Committee and say that it could be. He says the kinds of things that make people feel a little better. Of course, the stock market may drop a couple of hundred points, but, after it has gone up a couple of thousand points in the past two years, what is a couple of hundred points among friends? Is this as good as it gets?

The unemployment rate is around 5.3 percent, lower than we have seen it in a very long time. Of course, 5.3 percent is an aggregate unemployment rate; for certain populations, it is much higher. A short time ago, I read an article (fortunately I was reading in bed; it is best to be reading in bed when one gets surprised) in which the writer, a young man at the *Washington Post,* stated that unemployment was lower than it has ever been and that the only people disadvantaged were blacks and youth. He went on to the next paragraph as if this conclusion was insignificant, as if to say, "Life is good but a gnat bit me." Is this as good as it gets? If the overall U.S. population experienced unemployment rates hovering around 11 percent, as African Americans do, there might be some problem. African American people make up 12 percent of the population, which is not all that many, so we do not really worry about that. Latinos have an unemployment rate of between 8 and 9 percent; this too is not acceptable, except this too does not apply to the whole population. We would get upset only if it happened to the overall population. (Indeed, for the white population the unemployment rate in February 1998 was 4.7 percent, much lower than we have seen it in a very long time.)

So we see an economy that, on a macroeconomic plane, is expanding and looks good. People are talking about balancing budgets, although the balanced budget amendment failed. President Clinton gave up the company store when he agreed that we should balance the budget with or without an amendment. In doing so, he essentially foreclosed the possibility of social programs that would make interventions with regard to problems evident at the microeconomic level. The question remains, is this as good as it gets?

If, however, we are concerned about social change and social justice, we must ask ourselves what assumptions go into the notion that the only indicators worth paying attention to relate to macroeconomic growth. Number one, what assumptions are we buying into? Number two, how do those assumptions play out? Do they play out the same way for everybody?

Now, "everybody" is a interesting word. Let me tell you a couple of everybody stories. I was sitting on a panel one day with a man from the American Banking Association who said to me that, by the year 2000, everybody will bank by computer. I found that to be, quite frankly, a far-reaching assumption, but I listened to him because I was taught to listen before I went off. So I sat there and listened to him tell me why *everybody* was going to bank by computer by the year 2000. After he finished talking, I explained to him that only a third of white households and just 11 percent of African American households had computers in 1996. So unless there was some massive computer give-away program of which I had not been apprised—and I try to know about these things, since I have relatives who could use some free computers—I wondered how everybody was going to bank by computer. We began to bat around the meaning of "everybody," and finally the man conceded that it meant everybody who mattered—that is, everybody who had more than $20,000 to deposit. Understand that the average American family has an annual income of $42,000. What family, then, is actually going to be putting half of its annual income in the bank?

But "everybody" is a word that is used with some regularity. Let me put it to you more personally and maybe a little humorously. I am neurotic. It is not my fault. One of my books is entitled *Perspectives of a Mad Economist.* Is this mad as in crazy? Mad as in angry? Or mad as in Bellevue Hospital is just down the street? Who knows? In any case, one day I went somewhere that I did not want anybody to know I had been to, but I had to be somewhere thereafter that people needed to be sure I was going to. So the combination of not having been and needing to be led me to ask a limousine to meet me on the corner. Now, anytime you ask a limo to meet you on the corner, you know what is going to happen. Ebonically speaking, "They just ain't gonna be there." I am one of these high-strung, type A, "Where are you when I want you!" people. I waited about two minutes with my foot tapping on the pavement; finally I made my way to a pay phone. The young lady who answered the pay phone said, "Well, Ms. Malveaux, *everybody* has a cell phone." In other words, "Why are you so upset about having to walk two blocks; if your cell phone had been working, you wouldn't have been inconvenienced." If my cell phone had been working, I wouldn't have been having mental health problems in the first place. I did not have a cell phone and did not even know that I was not *everybody* until girlfriend told me that. I thought that I was just the universal black person, until she told me that *everybody* had a cell phone.

The term "everybody" crops up again and again in public policy. We have a Social Security Advisory Commission that has decided that the way to fix the Social Security shortfall is to raise the age of retirement and lower benefits. What is wrong with that? If you raise the age of retirement from sixty-five to seventy, with the understanding that the average black man dies at sixty-six, everybody, ebonically speaking, "ain't gonna get they money. Somebody gonna die before it happens." Now, who has made this decision? Probably somebody who is kind of fat, kind of old, sits at a desk, and has not done hard work in a while. If you do hard work, you understand that people who do hard work do not want to work past sixty-five. See those women at the buffet dinners wearing orthopedic shoes at fifty-eight; they are just barely going to make it to sixty-two. How can we make them work until age seventy? See the men on a construction site, hardly able to stand up, but pridefully doing their best. How are they going to work until they are seventy? Strom Thurmond, of course, can work into his nineties; what is he doing but sitting at a desk and having someone bring him papers that allow him to jam some more black people? References to everybody just disturb me, and it also disturbs me that the people who make policy are not the same people who live policy. When we talk about everybody, we are leaving a whole lot of bodies out.

We have it in our minds that everybody in America is a college graduate. In fact, 25 percent of all Americans over twenty-five have college degrees. Twenty-two percent of whites over twenty-five have college degrees, compared with 13 percent of African Americans, 8 percent of Latinos, 3 percent of Native Americans, and 38 percent of Asian Americans. In short, most Americans do not have college degrees. Have we become so myopic in the Boston–New York–Washington metroplex that we consider only the way we live when we make policy for everybody?

Although it should be apparent that I very much disagree with those who focus exclusively on the aggregate economic experience, the aggregate experience, quite frankly, should nonetheless frighten lots of people. A major economic transformation is taking place, and some communities are not paying attention to it. There is a parallel between 1896 and 1996, between *Plessy* v. *Ferguson* (which affirmed the constitutionality of the separate-but-equal doctrine) and California's Proposition 209. People talk about the political similarities between these dates, but we also need to talk about the economic similarities. The late nineteenth century was a period of industrial concentration in which robber barons consolidated economic power. The late twentieth century is proving to be the same thing, a period in which wealth is becoming more concentrated and falling into a very few hands. When an executive gets a severance package of $130 million (excuse me, but please!), questions about the meaning of work and worth should be raised. The same reports that announced the lowest unemployment rate in a decade also indicated that factory wages were down by fifty cents an hour. Although we have a "tighter labor market," workers do not have more money. In fact, workers are scared to ask for more money. This is the nature of the current economic conundrum. We have a president and a Congress that will celebrate six years of economic transformation that does not mean a whole lot to individuals. In the African American community, especially, there are questions about whether we can look at the current economic situation with jubilation.

If this is as good as it gets, what are we accepting? One, we are accepting economic gender gaps. We are accepting that women earn 70 percent of what men earn. Two, we are accepting economic racial gaps. We are accepting the fact that African Americans earn about 60 percent of what whites earn. Three, we are accepting welfare reform. We are accepting the idea that as many as five million people will enter the labor market sometime in the next two years. As they enter the labor market, they will have no protection. They are told that if they cannot find work, they simply will not have a social safety net. Two years and it is up or out. You get a better deal than that as a professor at a bad university. First they tell you that you are not going to get tenure. Then they tell you that you are *really* not going to get tenure.

Finally, they tell you that you have a year or so to find a job, but they will keep paying you. Why isn't this the kind of deal we cut for welfare recipients? Of course I am being flippant, but only slightly.

All of this welfare reform forgets a number of things. Not all people on public assistance are black: 38 percent are black; 40 percent are white; the remainder are Latino, Asian, or other. Most of these people have worked or had a job sometime in the last two years. The reason they are not employed is that something did not work out with their jobs (the transportation route changed or a kid fell from a swing, and they are back on assistance) or the job did not pay enough. We raised the minimum wage in a two-step process in 1996 from $4.35 to $5.15. At $5.15 an hour a woman—and I say a woman because 70 percent of those who earn the minimum wage are women and half of them are black or brown—will earn $10,000 a year. A woman who is responsible for one or two children who earns $10,000 a year is, quite frankly, extremely vulnerable.

The case I want to make is that the current economy is not okay. It is okay only for the people at the top who are benefiting from the growth in the stock market. Those people are a minority of all American people. Stocks are being traded on Wall Street, and investors are posting increased profits. The increases reflect a return to slavery wherein African American labor can be plainly and simply exploited. This relates to the breadth or magnitude of the current economic expansion. We would talk about these things if we thought the economy was in trouble, but because we think it is sound, we accept them as necessary conditions for maintaining our economic soundness.

The Fortune 500 companies employ the same percentage of the labor force as are engaged in temporary and part-time work—10 percent. Economic growth in the future is going to come from small and medium-sized businesses. When you see a Commerce Department excursion, you see several CEOs, but you do not see the heads of NANBO (the National Association of Women Business Owners), the Chamber of Commerce, or the NBA (the National Black Association). People who represent small and medium-sized businesses are not brought to the fore, because we have essentially bought into the notion that big businesses and large bureaucracies are models for economic success. Now, we know that is not the case, but are we prepared to change things?

When we buy into the notion that economic growth is a solution to contemporary problems, we are accepting a whole range of outcomes that we simply should not accept. In accepting that notion we are saying, "This is as good as it gets."

We have made a deal with ourselves that we do not want to talk about economic differences. For example, the Federal Reserve Board does not want to collect data on mortgage discrimination anymore. Why? Because the data is divisive? The data is the truth. The problem is not that we are collecting data that *shows* that something is wrong. The problem is that something *is* wrong. (Need I mention that the Federal Reserve Board does not have an African American, a Latino, a Native American, or an Asian American on it, although white women have been added to the board and thank goodness for that.)

In fact, we have a trifurcated economy consisting of Wall Street, Main Street, and the Side Street, or three different groups of people whose lives hardly ever seem to intersect. On Wall Street, we see the people who are benefiting from increased stock prices, the people who are celebrating the fact that the Dow Jones industrial average has been over 8000. I do not begrudge them the fruits of their investments; I only wish that they paid taxes on them. They represent at most 20 percent of the population.

On Main Street, we see the lines blurring between those who were once solidly in what we call the middle class and those who were considered a step below. These are the folks whose families make between $30,000 and $50,000 a year. They own homes. Many of them are middle-class because wives work. In the African American community, more than 45 percent of middle-class homes sustain their middle-class status *only* because there are two wage earners. This is not necessarily true for whites. Even white middle-class folks feel insecure and under siege. If they live in cities, they are paying tuition because they do not have any confidence in the public schools. If they do not live in cities, they are paying for other services. Many of them worry about what is happening to job security, a major issue for most Americans. These people at least see their lives validated by our politicians who talk about the middle class and how besieged it is.

But what about the poor? These are the invisible Americans. Among African Americans, they make up 30 percent of the population. Among whites, they represent about 15 percent. More than one-fourth of all American children live in poverty. They are on the Side Street. I call it that because we do not pay attention to these folks. They do not show up in our conversations about public policy. Less and less attention is being paid to the lives of many African American people on the Side Street; people who are productive in their communities and who have sustained the children who have gone on to higher education are being discounted in policy arenas.

We really need to demystify poverty and demonstrate that it is a failure of the system and not a failure of individuals. We need to talk about it and deconstruct these lies. People who aspire to grab public attention can do an awful lot to show what it means to be poor—that it does not mean that one is morally lax or somehow deficient; that what it means is that you just "don't have no money." That is what poverty is: "you don't have no money." It is not a magical, mystical state of being, as if somebody threw some magic dust on you and you became a lowlife. We have to keep talking about that, placing that idea out there.

People in policy discuss poverty only in terms of public assistance. There are other ways to approach poverty. We have a large number of people who could be defined as working poor. There are thousands, if not hundreds of thousands, of people who are homeless but work a full day. Ten percent of our labor force works at temporary or part-time jobs. To better serve these folks, we first need to talk about fair pay for fair work.

To the extent that a lot of people feel that poverty means having your hand out, we must begin to focus on those who really have a hand out. There is something called corporate welfare. A whole lot of people who get money from the government have not done anything to earn it. They need to be unmasked. We may well want to support national parks. I do not have a problem with that; I'm a California girl. But just as I want to support national parks, I also want to support people who do not have jobs. I do not see these things as different. There are people who say that they want to give money to national parks, but not to poor people. There are people who say that they want to give money to unemployed Lockheed engineers, but not to poor people. We must begin to take back those images in really, really clear ways, to make the concept of poverty one that is human, rather than inhuman and inaccessible.

Unfortunately, such inequality also raises questions about the role of government: Do we need an activist government or a passive government? What does government do for us? There is a widespread notion that the role of government should be reduced or shrunk. People have made the case that government distorts economic outcomes. There is just nobody who does PR (public relations) for government. Do you ride on roads? Government paid for that. Do you get your mail? Government paid for that. There are so many positive things that government does. I am not an advocate of big, big government, but I certainly think that government can alleviate the effects of predatory capitalism. Government can help with issues of distribution, and this is something that has been ignored. People who understand this have been silent or have said, "We don't want to talk about that."

Having laid out the economic landscape, I want to talk about solutions. What do we do given where we are now, at the cusp of industrial transformation? What can African Americans and others do to make sure that people are empowered? Let me start with two words: Circuit City. Not too long ago, a federal judge decided that Circuit City had been guilty of race-biased employment discrimination. He handed down one of the most comprehensive court orders against a discriminating company that we have ever seen. He said that Circuit City had to report to the court on all promotions made during the next five years. He said that it had to hire a director of diversity management to monitor compliance with the court's orders. He said that he did not trust Circuit City to be nondiscriminatory. He also suggested that the company was in deep denial. This is a judge sitting in the Fourth Circuit in Richmond, Virginia, the same circuit that produced the anti-set-aside decision *Croson* v. *Richmond*, in other words, one of the anti–affirmative action circuits.

This case is interesting because it raises questions about how we use our economic power. African American people have significant purchasing power, roughly $350 billion. It may not be what we are entitled to, but it represents an internal point in a production possibility curve. More efficiently used, that money could put us at the edge of a production possibility curve, generating more jobs and more opportunities. If we had our share, that curve could be pushed out. What do we do with concerns like Circuit City that discriminate? Do we work with them? Do we boycott them? People who believe that racial economic justice is important should also believe that we should not buy from people who discriminate, especially those who gleefully discriminate. That is point number one. Number two: even as we stop buying, we should also inquire about who manufactures and distributes the products and how we can create distribution processes inside the African American community. This is not just about African American people. African American economic viability serves America well. Targeted boycotts are something African Americans can do in concert with progressive white allies and with other people of color.

We have had boycotts that were successful and boycotts that

were less successful. Getting the word out there is crucial. With the Internet and other media, we are in a position fairly different from the one we have been in historically. The question, quite frankly, is whether or not we can build support for boycotts beyond the African American community, We represent 35 million people. If we want to bring Circuit City to its knees, we may need 100 million people. We are going to need significant numbers of equally outraged white people. We will kill racism when there are white people who feel as strongly about it as black people do and are willing to be as highly agitated and motivated as we are.

As for myself, I advocate the formation of a Boycott of the Month Club. Put the names of the Fortune 500 companies in a little bag and pull out a different one every month. Boycott each for a month. Why? Because we feel like it. Why? Because we want to. Yes, it is random. No, it is not fair. That's life. Discrimination is random, it is not fair, and there is not much else that we can do about it. It is called taking the matter into our own hands, putting it under our own control. It begins to make a point about the potential for black economic development.

In February of 1997, Kweisi Mfume released the results of a corporate reciprocity program undertaken by the NAACP. In a survey of sixteen major hotel chains, eight refused to answer a questionnaire about their relationship with the African American community. In light of that, the Boycott of the Month Club is not a bad idea. Heck, it beats revolution. It would say that we are willing to target our dollars. Indeed, there is a disproportionate African American patronage of certain goods and services. We are roughly 12 percent of the population, but we buy 40 percent of the Johnny Walker Red. Imagine what would happen if, just for one month, we decided that Johnny Walker could be black.

I am also a fan of entrepreneurial education for several reasons, even though I recognize the shortcomings of dealing with petty capitalism in the long run. If we look back at black economic history, Abram Lincoln Harris, who got his Ph.D. from Columbia in 1931, criticized the "Don't Buy Where You Can't Work" movement. Harris said that "Don't Buy Where You Can't Work" could not, in the long run, sustain itself, but he also said that, in the short run, it could make a point. As we contemplate shutting down large companies with our boycotts, it is clear that people of color will have to create their own employment opportunities through entrepreneurship. The people who will be able to weigh in on this are those who can tap into infrastructures that support entrepreneurial development.

When we talk about economic transformation in the African American community, we have to talk about the sense of community, the extent to which many of us do not see community, and ways to develop those spaces that "once upon a time" were communities. It is very difficult for people who have been peripheralized to suddenly decide to take economic control, because we live in an era of self-sufficiency, not collective sufficiency. We live in an era when people feel extremely and extraordinarily threatened, when even white men are saying, "It used to be better for me than it is now. So what am I going to do? Protect my own interest or look at the collective interest?"

There is an attitude held especially by younger African Americans that "I made it on my own, so I don't necessarily owe anything to some collective group." To the extent that this attitude prevails, you would not expect sports figures to say, "I've got $105 million, and I'm down for a million for this capital development fund, which represents essentially 1 percent of my earnings over the next seven years." You just do not expect to see that happen.

I would not put the weight only on sports figures. Issues of trust exist among older middle-class blacks. I wrote an article in *Emerge* in 1992 entitled "Power 2000," in which I talked about creating a capital development fund I called the Kumba Fund. I got two responses that really stood out. One came from a woman in South Carolina who thought that my idea was brilliant and wanted to buy into it; she enclosed a check for $1,000 made out to the Kumba Fund. Of course, I had to write her back and say, "Dear Sister, thank you, but the fund doesn't really exist." I also received legal papers from some man who said I had stolen his idea and should cease and desist from using it forthwith. These responses pretty much typify why it might be difficult for African Americans to come together. Many of us are caught somewhere between hope and suspicion. We all gain when people look toward the collective interest, but obviously I have a self-interest in making that suggestion.

The black middle class should be held to the same standard to which white capitalists are held. Whom do they hire? Whom do they promote? Where are the benefits? This is one of our contradictions. Consider the historical development of the black middle class. The cohort that arose after the Civil War basically depended on the community and so had to respond to it directly. In subsequent eras, elements of the black middle class strayed farther and farther away from the community, but we can apply the same kind of controls or sanctions against a remote or distant black middle class that we apply against anybody else. The African American community should not spend enormous political capital getting one job for one black person, especially if that one black person is not going to do anything for the community. There are exceptional instances in which we rally around an individual and a position because we feel that there will be a trickle-down benefit. It is very much like getting political accountability from an elected official. Voting is not the most we can do; it is the least we can do. Agitation around one position for one person is not the most we can do for her or him; it is the least we can do for them. The most we can do is stay in her or his face every week and ask, "What have you done for me lately?" And if we are incapable and unwilling to do that, then we get what we get.

There were hopes that the reelection of Bill Clinton and the appointment of blacks in high places would lead to improvement in the situation of African Americans, particularly with regard to economic outcomes, but little consideration was given to the structural impediments. Without second-guessing the ancestors, I want to suggest that the strategic decision we made to pursue *Brown* v. *Board of Education* and educational integration, as opposed to concentrating on a number of economic issues present at that time, may well have been a mistake. It was assumed that if we achieved educational equity, economic equity would follow. We know now, forty years later, that that simply is not the case. Given the representation of African Americans among state legislators in a number of places, as well as the Congressional Black Caucus and sizable majorities in some city councils, there ought to be ways to utilize set-asides to provide an economic leg up, but they might not be judicially defensible in an anti–affir-mative action era. Having used politics up to this point, we must now ask, How do we transform political gains into economic empowerment? Do we have any hope that this administration will adopt an urban policy? I don't think so. Is there anything we can do to make an urban policy happen?

I do not know a lot about New York, though I know a little more than I pretend. I know a fair amount about DC. I know about boarded-up buildings in downtown areas. I know that there are ways that private corporations, collectives, and others could, perhaps, reclaim some of those spaces and buildings. Some of the problems of homelessness could be solved if people were willing to simply take back some of that space. It would take a lot of work, but there are a lot of people willing to work. A little bit of government money, or foundation money, or private sector money could be used to transform neighborhoods and commu-nities.

There are some issues that we can definitely handle without government, and some issues on which we need to take govern-ment to task. I wish Bill Clinton would find someplace to worship other than the black church. Whenever the man gets into big trouble, he goes to the 'hood and sits in a black church. He starts singing and swaying. They have three kinds of fans in the black church: the Martin Luther King fan, the angel fan, and the Madonna and child fan. Guess which fan Clinton gets? The Mar-tin Luther King fan. He stands by the camera with a Martin Luther King fan and holds it up. My grandmother watches him and says, "Oh, Bill Clinton; he's cool. He's got a Martin Luther King fan." He waves the fan. And he sways. And he sings. And he sways. And he sings. And he sways. Then he goes out into our community and eats. He starts off at Mrs. Jones's Rib Shack and makes his way down to the Florida Avenue Grill. We all know that it takes more than a walk through the 'hood to make you a homey and more than a genuflection at the black church to make you cool. The bottom line here is that, in terms of an urban policy, we have seen a great deal of genuflection but not a lot of action.

When people do good things for cities, they do good things for African Americans. Cities are blacker, browner, older, younger, and more female than the rest of America. When public policy is directed toward urban spaces, it is directed toward the people who sit at the margins. President Clinton has ignored these spaces partially because of his commitment to a balanced budget. This has meant that we do public policy via demonstration programs. Enterprise zones became the great American "pity party," in which cities wrote grant proposals making themselves out to be so pitiful, more pitiful than other cities, in justifying their need for more money. Cities should not have to compete with each other on the basis of poor demographics. Instead, we need to realize the aggregative or cumulative economic benefits that we get from having cities and urban development. If you live in New York, DC, or LA, you already know it. We city dwellers with positive energies contribute to the arts, to culture, and to society. There would be no subways without us. So many exciting things would disappear without us. For that reason, we need to look at the key role that cities play in American society and vitality. It is important when we talk about solutions to keep cities central in our thoughts, and to talk about ways we can deal with urban development.

Equally important is the issue of employment development. Welfare reform will erode existing public service jobs. Libraries were not closed during the Great Depression; we began to close them in 1986. We can provide jobs for people that serve a greater community, if we decide that we want to do that. We do not talk a lot about those Side Street jobs, about the fact that 45 percent of African American women hold jobs that pay less than $7.50 an hour. That is a frightening statistic. Comparable numbers are 38 percent for white women, 25 percent for black men, and 10 percent for white men. At $7.50 an hour, are people earning a living wage? Should the market really determine wages and thereby the terms and conditions of people's lives, especially given that we say we do not want any more dependency? If we do not want dependency, but want to pay low market wages, then we are essentially institutionalizing and criminalizing poverty, because if you are poor, there is something wrong with you, not with the economy. To the extent that we demonize poverty, we exclude a number of people from the mainstream of our society.

Welfare deform—I use the word "deform," not "reform"—has essentially placed women in a very precarious position. From a feminist perspective, the failure of white women to rally around people on public assistance is extremely problematic. In addition, that community college professors have not understood the extent to which their livelihood, in the face of dropping enrollments, is dependent on women on public assistance going to college is very shortsighted and frightening. I have no problem with people "working" for their welfare checks, but it seems to me that college attendance is a form of work. Should someone with three children be treated like someone with none? I would not impose a twenty-hour-per-week work requirement on a woman with three children in school who is going to school full-time herself. Those who take draconian positions on work for students on welfare fail to understand that these people have taken a first step that many others in their circumstances have not taken. They should be applauded, and not punished, for doing so.

As we talk about solutions, on some level and in some ways, we have to look beyond the domestic environment and at the international environment. We have to examine the extent to which we export poverty to other societies. When we decide that we will import products from China that are produced by people earning less than a dollar an hour, and grant their country most-favored-nation status (political contributions notwithstanding), we are deciding to make American workers who must earn the minimum wage compete with them. I am not suggesting that we close the doors to China or to Mexico, but I am suggesting that we look very carefully at the web of international relationships that we are creating. At the very minimum, we should under-stand that we have two choices in our country: we can raise world living standards by exporting those standards, or we can lower living standards—not only the world's but also our own—by deciding that it is acceptable for the products of exploited labor to enter this country.

Disgustingly, while we absorb the products from China, we have written off major parts of the world population. We have written off Africa. (Senator Mitch McConnell of Kentucky said that giving money to Africa is like throwing it down a black hole. What symbolism!) Latin America is rarely discussed in our inter-national conversations. Yet we know that significant populations exist in both places; as we talk about solutions, we have to talk about them. The North American Free Trade Agreement could and should be expanded to include the Caribbean basin. If we are prepared to give deals to people, they should be available to those in our hemisphere. More than that, we have to address our participation in a set of structural adjustment policies which have made developing countries extremely vulnerable. This includes countries in West Africa that essentially risked their environmental survival to pay back, at appreciated rates and unfair interest levels, loans that they entered into unwillingly.

Is this as good as it gets?

The status quo we see today is a very flawed. It seems fine macroeconomically, but beyond that lies a microeconomic deficiency that is best explored through the prism of Wall Street, Main Street, and the Side Street. A minority of Americans are doing very well, a majority are in precarious positions, and many are doing extremely poorly. When we disaggregate this by race, we find that the African Americans are more vulnerable, poorer, and less likely to be occupying a Wall Street position. As for solutions, we must think about concerted action that comes not only from the African American community but also from the population at large. Let's face it, this is not South Africa. African Americans are in the minority. We have to make strategic alliances with other people in order to have economic self-sufficiency. That is not impossible. If people find Circuit City as reprehensible as I do, they do not have to be black to boycott it. If people find Texaco as reprehensible as I do, they do not have to be black to boycott it. If people decide that they want fair wages from the people with whom they have strategic economic partnerships, that decision need not be based on race, but might simply be a matter of fairness.

America is ours as much as it is *theirs*. We have to be clear about that. What Du Bois said about two warring souls in one black body, about the duality of our African and American presence, is extremely important. We own this country as much as white people do. In fact, we built this country more than they did. We are not guests at the table called America. Not when we carved the table, polished it, put the food on it, and did everything else. From that perspective, you know we own this, and in owning it we decide how we press a claim and also how we make our mark. On the mall in Washington, we genuflect to the Vietnam Veterans, to Lincoln, to Washington. There needs to be a slave memorial on the mall. There needs to be a public thank-you to our ancestors for the fact that we built this country. It will clear their consciences. It, quite frankly, will lift our spirits. It will allow our young people to understand what our place in history is and that it is not inferior. Then we will not have to talk about whether to live in, for, or with America, but about the fact that there would be no America if it were not for African people.

The problem is that you cannot simply measure growth or well-being by increases in GNP, although this is what people are essentially attempting to do. I have tried to point out the many limitations of doing that. Unfortunately, those limitations are not universally recognized. Nothing is coming from Congress, the state legislatures, the United Nations, or any one of a number of other responsible bodies or entities that suggests that predatory capitalism is not the only way to measure well-being.

Whenever people talk about the good old days, I want to ask them, "Good for whom?" In 1940, some 70 percent of all black women were maids. Good for whom? In other words, is this as good as it gets? The economy is better than it was in the 1950s, but frankly it is simply not good enough.

Joycelyn Elders, M.D.

Dr. Joycelyn Elders is a woman of courage and determination who has used her extraordinary intelligence and initiative to become the nation's leading black public health advocate and educator. Ignoring taboos that are strong in our communities—taboos born of ignorance, misguided religious fervor, and fear—she has spoken out about and tackled problems that pertain to human sexuality, including teenage pregnancy, child abuse, AIDS, and other sexually transmitted diseases. The urgency and energy she brings to her roles as teacher and preacher for black public health demand that we grapple with problems we are reluctant even to discuss, though our very lives depend on it.

Dr. Elders's dedication, passion, and effectiveness are in part attributable to the fact she knows firsthand what it is to be black, female, and poor. Born Minnie Jones in Schall, Alabama, on August 13, 1933, the eldest of the eight children of the sharecroppers Haller and Curtis Jones, Dr. Elders attended Philander Smith College, in Little Rock, on a full scholarship. Her family took to the cotton fields before the harvest began in order to raise the five dollars required for her trip to Little Rock. She financed her medical education through the GI Bill by enlisting in the U.S. Army. After a three-year stint as a physical therapist in the military, she entered the University of Arkansas Medical School in 1956. On Valentine's Day 1960, she married Oliver Elders, then basketball coach of black Horace Mann High School. Upon graduation from medical school, Dr. Elders interned in pediatrics at the University of Minnesota and returned to the University of Arkansas as a pediatric resident and ultimately chief resident in pediatrics. She went on to become a researcher and professor in pediatric endocrinology and an expert on childhood sexual development and diabetes.

In 1987, the course of her professional life changed. She "found her calling." She became the head of the Arkansas Department of Health, a position she held for six years. As an outspoken public health advocate and tireless administrator, she worked to implement policies that would make a real difference in the lives of the poor, both black and white, of her home state and eventually the nation. In the face of stiff opposition from the radical right, the department undertook controversial programs aimed at preventing teenage pregnancy and creating school-based clinics. When Arkansas's Governor Bill Clinton was elected president, he asked Dr. Elders to become the surgeon general of the United States.

Her tenure as the nation's so-called First Doctor was short-lived. During her fifteen months in office, she continued to speak out about highly charged issues in ways that riled the radical right and ruffled members of the Clinton administration. In response to a question posed by a reporter after she made a speech at the National Press Club in Washington, D.C., she said that the crime rate might be lowered if drugs were legalized, but that the consequences had to be studied. Eight days later (and apparently not coincidentally), a warrant was issued for the arrest of her son on charges of selling cocaine, under circumstances that suggest entrapment. Finally, at a World AIDS Day conference at the UN, a psychiatrist asked her about masturbation in the context of an exchange about the necessity of breaking down barriers against discussing sex. Dr. Elders replied that she was a strong advocate of complete, age-appropriate comprehensive health education, and since masturbation was a part of human sexuality, it should perhaps be taught. She thought the statement was fairly innocuous. The secretary of health and human services and the president's chief of staff thought differently. The president asked for Dr. Elders's resignation, and she complied. She returned to the University of Arkansas and her position as a professor of pediatric endocrinology.

It is hard to understand the fuss that Dr. Elders can cause anytime she opens her mouth. She speaks with the pragmatism and rationality of a physician and medical researcher, the folk wisdom of a revered female elder (as her very name suggests), and the elegance of a black preacher. She tells the truth, in simple, straightforward language, and crusades on despite the consequences. She is a lifesaver. There is black genius in that.

REGINA AUSTIN

EDUCATING ON BEHALF OF
BLACK PUBLIC HEALTH

A System Delivering More Sick Care
Than Health Care

Our society is sick. We know that it is sick. It has been sick for a long time, and it should not be sick. It should not be sick, because we have the technology, the resources, and the know-how, yet we lag behind many industrialized countries in terms of health. We have the best sick-care system in the world; you just have to be sick enough to get into it. The sicker you are, the better we doctor. The problem is we do not have a *health care* system. The United States is one of only two industrialized nations that do not have universal access to health care for all of their citizens. South Africa is the other, and it is working very hard to provide health care for all its people.

We have seen many changes take place in our health care system as we prepare to go into the twenty-first century. We have seen advances in medical technology. We have seen advances in biosynthetic hormone research. When I started doctoring, we used to get growth hormone from human pituitaries. Now it can be made biosynthetically, which is wonderful. We have lasers so powerful that we can read a license plate in Japan. Right in our own living rooms, we watched a war being fought in the Persian Gulf as it was happening.

Yet, our society is not able to prevent the consequences of tobacco smoking, to prevent teenage pregnancy, to immunize or even to feed all the children, or to prevent premature birth and premature mortality. Furthermore, we are still unable to prevent the spread of HIV disease or AIDS. We watched AIDS start out as a white gay male disease, and then spread from our two coasts to throughout our country. We watched it evolve from being a political football to being a disease. (For a while, it was not even allowed to be a disease.) We watched it when it was a fatal infection. Today AIDS has become for some a chronic disease that we are teaching people to live with, rather than to die from, which is a good thing. Yet, now we are watching it move through minority communities, among heterosexuals and particularly among black women. While African Americans make up 14 percent of our population, 59 percent of the women wih HIV disease are black.

We have seen the cost of our health care system (or our sick-care system) go from 5.1 percent of our gross domestic product in 1960 to 14 percent in 1994. If the pattern continues, costs are projected to reach 19 percent by the year 2000. With expenditures of more than a trillion dollars, we spend more on health care than any other country, yet we do not have the best statistics when it comes to health. Even with regard to our best-off, our white women, we rank behind other industrialized countries.

The statistics concerning African Americans are staggering. I often say that if you take any negative statistic that you want and multiply it by two, you will come close to what the figure is for black Americans. Take infant mortality. In 1993, the infant mortality rate was 16.5 percent for black babies and 6.8 percent for white babies. The life expectancy of a black male child born in 1994 was 64.9 years, while that of a white male was 73.2 years; of a black female, 74.1 years; and of a white female, 79.6 years. When we consider some of the diseases that afflict Americans, we also see a wide variation by race. Blacks with cancer are thirty times more likely to die than whites with cancer. The black cancer rate is not higher; blacks just get into treatment later, and when they get into treatment, they may not get all of the services that others tend to get, or they may not know to ask for or demand the services they need.

When we consider our young black men, we find that their rate of death from homicide since 1985 has increased 39.5 percent. We are losing a very valuable part of our human resources. We know that unemployment is three times higher among black males than among white males. Blacks are twice as likely not to have insurance as whites. When we look at our young black women, we find that we are very often losing them to poverty, ignorance, and enslavement because of our failure to educate and our failure to get involved. "Well, Dr. Elders, what does that have to do with health?" I am asked. Health is more than the absence of disease. Health is about jobs and employment, education, the environment, and all of those things that go into making us healthy.

Finally, consider the fact that blacks seek health care from our black health care professionals. Of 261 million Americans, approximately 32–34 million are black or African American. But look at our representation in the health care professions. Blacks constitute only 3 percent of doctors, 5 percent of pharmacists, 4 percent of nurses, and 4 percent of dentists. That tells me that something is wrong and that we have got to do something about it.

We have a multiheaded dragon in our midst that for too long has been waging a domestic war on our young, our poor, our elderly, and our underserved. The faces of this dragon sometimes manifest themselves as poverty, the source of the most pervasive health problem we have in America. Sometimes they manifest themselves as diseases such as AIDS, sometimes as violence, and sometimes as racism, sexism, and classism. For too long our "isms" have pushed our young, our poor, and our minorities to the back of the social justice bus. I think it is time for us to ask the question "Do we feel that every American should have a right to health care?" In our society, we feel that every criminal has a right to a lawyer. Shouldn't we feel that every sick person has a right to a doctor?

If I Had It to Do All Over Again

Most of you know that I was your surgeon general, and I want to tell you that I loved being your surgeon general. I did the very best job that I knew how to do. I also want you to know that if I had it to do all over again, starting in the morning, I would do it exactly the same way. I feel I did it right the first time. I felt that the issues I was talking about were the issues that we need to talk about. They are issues that our community is facing every day. I was out there saying that we need to have health education as part of our school program. Let's educate young people about how to be healthy. Of course, that was misinterpreted, and it was said that I wanted to teach young people how to have sex. Well, we all know that nobody ever needs to teach anybody about how to have sex. God taught us how, so we do not need to be taught *how*; but we do need to be teaching young people how to be responsible, rather than sitting around trying to legislate their morals. That was what I was about.

When I was out there saying I wanted to prevent unplanned, unwanted pregnancies, of course, that was interpreted that I wanted women to have abortions. Well, you know, I tell people all the time I am not about promoting abortions. I have never been about abortions. I am about preventing unplanned, unwanted pregnancies. If you prevent unplanned, unwanted pregnancies, there is never a need for an abortion. I have never known any woman to need an abortion if she was not already pregnant. We need to deal with the real issues, rather than all of those side issues.

We get involved with all this blue smoke and mirrors. People out there talking about abortion do not have to deal with the problem of access to health care, for example. Let me talk about Arkansas and the South because I do not know about every place else. People in the South fought so hard, absolutely fought against desegregation and integration. They invoked all of these Bible verses that supposedly said that integration of the races was wrong and that children of different races should not go to school together. Well, these are the same people who are now fighting so hard and talking about the right to life. Think about whom they are fighting and whom they are hurting. Women who have had abortions for the most part are women who can afford them. If you have the green, you can get an abortion whenever you please. The only people the antiabortion forces really hurt are the young, the poor, and the ignorant. These abortion opponents say they want to help the little babies, but they do not want them to get welfare, they do not want them to get health care, and they do not want them to get any early childhood education. They want to make sure the babies endure and perpetuate another cycle of poverty, ignorance, and enslavement.

We have to step back and ask what the real issues are, what do we really need to be talking about. I have come to understand that the best way to reform welfare is to prevent the need for welfare. I have never known anybody you could pay to be poor, so let's be real. We need to be certain that we actually understand and know what is going on. Look at prison construction. We have built more prisons in the past ten years than schools. Can you believe that? The average cost of keeping one inmate in prison for one year is $35,000. I bet a prisoner could go to NYU for less than what we pay to send him or her to the penitentiary. We hear all this talk about family values. Let's talk about family values. If one genuinely believed in family values, one would support those institutions that support families, like those that assure secure jobs, safe schools, safe communities, and safe families. I think those are the things that we have to begin to speak about.

Most of you know that I once mentioned that I felt that we should study the legalization of drugs. I said *study* it! We spend

$17 billion a year on a "war on drugs" that is failing. We need to know what we are doing. Of course, the administration said that it was not going to study the matter, and it rained all over me. But, as far as I am concerned, we need to know how to approach drugs. I did not say *legalize* drugs, but if that is an option, if we can do better to help our people by legalizing drugs, then as far as I am concerned, we should do what makes good sense and what makes for good public health. I essentially said let us look at all the options. Other countries are looking at other options. Our present policies have made Uncle Sam the world's biggest jailer. We have gone from fewer than 2,000 people in prisons or jails in 1970 to 1.5 million people by 1996. Sixty percent of all incarcerations are related to drugs, and you know who the incarcerated are. Young black men are fourteen times more likely to be incarcerated than any other group. We send whites to treatment programs and blacks to prison.

We have got to look for things we need to do to make a difference and stand up and fight for them. I know that we have had a lot of problems and a lot of adversity and diversity, but we cannot let that prevent us from healing, organizing, and moving forward. My brother tells me, "You've got fifteen to twenty years of schooling, and our mom only finished the eighth grade, but our mother sometimes uses a lot more sense than you do." Indeed, some of the things that my mom told me really helped me to survive. That is what parents give you, the Bible skills. There are four proverbs or sayings that my mom gave me that really helped when things got tough. The first thing she told me was "If you want to get out of the cotton patch, you've got to get something in your head." She meant you have got to get an education. Most people have never picked or chopped cotton, so you probably do not know anything about that, but I can tell you the prospect of working in the cotton fields was a real inducement to getting an education. Another thing that my mom told us was "You have to recognize the truth and speak out. The day you see the truth and cease to speak out is the day you begin to die." You can tell I am going to live a long time, because I am always speaking out. My mom also told us, "Always do your best; that's good enough." I rely on that one a lot. The fourth and final thing she said was "Don't ever throw away your tomorrows worrying about yesterday." When I got kicked out of public office, I had to say that to myself many times in order to be able to survive the ordeal.

I have thought about what I said many, many times since leaving the position of surgeon general, I want you to know that if I held the same job and were asked the very same question about masturbation that led to my departure in the same way today, I would give the same answer. I thought I gave a smart answer. I thought I gave a correct and proper answer to a question asked by a physician, of a physician. Nobody has ever had to teach children how to masturbate. Ninety percent of men say they masturbate, 80 percent of women say they masturbate, and the rest lie. We need to stop lying to children. We need to stop telling them that hair will grow on their hands if they masturbate, or that they will go crazy, or that they will go blind. We really need to begin to be honest and tell the truth. That is among the things I was fighting about. Dealing with and talking about the facts has never given anybody AIDS, and it has never gotten anybody pregnant. It is not all bad.

The Health Status of the Least-Well-Off among Us

We are facing many problems as we move into the twenty-first century, especially in terms of health and very especially in terms of minority health. If we fix health care for everybody and make it accessible to all people, we will have made health care accessible to the least of them.

Fifty percent of the causes of premature death are social and behavioral problems, like drug usage, risky sexual behavior, and alcohol consumption. Twenty percent are environmental, 20 percent are genetic, and only 10 percent are related to access to health care. Consider how our life expectancies have been extended by thirty years since 1900. Just think, every year our life expectancy increases one month. Every week it increases seven hours, and every day it increases fifteen minutes. If one gets past the age of fifty—that is, if one gets past the early years of life— then one will very likely live to a very ripe old age. Doctoring and all of our fancy technology have increased life expectancy only eleven years. The rest of the increase is attributable to the things you do for yourself, like maintaining good nutrition, not smoking, not drinking, not driving while drunk, not engaging in high-risk sexual behavior—in other words, avoiding the activities that relate to and cause premature death.

Much of the increase in life expectancy is related to things that we take for granted, like clean drinking water, putting screens on windows, and immunization. Immunizations, for example, have probably saved more children than anything we have ever done. Certainly there are side effects, but their incidence is very low. If we could get 90 percent or more of the population immunized, enough to get herd immunity, we would not have any problem. But if we allow parents to just decide indiscriminately who is going to be immunized, the percentages could drastically change, and we would start seeing cases of polio, measles, and whooping cough. There is no question but that, if parents will not immunize children when they are babies, they will have to be immunized before they go to school. It would be much better if children were immunized on time. In some cases, children are not even allowed into day care unless they have been immunized.

We have to deal with the problem of poverty, especially as it regards our children. Thirty percent of the minority population is poor. If we look at children in general, we find that in 1970 one child in seven was poor; in 1990 it was one in five; and in 1992 it was one in four. If you look at minority children, the rate is one in two; 49 percent of minority children under six years of age are below the federal poverty line.

Children who are poor will be members of only one club in their lives. We call it the 5-H Club. 5-H children are hungry every night, though they live in the richest country in the world. Between 3 and 5 million American children go to bed hungry. 5-H children are healthless. Out of 261 million Americans, 43 million have no health insurance. Roughly 58 million people have no health insurance sometime during the year. Moreover, 133 million Americans have insurance with significant caps on coverage. That means that when their medical bills reach a certain amount, usually when they have contracted a bad disease and need health insurance the most, they lack sufficient coverage. Moreover, most of our health insurance is related to our jobs.

When we get sick and lose our jobs, we often lose our health insurance. We have children who are homeless. When mothers are homeless, children are homeless. We have children who are hugless. We have children who find it easier to get drugs than hugs. We have children who are hopeless. When hope dies, moral decay cannot be far behind. So there you have it: hungry, health-less, homeless, hugless, and hopeless children. The members of the 5-H Club.

We, of course, have a tobacco industry that attacks our young every day. It daily recruits 3,000 young people to start smoking. According to Centers for Disease Control statistics, the overall rate of teenage smoking in 1995 was 34.5 percent. In a departure from the usual pattern, the rate of adolescent smoking is lower among blacks than among whites: 19.2 percent to 38.3 percent. (The rate for Hispanic youth, however, is 34 percent.) Smoking among young black males has increased (to 28 percent), though it is below the rate for whites and Hispanics. We do not really know why black adolescents smoke less. When I suggested that they don't have the money to buy cigarettes, I was told, "Dr. Elders, they've got money to buy everything else. Why don't they have the money to buy cigarettes?" We know that 90 percent of the people who smoke started before the age of nineteen, so if we can keep teens from smoking before they reach the age of nine-teen, they will probably never smoke. We need to keep going whatever is working for black kids.

A major source of poverty, ignorance, and enslavement in our society is children becoming parents before they become adults. If we can get our arms around that problem, we can begin to deal with some of the other issues influencing health. More than one million teenagers become pregnant every year. Black teenagers are twice as likely as white teenagers to have a pregnancy before the age of twenty. But what many of us never talk about is that 84 percent of teenagers under fourteen who become pregnant were made pregnant by somebody in their own home. Eighty-four percent! That to me is a real problem. Seventy percent of the teenagers who become pregnant were abused at sometime in their life, and 70 percent of their abusers were adult men. I tried to get a law passed in Arkansas that would have required that any girl aged 14 or under who became pregnant be evaluated for possible sexual abuse. I did not say that these children had in fact been abused. I simply said that the matter should be evaluated or looked into. "Dr. Elders, what if she's lying?" How much lying can a girl fourteen and pregnant do? We know that there is a real possibility of statutory rape in such situations.

We are not talking about children having sex with children today. The Alan Guttmacher Institute, which has done wonderful research, tells us that more than 70 percent of the children born to teenagers are fathered by adult men, not teens, yet we do not make much of that. On the other hand, there was a story in the newspaper a while ago that really disturbed me. An eighteen-year-old man in Milwaukee got his fifteen-year-old girlfriend pregnant. He quit school to go to work in order to take care of his child, and the authorities wanted to prosecute him and send him to prison for forty years. Can you imagine? An eighteen-year-old and a fifteen-year-old. We want to punish children who are trying to be responsible. Yet, we do nothing about the abuse of adult men that results in the majority of teen pregnancies that we see going on out there in our society.

We spend more than $30 billion a year for public assistance, food stamps, and Medicaid for children born to children. Still, we do not want to spend $200 million for family planning for all the poor women in America. Roughly half of all pregnancies in the U.S. each year are unintended. We have the highest teenage pregnancy rate in the industrialized world—twice as high as England's and Canada's; ten times as high as Japan's. A single act of unprotected sex carries a 1 percent risk of HIV, a 30 percent risk of genital herpes, and a 50 percent risk of gonorrhea. That to me is a real problem.

Strategies That Might Make a Difference

So, what are some of the strategies that we must pursue if we are really going to make a difference? I think that we have to strengthen our personal health care system. The system we have now is not coherent, is not comprehensive, and is not cost-effective. It costs too much and delivers too little. We do not have choice; we only think we have choice. When employers pick the doctors they are going to use, we have to pick from what they've picked. The system is not equitable. It may be equitable if you have enough money to pay for it, but if you do not have the money, you have to go where you can. The system is certainly not universal.

We have to strengthen our public health system if we want to save our society. We have to deal with the three P's—poverty, population, and pollution. We are not doing very well with any one of them. We've got to make every child born in America a planned and wanted child. We know how, we have the resources, and we must make the commitment to get it done.

Nothing saves more money than keeping people healthy. One low-birth-weight baby can cost more than health education for an entire school system. We still prefer to keep people in prison, care for people after they contract AIDS, nurture low-birth-weight babies after they are born, and treat measles in children after they get the measles, rather than prevent any of this. We have to start thinking prevention. We have too much intervention.

I have often accused our churches of not doing the things they need to do. They have been moralizing from the pulpit and preaching to the choir. When I was state public health director, I did a lot of work with churches (though when I was in Washington I was called an atheist). The ministers said of the reforms I advocated, "Dr. Elders, it's just morally wrong." When they wanted to talk about what is morally wrong, I reminded them that it is morally wrong for children to be hungry, morally wrong for children to be cold, and morally wrong for children to be abused. The ministers saw what is happening in our society and never said anything about it. We take these hard lines with regard to some issues and say nothing about what is going on over here that is or ought to be equally disturbing. It is time for the churches to get out into the streets, get involved, and begin to make a real difference. They have the power, the prestige, and the position, and they need to use these to begin to make a difference, especially in our black communities.

We have got to educate, educate, educate. We've been making smart bombs, while Japan was making smart children. We have young people graduating from high school with shoes that light up when they walk and brains that go dead when they talk. We cannot keep a person healthy, if she or he is not educated. We've got to start early. We've been doing too little too late. Only 18 percent of poor children—those on Medicaid, the poorest of the poor—ever have any early childhood education. Eighteen percent! Almost 80 percent of other children, the nonpoor, get early childhood education. The nonpoor children don't have to go to Ms. Janes's Schoolhouse. They could get it right there at home. We've also got to have comprehensive health education in our schools from grades K through 12.

We have to educate parents. Parents are doing the best they can; they do not know any better. We have a lot of dysfunctional families. We have to teach those families how to be healthy. Just because the parents are ignorant does not mean that we must commit their children to the same fate. As a function of community life, we need to make a difference. We have to make services available to people wherever they are. Schools are a wonderful place. We have 50 million children in school every day. Why can't we take the services to where the children are? We have to offer all of our young people hope, hope for the future, if we are going to make a difference in our society.

So what is your role? What is your role as a black leader or as a white leader or as somebody who wants to make a difference for the twenty-first century? What should you be about? How can you make a difference? I think we all have to decide whether we want our society to fly up and soar with the eagles or whether we are going to continue to crawl with the snakes. We have to have leaders who are willing to lead. We have an awful lot of leaders who take a poll, find out which way the wind is blowing, and jump out in front. We have to begin to be real leaders, leaders who can make a difference in our society. We have to recognize the source of our power. You know, too many of our young black men carry their power in their pockets in the form of a weapon, as opposed to an education in their heads.

We have to educate, educate, educate. We've got to educate our communities, educate our schools, educate our teachers, educate everybody, so we can begin to do the things we must do to educate our politicians. I tell you they are educable, but they are slow learners. Just keep working on them. We've got to become aware of the problems, become advocates for solutions, and develop an action plan that is right for our country and right for our world.

We've got to make health services available, accessible, and affordable. Once we do what is right, all of our people will be able to get on board. You know, some of us could go out there and swim across the river, but many of us need a bridge to get across. We need to make sure that all of us will be able to get across. We've got to be dedicated to programs that support prevention, rather than just intervention. We have to empower people, and we empower people through education.

Accepting Responsibility

We each have to reach out and be responsible. I'm going to be responsible, if nobody is responsible but me. Sometimes it is a lonely road. When you try to make changes, always remember that it is difficult. The most dreaded "C" word in the English language is "change."

When I went to Washington, I was trying to make changes. People said, "Dr. Elders, the time is not right." "The people are not right." "The place is not right." "The money is not right." And, of course, you know what they finally said. They finally said, "Dr. Elders, you're not right." We have to keep going in spite of that; just because "they say" does not always mean that you are wrong. Always remember that one person with courage makes a majority. We have to be successful. We cannot afford to fail. The lives of our most valuable resource, our bright young people, are at stake. A society grows great when old men plant trees under whose shade they know they will never sit.

One of the things I held on to when I was being criticized so much was something my bishop said. He said, "Dr. Elders, always remember that the work you're doing is like dancing with a bear. When you're dancing with a bear, you can't get tired and sit down. You've got to wait until the bear gets tired, and then you can sit down." I am always out there trying to get some new partners to help me dance with that old bear, so I can sit down.

Angela Davis

Angela Y. Davis, teacher, writer, scholar, organizer, and activist, has been an inspiration to participants engaged in liberation struggles throughout the world. As a young woman, she stood up to injustice in America and prevailed. Her very image at the time—tall, elegant, proud and defiant, serious and intelligent—still arouses our spirits. For almost thirty years since, she has remained a staunch advocate of black equality and a champion of the socially excluded and the maligned.

Angela Davis first came to national attention in 1969 when she was removed from her teaching position in the Department of Philosophy at UCLA because of her activism and membership in the Communist Party, USA. She fought the dismissal and was reinstated. Her involvement with the imprisoned Soledad Brothers, W. L. Nolan and George Jackson, and George's brother Jonathan, led to her being placed on the FBI's Ten Most Wanted List. After two months under-

ground, she was arrested and spent sixteen months in jail. A massive international "Free Angela Davis" campaign led to her release on bail. She was ultimately acquitted of all charges. Her defense committee became the National Alliance Against Racism and Political Repression, which continues its work today.

Former California Governor Ronald Reagan once vowed that Angela Davis would never again teach in the University of California system. Time has proven him wrong. Angela Davis is currently a professor in the History of Consciousness program at UC Santa Cruz and was recently awarded a University of California Presidential Chair in African American and Feminist Studies. Professor Davis has lectured throughout the world. She is the author of numerous articles and six books, including Angela Davis: An Autobiography, Women, Race & Class, *and, most recently,* Blues Legacies and Black Feminism: Gertrude "Ma" Rainey, Bessie Smith, and Billie Holiday.

Angela Davis has been in the vanguard of activists working on the significant social issues of our time. At present, when blacks are experiencing unprecedented rates of incarceration, she is focusing her energies on penal reform and racism in the criminal justice system. She has been unflagging in her effort to bring attention to the situation of women prisoners in particular. Willing to analyze the full implications of the injustices created by the "prison-industrial complex," she cogently and fearlessly advocates in the essay that follows what many will find a frightening prospect—the abolition of jails and prisons.

Angela Davis radiates a black confidence that she puts to the service of freedom and truth telling. Approachable and without pretense, she generously lends her prominence to the causes of others. She has never disappointed us by making compromises with middle-class values. More than smart, she is a radical thinker, one of the few black intellectual leaders who capably tackle subjects ranging from feminism and sexuality to African American music and prisoners' rights. To this day, she remains a truly committed warrior against oppression in America and throughout the world who is respected even by those who find her positions anathema.

REGINA AUSTIN AND MANTHIA DIAWARA

PRISON ABOLITION

I was initially somewhat put off by the title of this collection, especially by what I interpreted to be its elitist implications. But Walter Mosley convinced me that this deliberately provocative title is meant to urge us to think about genius in essentially less elitist and more inclusive and collective ways. Well, that sounds all right to me. I will see what I can do to help summon up the collective genius of our community.

I want to focus on the prison-industrial complex and its very specific impact on black communities. I want to urge you to think very deeply about our reluctance to engage in serious discussions about the impact of jails and prisons on the black community. In particular, think about the fact that black women are being incorporated quietly into this complex, and consider how contemporary developments such as the disestablishment of the welfare system will escalate the feminization of prison populations.

Civic Death and the Objectification of Black Prisoners

How many of you, my black readers, know someone who is or was in jail or prison? Or perhaps I should ask, How many of you do not know anyone who has been touched in some way by the criminal justice system? Most of us have family or friends whose lives have already been claimed by jail or prison. When I asked these same questions twenty years ago, there were fewer than 200,000 people in prison, which at the time seemed an enormous number. Now the incarcerated population is about 1.5 million. Cousins of mine are currently doing time or previously did time in some of California's most notorious prisons. And I guess I have to say that I myself have been touched by the system as well.

With all of your connections to incarcerated black people, how does prison figure in your everyday conversations? Do you have discussions about prison experiences or prison life with members of your family, friends, and colleagues, or are your imprisoned friends and relatives treated as if they have somehow disappeared into a void that is at once so frightening and so shameful that you are unwilling to acknowledge its existence?

Of course, prison is a frightening phenomenon. When I was arrested many years ago—in 1970 I guess it was—something happened that taught me about the way people tend to treat those who are claimed by the penal system. A bunch of my friends went to my apartment and divided my stuff up among themselves. Afterwards, when I got out of jail, I would visit my friends' apartments, and see things that belonged to me. I think they thought that I was gone in a way, that somehow I had died as a result of having been claimed by the system. We often treat people in jail or prison as if they were dead or as if they had suffered a kind of civic death when they were sentenced. It is true that prisoners do suffer a civic death in that the vast numbers of people who have been convicted of felonies temporarily or permanently lose their right to vote. But we do not have to treat them the same way the system does. Unfortunately, prisoners suffer another kind of civic death at the hands of those of us in the "free world," which is what life out here is called by those who are on the other side. This second death is created by the collective silence with which we in the "free world" respond to their predicament.

Our collective amnesia vis-à-vis the imprisoned population is reminiscent of another amnesia—our historical tendency toward willed forgetfulness regarding slavery. We have inherited a fear of memories of slavery. It is as if to remember and acknowledge slavery would amount to our being consumed by it. As a matter of fact, in the popular black imagination, it is easier for us to construct ourselves as the children of Africa, as the sons and daughters of kings and queens, and thereby ignore the Middle Passage and centuries of enforced servitude in the Americas. Although some of us might indeed be the descendants of African royalty, most of us are probably the descendants of their subjects, the daughters and sons of African peasants or workers. Naturally, people would rather imagine themselves the progeny of nobility than the offspring of servants.

Important as it might be to affirm our connection to Africa, the Africa that is created in the popular imagination is not the historical Africa that our ancestors produced. Besides, the emphasis on Africa to the exclusion of the experience of slavery often reflects a very masculinist notion of black history, one which ignores the experiences and contributions of women. It is impossible to engage the history of slavery without acknowledging the part that women played in ensuring the survival and liberation of our communities.

I remember when Toni Morrison's *Beloved* and Sherley Williams's *Dessa Rose* were published. These novels asked us to imagine what it might have been like for black human beings, women as well as men, to have experienced slavery and to have constructed their own lives within the confines of that institution. Haile Gerima's film *Sankofa* poses the same question to us. Imagine life behind the walls, and fiercely challenge the tendency to turn hundreds of thousands of black people who inhabit the prisons into abstract versions of the "criminal," just as Toni Morrison's work challenged us to be self-critical of our habits of envisioning slave women and men as abstract versions of the "slave."

I recognize that restoring the personhood of black prisoners is a tall order, given the role popular culture plays today in criminalizing communities of color. Both mainstream reality-based police programs on television and the lyrics of black rap or hip-hop portray blacks as criminals. *America's Most Wanted* has actors re-creating crimes, including violent ones, in order to persuade viewers to join in what the narrator frequently refers to as the "manhunt." A show like *Cops,* on the other hand, is not just reality-based; it presents actual footage of pursuits and arrests. It is a frightening fact that such programs provide "entertainment" for millions of Americans. Of course, there is the argument that

America's Most Wanted has resulted in the arrest of numerous fugitives, but in my mind these productions have one overarching impact and that is to further separate the presumably law-abiding citizens who are staring into the television from the "criminals" who are caught "in the act" on tape or as represented by actors. The entertainment industry thrives on glorified violence, which results in the desensitization of the viewing public to violent acts, blood, gore, and the like. Thus, Jane and Joe Q. Public who sit in their living rooms watching *Cops* and *America's Most Wanted* are not so much aghast at what they see as they are pacified, entertained by the action, and relieved that the streets are being made safe by "the law." This is a very complicated matter because "the law" includes the television program! But the most insidious effect of reality-based shows is that the myth of rampant crime is reinforced, and the repetitions of "criminals" that flash across the television screen become symbolic objects in the viewers' minds that then translate into fearful and racist responses to certain types of people, often people of color, who are criminalized by these representations. Finally, the specter of crime that is suggested by politicians and these sorts of television shows is, I think, always greater than the reality.

As for rap or hip-hop, in the weeks following the fatal drive-by shooting of the rapper Notorious B.I.G. (a.k.a. Biggie Smalls) in Los Angeles, the media reported speculation as to a possible connection between this senseless killing and the murder, by similar means, of Tupac Shakur in Las Vegas. Meanwhile, Tupac's friend and associate Shug Knight was given a nine-year sentence for violating his parole by allegedly getting into a fight just hours before Tupac's murder. Tupac had just been released from prison himself not long before he was killed. Biggie also had his own run-ins with the law from his days on the streets of Brooklyn.

I would not agree that rap music glamorizes prisons, or rather the prospect of spending time in prison. With all of the brothers who did or currently are doing time, I do not think any sane black man would glamorize the prison experience. But, at the same time, I think it is fair to say that to some degree the "gangsta" culture—for which Tupac, Biggie, and numerous other rappers (some, by their peers' standards, less "legitimately" than others) have been self-proclaimed spokesmen—does reinforce certain practices that tend to land people, namely young black men, in jails and prisons. Guns, violence, and to a lesser degree drugs are integral props for many rap acts, the lives of whose members have been shaped in part by an outlaw subculture that too often is the only access to "power" (guns, money) they can conceive.

This aspect of rap/hip-hop culture is unfortunate because the medium does have revolutionary potential, but it is merely a reflection of a larger society that, through its increasing disregard for what it considers the throw-away populations of the inner city, perpetuates the self-destructive activities in which those populations often engage. From the perspective of many an inner-city youth, however, the name of the game is survival, by whatever means necessary. Drugs are big business in the ghetto, and the violence that comes along with establishing, protecting, and expanding that business translates into power. But we are talking about power over the very people—youths, families, single mothers—who are struggling daily to have a chance of life beyond the boundaries of the ghetto. It is a very vicious cycle, indeed.

The problems do not begin with gangsta rappers, but these brothers certainly can become a part of the problem. By the same token, however, they can become part of the solution, and more and more of them are striving to do so. Ice-T is an excellent example of a brother who has maintained his "legitimacy" among his peers and his audience alike, while simultaneously doing some very important work to stop the violence and to address issues like unemployment. Also, I saw a public-service message on Fox during a break in *New York Undercover* in which Method Man was speaking out against violence. Mainstream hip-hop generation publications like *Vibe* are becoming more and more politicized, and there continue to be grassroots publications on urban culture that can serve to bring people together around important issues affecting young people of color.

I hope that, in the wake of Biggie's murder and the dialogue that followed, rappers from both coasts will renew their efforts not only to bring peace to the hip-hop community but to work for peace in the communities from which they hail, and for social justice in the larger society. With their access to the media, these brothers have a lot of power to speak to a lot of people. This is where hip-hop's revolutionary potential lies, for it can function as a tool to facilitate the subjectivity of its audience, which is largely objectified by the mainstream media. The important contributions of many women rappers who in their work have challenged misogyny are excellent examples of this process.

Black people must recognize that they may be reproducing the very ideologies that are used to dominate us. If we are not vigilant, black people can be persuaded to participate in the process of reproducing racism. Consider the fact that there are corporate criminals who are responsible for the deaths and maiming of thousands and thousands of people or for assaults on the environment, yet they end up perhaps paying only a fine. When we walk down the street, however, and see someone who could be one of those corporate executives in his three-piece suit, we are not frightened. We cannot imagine being afraid. Yet when we see a young black brother walking down the street, the fear immediately takes hold. There is very important work to be done, and part of that work is trying to regenerate among our people a sense of collective struggle. This is a challenge which must be met particularly by and among our youth. It is the young people who will generate these new movements, whom we can draw upon for sustenance, in order to nurture our courage, and develop the collective possibility of assuming radical positions. We have to become radical again.

Slavery and the Penal System: Powerful Analogies

Indeed, we can do much more to combat the prison-industrial complex which is ravishing our communities if we recognize its historical connection with slavery and look at the nineteenth-century abolitionist movement as an inspiration for a late twentieth-century abolitionist movement that will work to reduce and ultimately abolish the use of imprisonment as the main means of addressing (or rather not addressing) social problems that are rooted in racism and poverty. Moreover, we may be able to use historical similarities, parallels, and conjunctures in the activist work that we must do to foster the abolition of prisons. We have to do something. We have to figure out how we are going to persuade vast numbers of people to stand up and oppose the expansion of the prison-industrial complex.

In the rest of this essay, I want to elaborate on the historical connection between the institution of slavery and the institution of prisons. First, I will consider some of the structural similarities between slavery and the penal system. Second, I want to discuss further the relationship between slavery and prisons on an ideological level. This time I want to focus on how we have learned to think or avoid thinking about these institutions in a way that renders women especially invisible. Finally, I want to explore parallels between the historical social movement that helped to abolish slavery and a possible new mass movement calling for the disestablishment of the prison system as we know it today.

There were not many black people in prison during slavery. The system of slavery was in fact a system of incarceration because it constructed walls around those it enslaved and determined their possibilities of physical movement. (By this definition, the reservation system, which crowded large numbers of indigenous peoples, Native Americans, into confined spaces, was also a system of incarceration.) The slave codes strictly defined what black slaves could or could not do; they often did not permit them past the boundaries of the plantation or farm without written permission. Even the slaves' most private and sexual relationships were regulated by their masters.

Slavery, then, was its own prison. But as soon as slavery was abolished, the population of southern prisons became predominately black. Between 1874 and 1877, the black imprisonment rate went up 300 percent in Mississippi and Georgia. In some states, previously all-white prisons could hardly contain the influx of African Americans who were sentenced to hard labor for petty offenses—offenses as bogus as impudence or failing to look down at the street when passing a white person. It was during this period that the convict lease system emerged. Under this system, black people were arrested for the most negligible crimes and then were "leased out" to work on plantations and farms doing the same work from which they had just been liberated as a result of emancipation. Thus, the penitentiary system allowed for the continuation of slavery. The Thirteenth Amendment abolished involuntary servitude only for those who were not convicted of crimes.

The connection between slavery and the penal system is evident in the parallels between the representations of female slaves and their contemporary counterparts, our incarcerated sisters. I was in jail when I wrote my first article about slave women. It did not occur to me until much later that I was drawn to doing research on black women and slavery precisely because I was experiencing something very similar in 1970. I had engaged in a number of conversations by mail with people like George Jackson and others who at that time were very much influenced by the masculinist propaganda of the period. For example, the Moynihan report argued that the real problem in the black community was the matriarchal structure of our families. It was very clear to me that there was a connection between the way black women were being represented in the society and Daniel Patrick Moynihan's attempt to make them responsible for what he called "a tangled web of pathology" within the black community. So I decided to do research on slave women.

However, I was only allowed to have books in my cell that related to my case. I had been recognized as my own attorney. I had other attorneys as well, but I had argued that I should have the right to defend myself. I had to argue that the works I needed in order to do the article on women and slavery were required by me for the preparation of my case. Interestingly enough, it turned out that I did need those materials. Unaware of it at the time, I later recognized how important it was to talk about the intersection of gender and race in order to develop a compelling case.

I also discovered how few people acknowledged the fact that there were women slaves. People, scholars even, often assumed that, if there were women slaves, they were house slaves. There was also the popular myth that somehow or other black women slaves were in collusion with the white masters against black male slaves. (Regrettably, I think we may be experiencing some contemporary versions of this story.) Since that time, a number of really important historical studies, novels, and other literary works about black women and slavery have appeared, but it occurs to me now that there is a similarity between our historical tendency to render slave women invisible and the way we tend to talk about the penal system as if there were no women in prison.

In focusing on the relative invisibility of women prisoners, I am not calling for some kind of gender-based equality within regimes of incarceration. In September of 1996, I saw a picture in the *New York Times* of three women prisoners in Phoenix, Arizona. The photograph foregrounded their combat boots, which were linked together by chains, and the accompanying caption read "A Chain Gang of Women." The article said, "The nation's first female chain gang began work yesterday, picking up trash and pulling weeds in downtown Phoenix. The 15 women were chained at the ankles in groups of five." The article goes on to quote Sheriff Joe Arpaio: "I don't believe in discrimination in my jail system." He in essence claimed that he was combating gender discrimination by giving women the opportunity to work on chain gangs. Of course, that is ridiculous. But it says something about the way in which we have to guard against formulating issues within what I would call a framework of bourgeois democratic equal rights, because it creates as many problems as it solves, if not more. In a sense, a call for equal rights for women prisoners only reinforces the punishment industry.

Vast numbers of women, and black women in particular, are heading toward the prison system. The rate of increase in arrests, convictions, and imprisonment is much higher for women than for men. In absolute numbers, a much smaller cohort of women than of men is currently behind bars, but the rate of construction of prison space for women far outstrips that for men. Think about the historical trajectory. Think about what the prison population will be like ten or twenty years from now.

The feminization of the imprisoned population is partly the result of the disestablishment of the welfare system, which is prompting increasing numbers of women to participate in alternative economies, like the drug trade and the market for sexual services, which lead them directly into the criminal justice system and into prison. This is one of the most striking implications of Clinton's disestablishment of the welfare system. Moreover, there is a history of black women being locked away in mental institutions, rather than receiving the kind of treatment and/or assistance they need. With the disestablishment of mental institutions, prisons have become the repository for these women. Furthermore, because drug use is higher among women in black communities (the reasons behind this reality are too numerous to go into here), many black women are incarcerated when they should, in fact, have access to drug rehabilitation programs. (Of course, all sorts of preventive measures should be in place to keep people from reaching the point of drug abuse, but that is an entirely different conversation.)

The Prison-Industrial Complex

It is important for us to think about the penal system as a prison-industrial complex. I am not one to nostalgically invoke the sixties as others do, because I do not want to go back there—it was too crazy then. But I think we can learn from them some lessons that are useful for the work that we need to do today. There was a time, back in the sixties, when a few people used the term "military-industrial complex." I can remember the conscious efforts to politicize and educate people, on a popular level, about the concept; they succeeded to the point that the phrase became a term sisters and brothers used regardless of whether they were doing work within educational institutions like universities or in similar institutions like prisons.

I remember in the late 1960s, when black activists first began to do political work on behalf of political prisoners and then expanded their area of concern to include the prison system in general, there were perhaps 150,000 people in prison. In 1980, there were approximately 500,000 people in federal and state prisons and in local jails. Five hundred thousand, and that was quite a lot. In 1995, there were over 1.5 million people in prison. That represents a tripling of the incarcerated population in fifteen years. In addition to the 1.5 million people at present in prison, some 700,000 are on parole and 3 million on probation. So we are talking about 5.4 million people under the direct supervision of correctional systems. In 1980, the figure was 1.8 million. We obviously have a serious problem.

Compare the numbers of people who are incarcerated here with the numbers in other countries. Recently, I conducted a series of interviews with women imprisoned in the Netherlands, outside of Amsterdam. The percentages with respect to women of color were roughly the same there as here. Half the prison population consists of people of color from the former Dutch Caribbean and South American colonies; vast numbers of people from what is now the South American Republic of Surinam are in prison. But in the Netherlands there are 55 people per 100,000 in prison. In England there are a few more, 96 per 100,000. Do you know what the figure is for this country? Six hundred per 100,000! America's incarcerated population is the largest both proportionately and absolutely. America operates the largest prison-industrial complex in the world.

I refer to the "prison-*industrial* complex" because the prisons do not stand alone. The right-wing politicians who participate in the process of crimininalizing minority and poor populations are not the only ones with stakes in the continuation and growth of prisons. There are corporate stakeholders as well. Prison construction is the most profitable segment of the construction industry. Moreover, because of the deindustrialization of the U.S. economy and the movement of vast numbers of corporations to the Third World in search of cheap labor, many Americans have been left jobless. One of the reasons that so many people of color and poor people are in prison is that the deindustrialization of the economy has led to the creation of new economies and the expansion of some old ones—I have already mentioned the drug trade and the market for sexual services. At the same time, though, there are any number of communities that more than welcome prisons as a source of employment. Communities even compete with one another to be the site where new prisons will be constructed because prisons create a significant number of relatively good jobs for their residents.

Also to be factored into the equation are the privatization of prisons and the joint venture programs that make use of prison labor in a way that recapitulates the convict lease system, which represented the continuation of slavery through the prison system. In California, for example, a joint venture program invites corporations to come into the prisons and make use of prison labor on-site. This program is publicized in a brochure that essentially tells corporations, "There is a perfect labor force for you here." First, there is no need to worry about vacation benefits, health benefits, or any kind of benefits at all. Second, there are no child care problems. And then, of course, prison workers are not organized into unions and therefore have no collective autonomy; they can be used in the same way corporations attempt to use workers in so-called Third World countries. The trade union movement certainly ought to get involved in challenging the importation of jobs into prison.

Thus, the stakes are really much higher and more diverse than they might at first appear to be. We must begin to talk about the prison-industrial complex.

It is very clear that prisons have not solved any problems. They have not helped to eliminate the material conditions in poor communities and communities of color that create the trajectories that lead their members into the criminal justice system. The whole notion of prisoner rehabilitation has become obsolete. It has been replaced with a goal of punishment across the board. Educational opportunities are being cut. Prisoners are not even supposed to lift weights. The history of the prison system in this country reflects pendulum swings between policies of rehabilitation and reform, on the one hand, and policies of punishment and retribution, on the other. Reform does not work, because prisons cannot be reformed in a way that would assist them in rehabilitating human beings. How can you rehabilitate individuals when you do not allow them even a small measure of autonomy? How can you rehabilitate them when you do not treat them as human beings? Prisoners are told when to get up, when to brush their teeth, when to take a shower, and when to eat. Nearly every possible choice that one might make about one's life is taken from them. And how do you expect people to feel? I can remember how I felt after experiencing such control for sixteen months. It was really difficult to have to learn again how to make simple decisions. I can imagine what it must be like for someone who has been incarcerated for ten or twenty years. I do not think, even if we were pursuing it now, that rehabilitation would actually be possible in the prison environment. Perhaps it might work in community-based situations where small numbers of people live in houses, but not in huge institutions.

In order for any antiracist theory or practice to be successful, it must counter the widespread assumptions that prisons are here to stay and that we are powerless to affect their consumption of the social resources that ought to be directed toward education, health, housing, and other antipoverty initiatives. We can take inspiration from the fact that as eternal as the American system of slavery was assumed to be by its defenders, and those who profited from the labor of Africans, it nonetheless could be and indeed was abolished. Of course, northern industrialists recognized that wage labor could be much more profitable than slave labor; that was one of the reasons why the capitalists joined with the abolitionists against the slavocracy.

I went to the exhibition of artifacts from the *Henrietta Marie*, a British slave ship that sank in waters off the coast of Florida, when they were on display in Charlotte, North Carolina. The wreck was discovered in the 1970s. It is one of just three sunken slave ships discovered in America, and the only one in the world from which artifacts have been recovered. Among the artifacts I saw were shackles for children. It was very moving. But a ship like the *Henrietta Marie* should serve as a reminder not only of the historical pain and suffering of slavery but also of the impermanence of the institution. I want us to imagine the possibility of future generations visiting prison museums. Imagine a time when these fortresses no longer occupy their present place in society.

I am sure you are asking yourselves, "What about the rapists and murderers?" That question always comes up. That is where our concern takes us when we think about abolishing prisons, isn't it? Be honest. Because we immediately worry about what will happen to the people who have committed horrendous crimes, it is possible for vast numbers of people who have not committed such crimes to be locked up and treated as less than human beings. The vast majority of women are in prison for what we call "victimless crimes" like prostitution, yet no one does anything about their incarceration, because of the specter of turning loose murderers and rapists. This ideological bind serves to support the expansion of the prison-industrial complex.

The idea of abolishing jails and prisons grows out of the belief that the social ills these institutions are supposed to address have roots outside of the individuals who are locked up and punished. I am not advocating that we do away with all correctional facilities and let violent offenders roam the streets. Perhaps we do need to lock up the murderers and the rapists, but these are not the only people in jails or prisons, yet the stereotype that they very nearly are causes many citizens to balk at the notion of prisoners' rights. Many people who commit violent crimes need psychological help, but these people should not be the basis for a discussion of abolition. Consider, rather, the many nonviolent offenders, like drug abusers, whose crimes harm only themselves. We need to take the discussion to another level. If we talk only about violent offenders—the worst cases—there will never be any forward motion in the direction of prison abolition. Instead, we need to focus on creative dialogue around the possibility of abolishing jails and prisons as the knee-jerk response to every form of crime. We need to advocate such alternatives as community-based programs and the decriminalization of drugs and prostitution.

We must come up with some solutions. I do not have any answers, but I do know that we have to try to break down the ideological and material walls of the prison system. Everyone of you must ask yourself what you can do from where you are. I am appealing to all of you to become prison activists.

Many of us assume that activism involves a calling—that one is "called" to activism the way one is "called" to the ministry. For years and years, people asked me, "When were you called?" I tried to remember if I had experienced a moment of conversion, an epiphany. Was it this time? Was it that? No, it couldn't have happened then, because I was already active. Finally I realized that activism is not a vocation or a calling. It can be the way we live our lives. It was just how I learned to be in this world, how I learned to live my everyday life. Large numbers of movements in this country have emerged as a result of people's approaching activism in the same way, especially women. It is not a big deal. It is not anything extraordinary. It is not anything for which we seek or deserve applause or acknowledgment.

We have to begin to think about those of our sisters and brothers who are on the other side, and to figure out how we can prevent the expansion of the monstrous prison-industrial complex. All of us can do the work of dismantling this complex whether we are students, educators, artists, writers, or trade union members. If we do not manage to bring everyone into this campaign, increasing numbers of us will find ourselves on the other side.

Farai Chideya

Farai Chideya is a correspondent with ABC News and a former CNN Generation X political analyst. She joined CNN in February 1996 and was immediately named to the New York Daily News Dream Team *of television analysts and reporters covering that year's election. The newspaper also called her that year's most promising newcomer. Before joining CNN, she worked for MTV News from 1994 to 1996; there she helped launch MTV's 1996 Choose or Lose: Voter Awareness Effort. Before that, she was a reporter for* Newsweek *in New York, Chicago, and Washington for four years. In 1995, she wrote* Don't Believe the Hype: Fighting Cultural Misinformation about African Americans, *based mainly on information from government sources.*

As a freelance journalist, Chideya has written extensively about music, books, and pop culture for the Village Voice *and* Spin, *among other publications. She has also profiled white supremacists for* Mademoiselle, *examined child sexual abuse allegations for the* Los Angeles Times, *and written on affirmative action for the* New York Times. *In addition, the Freedom Forum, a nonpartisan international foundation dedicated to protecting the free press and free speech, has granted her a fellowship to investigate why people under thirty watch less television news than older people do.*

Chideya graduated magna cum laude from Harvard College in 1990. She's done a lot since then, I see. She resides in Manhattan, where she is working on her second book, about youth and national identity. Her father is from Zimbabwe, and her mother is from Baltimore, where Chideya was raised.

I just want to say a little about my relationship with Farai. Mainly, we argue. We fight. Whenever we are together for more than seven minutes, we start arguing about things. I look at it kind of optimistically: I think we argue over small things while agreeing on larger issues.

The last time we got together, we were at a play together and sat down and discussed democracy and the vote. You'd think that we would agree, but we were fighting. We were yelling in this restaurant. I'm telling her that I believe that all politicians are the same. All of them. All that matters is their constituency, and their constituency isn't necessarily the voter. Farai is really mad at me about that. She's like, they're not all the same. I'm talking about George Wallace, and she's saying, Who is that man? And we're fighting. It was really funny.

The first time we argued it was about the notion of black genius. I spent a lot of time trying to say to her that my idea or my notion of black genius is not a hierarchical notion. And she was very leery. Very leery. And no matter what I'd say, and no matter how I tried to make it sound better, she says, Hmmm. And I think that's one of the rea-

sons I wanted Farai to contribute to this collection, because of that healthy kind of leery attitude she has about me, because it's the same feeling I have about myself really.

But I want to tell you what my idea of black genius is and why I think Farai represents an important element in that. Black genius for me is the spirit of the times. It is not in any one person but the shared knowledge of a possible destiny among a whole group of people: city people, blues people, people who recognize the specter of homelessness in their bathroom mirrors in the morning. Black people are not all black; they are white people and yellow people, red and brown people, who feel the beat of history in their blood while they witness the barbarism of hierarchy. One of the major elements of genius—black genius specifically in this case—is youth. Because youth adapts and more quickly understands the nature of danger and possibility. Youth is foolish and reckless, and without this foolishness and recklessness, we could never advance.

And if you want to understand what I mean by reckless fool—I'm not trying to say that's Farai necessarily, though it may be—it's a young person who might refuse to fight Vietnamese Communists. It's a person who refuses to invade a foreign land, a person who will accept that black mark on his or her file rather than do the wrong thing. It's a person who will break the law rather than do the wrong thing. And that's genius. That's the genius of survival and that's very important for us, black people in America. Black people whether or not we're black.

WALTER MOSLEY

HOLDING THE MEDIA
ACCOUNTABLE

There is a degree to which mediocrity becomes the norm in most large systems, the government being one of them and the media being another. We are not getting the truth from the media on racial issues in particular. I want to discuss how we might go about searching for that truth, how we might go about controlling the media by calling it to account. Before I consider various means we can employ to control the media, I want to reflect on why we should want to do so in the first place.

Assessing the Media's Impact on You

Let me start with a quiz. Determine whether the three statements I am about to make are true or false. The first statement is that 45 percent of America's newspapers have no black, Latino, Asian

American, or Native American reporters. True or false? The Second, there are more young black men in prison than in college. True or false? Finally, only 1 percent of prime-time television characters are Latino. True or false?

Well, the first statement—that 45 percent of America's newspapers have no black, Latino, Asian American, or Native American reporters—is true. Only 5 percent of America's newspaper reporters are black and only 3 percent or so are Latino. Population-wise, of course, the picture is very different: 13 percent of Americans are black and 10 percent are Latino. There is a huge gap between the people represented in newsrooms and the population of America as a whole. It follows that there are huge gaps in the portrayal of blacks, Latinos, and most nonwhites by and in the news media. Keep in mind, then, as we proceed that roughly half of America's newspapers have no nonwhite reporters.

The second statement is false. There are *not* more *young* black men in prison than in college. I stress the word "young" because it makes for a trick question. There are three times as many young black men in college as in prison. Yet, overall, there are more black men in prison than in college, a circumstance that should absolutely appall us. Moreover, a third of young black men are in prison, on parole, or on probation, and that is way too many. But when we compare apples and apples and consider where young black men are today, in college or in jail, we find there are three times as many young black men in college. Even though many serious negative trends affect the African American community, we have cause for hope and need to keep in perspective the breadth of our experiences, not just the negatives.

The final statement was that only 1 percent of prime-time television characters are Latino. That is true. The media that I will discuss is mainly the news media, but not exclusively. The entertainment culture has a huge influence on how we think, how we perceive race, and how we perceive community. When we consider that 10 percent of this country is Latino, but only 1 percent of television characters are, we should recognize that an entire ethnic population is being rendered invisible.

As for black characters, 18 percent of television characters during prime time are black, but they are almost exclusively on black shows. There are black shows and white shows, but blacks and whites are rarely on the same shows. We seldom encounter blacks on shows that start at or after 9 P.M., which is when hour-long dramas are shown. There are black people in sitcoms shucking and jiving; anything other than that is impermissible.

What, then, are we to make of the results of my quiz? Three propositions become clear: first, there are not enough nonwhites in the newsroom; second, certain fundamental issues like education and criminal justice are not being covered well when it comes to race; and finally, even the entertainment culture does not produce a true portrait of the nation's diversity. All of these propositions contribute to a common problem—a problem of perceptions. We cannot live without perceptions. We all have perceptions. We all live and die by them in a certain sense. If you perceive a car coming toward you, you step out of the middle of the street. It is not a bad idea to have perceptions, but it helps enormously if they are true. This is where we turn to the news media. We trust, or many of us trust, the news media to deliver at least an approximation of the truth, to deliver something which is a touchstone to reality in a nation we cannot personally assess because of its breadth. We cannot individually know what is happening in Albuquerque, what is happening in Chicago, and what is happening in Dubuque. We need to rely on the news media to paint a picture of the society in which we live. On the basis of that picture, we draw assumptions that influence everything from how we vote to whom we choose to live next to.

But suppose the picture is not accurate. Consider the pervasive images of black life in the media. According to one very hard-bought study—which taped and analyzed an entire year's worth of nightly news coverage—60 percent of the images of African Americans were negative in tone; 60 percent of the images were either of people who were victims (people without jobs or people who had been robbed, beaten, or abused) or of people who were the abusers and the victimizers. If viewers see that 60 percent of the people of one group are living lives of degradation, they will make assumptions about the worth of those people, their value, and their ability to succeed. If viewers see only the portrayals in the news media and never interact in a meaningful way with a black person, they probably will not want to live next to a black person or be friends with one. They will not even necessarily want to share much of their workday with a black person. The reality is that most Americans live largely within their own racial groups. Blacks live with blacks, whites live with whites, and so on. The viewer who looks at the black community from the outside through the prism of the news media is very likely seeing a group she/he would not want to associate with. That is the crux of the problem. This explains why we should want to control the news media.

Understanding How the Media Works

Now, how do we control the news media? Well, the first step is to understand how the news media works. I have been very privileged to work for three different corporations with different views on doing the news and different approaches to news judgment. Exercise news judgment, that is what editors do. They determine what is and what is not a story. They decide what deserves ten minutes and what deserves two minutes. They designate the stories that merit a whole page, a series, or no coverage at all.

My first job was at *Newsweek* magazine. I was fortunate enough to get a minority internship that paid. Mark Starr was the first boss I had at *Newsweek,* and he is still my mentor. Starr is head of *Newsweek's* Boston bureau and the national sports correspondent. That he himself was willing to supervise a minority intern was extremely important. Starr had a South Asian, an Asian, and a Latina as well as myself go through his office. Realistically speaking, few students of color would have similar opportunities to work forty hours a week (and that was sometimes what they asked for) for pay at the daily newspaper. At one point, I had two work-study jobs. Most of the time, I packed and shipped books. Now, that is not exactly brain work, but it helped me to pay my tuition. Paid internships that target blacks and Latinos really help to diversify the media. Internships that pay are especially important for minorities because of their socioeconomic positions. I was given this chance. I did not have the same qualifications as a "Crimson jock," someone from the Harvard

University newspaper. But I walked in there, and Mark Starr took the time and trained me.

The first experience that brought home to me the power of the media occurred when I went to a women's prison for a story on which correspondents from all over the country contributed. I interviewed two women, both murderers who had killed their abusive spouses. I talked to these women and tried to get to the heart of what they had done, how they had come to feel about it, and whether they felt that their incarceration was unjust, because they had acted in self-defense. I realized that if I were of one mind-set I could portray them completely as victims of abuse and an unjust system. If I were of another mind-set, I could say that the outcry against the abuse of women in such cases is complete poppycock; these women killed their husbands while they were sleeping or going out to fix the car and are hardly deserving of sympathy. The portrait that I painted was, I felt, a little bit more nuanced. Their decisions were not ones that I would have made, but it is easy to understand how these women made them. In many cases, such women were given mid-range sentences, not acquittals, but terms lighter than those meted out to a cold-blooded murderer. Simply by writing what I saw as the truth, not one sensationalized version or another, I was affecting the perceptions of the four to five million people who read *Newsweek*. And when there was a case in their hometowns that had an element of domestic violence, they would probably rely on some of the stories, images, and tales reflected in the media's representation of previous cases to make up their minds.

Every day, when we read the newspaper or watch the television news, we bank a series of images, phrases, and words for future use that can be invoked when we choose to interact with government officials or decide whether our criminal justice system is fair. We use the media as a way of creating a common bank of experiences that we have not witnessed firsthand. We have not been, all of us, to these prisons. We have not been in the halls of government, but we get a sense of them through what journalists tell us.

If journalists walk into the different situations that matter to us as a nation with a series of preconceived notions, particularly about a specific race, then the reporting we get is simply not going to be very accurate. There are several different ways in which the reporting on race gets completely screwed up. Preconceived notions can make the reporting outright racist. Sometimes, a reporter will visit a neighborhood in the aftermath of a violent event and look for the person who has the worst, most screwed-up, "in your face," "gonna kick your ass" attitude, because it makes for good television. Such a move reflects a racist attitude since it tries to portray an entire neighborhood, or even an entire race, through one such individual. And yes, we need to just keep in mind that every black person on television stands for every other black person in America. To knowingly search out the person who represents the worst of his or her community is to actively degrade your ability as a reporter to present the issues fairly.

Discussions about the issue of race in the media raise the whole issue of political correctness and what it is that blacks want. Blacks certainly do not want nothing but positive stories. Most victims of black crime are black people. Most victims of white crime are white people. Not reporting the negatives does not do the black community any favors. But we need to be mindful that the reporting be accurate. For example, William F. Buckley, a well-known conservative syndicated writer, in a column on what he very broadly called "the black problem," said that most whites are killed by blacks. Most white victims are killed by blacks? No, in fact, 70 percent of white murder victims are killed by whites. Eighty percent of black murder victims are killed by blacks. People tend to kill their own. When his error was brought to his attention, he never ever replied, responded, or apologized. That is an example of complete racist inaccuracy. Buckley did not simply print something about which he knew nothing; he also had the audacity not to acknowledge that he had been wrong.

In addition to racist inaccuracies by the news media, there is the even more pervasive problem of racist omissions, as exemplified by the near-invisibility of blacks, Latinos, Asian Americans, and Native Americans everywhere except in the crime coverage. As a working journalist, I find it easy to understand the root of this problem. First of all, most journalists are overworked. It has not been a very kind decade in the business. A number of companies are operating with a staff that is too small, working that staff too hard, putting money into glitzier advertising schemes and not necessarily into developing their reporters. Put yourself in the place of the typical overworked newspaper reporter who has been given exactly six hours to produce a story on buying a first home. Say something else has fallen out of the section, the edition is closing at four, and your editor needs a story from you by then. The first thing you think is not "Oh gee, I think I should interview a wide variety of people in the community." You need to find some people who are buying a first home, fast. So you rush out and, whatever color you are, instinctively turn to people of that color. You call your friends and ask who is buying a home. Or you call the real estate agents you have heard of and ask them for the names of first-time home buyers. If roughly 80 percent of America's reporters are white, they are likely to turn to white first-time home buyers. This is for a story that is completely outside of the racial context. As a consequence, every day the newspaper reader will see black people in the crime coverage, black people in the stories on welfare, and black people in the stories about failing schools, but they will never see black people in the stories about buying a first home, petitioning a city council representative, or installing computers in the schools. Readers are bound to get an impression if they never see African Americans or other people of color in the routine, everyday coverage that makes up the bulk of what a newspaper or television station offers. Remember that 60 percent of network news coverage of African Americans was negative in tone. African Americans are concentrated in stories about crime and welfare dependency and are rarely seen anywhere else. There is no balance.

The ninety-second to two-minute news stories shown on the local and national nightly news programs also lend themselves to racist treatment of African Americans, Asian Americans, and other groups. The structure of television news in particular is completely based on confrontation. If there is no confrontation, there is no story. Good news is seen as soft news. Bad news is seen as being good news for the television station. Ergo, the adage "If it bleeds it leads." If there is a shooting in the inner city, run right over and tape that as opposed to talking to people in the community and getting a more nuanced version of what goes on there on an everyday basis. Pieces on your money, your family, and everyday life tend not to involve blacks, Latinos, or Asian Americans, because the stories are not assumed to deal with race. When black people do get into a story, it is about a "bang, bang shoot-em-up," "drug using and dealing" minute and a half. I call this "drive-by journalism."

Not only do we get a dearth of images of African Americans throughout the breadth of news coverage, but we also get an extreme overemphasis on the negatives. For example, a reporter assigned to do a story on welfare may or may not know that the largest number of welfare recipients lives in the suburbs. Regardless, she/he cannot walk down the streets of a suburb asking people if they are on welfare, but she/he can go into an urban housing project and be pretty sure that if she/he knocks on enough doors she/he will find someone who is receiving welfare. There is a kind of fish-in-a-barrel assumption that leads reporters back to the inner city again and again for stories on crime and dependency, when they should realize that it is their job as working reporters to portray the true face of the problem if it goes beyond the inner city.

The same is true of the portrayal of drug use. William Bennett, another well-known conservative, who was the drug czar under President Bush, has said that the average drug user in America is a fully employed white male in his thirties. According to drug statistics, blacks and whites have an equal likelihood of being frequent drug users, but that is hardly the image portrayed in America's newspapers. There is a relentless emphasis on black and Latino drug users and drug sellers. There are many more drug sales in inner city neighborhoods than elsewhere, but a large portion of them involve people who drive in from the suburbs to pick up what they need and return home. We do not see these "innocent drug users" in the news coverage, however.

Asking the media to do a better job of presenting our lives, of course, deals only with the problem of how we are portrayed and how people perceive those portrayals. It does not solve the drug problem or the crime problem. Nevertheless, it is important to deal with the media because, for example, citizens who believe that black kids cannot learn because they are genetically intellectually inferior will not vote to invest in the public school system, since black kids cannot learn no matter what. That is one example of what the media's impact is. It would be helpful in grappling with social problems like drugs and the deterioration of families if there were better portrayals of individual struggles. Take the struggle of a woman who is receiving welfare. Suppose she has relatives who are using drugs and some kids who are struggling through the public school system. A quick hit might say, "Well, like most people's lives in the inner city, hers is a mess." That presents one image. An alternative approach would explore the ways in which she is struggling and realistically tell the audience what is working for her and what is not. Then we can try to replicate the success and jettison what does not work. Better media coverage would take some of the pain that we are experiencing and pull out of it ways of moving on.

There is a substantial difference, then, between what we read in the newspapers and see on television and the reality of the black experience, the Latino experience, and the Asian American experience. It is interesting that Asian Americans are often separated out of the herd of people of color. There are certainly differences between the experiences of Asian Americans and the experiences of blacks and Latinos, but Asian Americans earn less than white Americans though they are more likely to have college degrees. Why is this important? Look at a book like *The Bell Curve*—one of my favorite books—in which Charles Murray analyzes the earning differences between blacks and whites. He concludes that, judged by educational attainment, blacks are underpaid, but if IQ is considered, the difference disappears. Well, actually, there are black Americans who have IQs equal to those of whites but who still earn less. Moreover, they are 32 percent more likely to have a college degree. It seems to me that Charles Murray has proven that there is employment discrimination, and it must really exist because he has no stake whatsoever in backing me up. Beyond that, if he thinks that the racial wage gaps are a matter of IQ or educational achievement, the data on Asian Americans suggests quite the opposite. Murray says that Asian Americans are the racial group with the highest IQs, and U.S. Census Bureau statistics indicate that Asian Americans are the racial group with the highest college graduation rates, yet they still earn less than white Americans.

People of color—blacks, Latinos, Asian Americans, Native Americans—have been bearing the burden of racial discrimination and probably will continue to do so. The only reason I bother to mention something that seems so commonplace is that, right now, reverse discrimination is one of the media's new pet peeves. You have seen the stories on white men who cannot find a job because black people and women are taking them all. Yes, reverse discrimination exists; I would be the last person to say that it does not. Every single form of discrimination exists, but discrimination against people of color, women, gays, and lesbians is still the norm. It is not the reverse discrimination in favor of these categories that is the pervasive problem. If we look at the statistics we can see that. But there is a certain amount of trend spotting within the media that influences the way African Americans are portrayed. Racial discrimination has been around for three hundred years; readers and viewers need something new, so reverse discrimination is the trend of the month or the year, and ten stories on reverse discrimination follow. This makes sense from the perspective of America's newsrooms, but suppose you are the reader or viewer who is treated to ten stories in one month on reverse discrimination and none on commonplace racial discrimination, gender discrimination, or discrimination against gays and lesbians. You might come to believe that the true story is the one on reverse discrimination. The media does not benefit us when working journalists decide that they are going to focus purely on one issue, to the exclusion of others which are no longer deemed sexy.

Raising Hell: Resistance Tactics for Journalists

I suppose this explains why I almost always feel conflicted when doing a commentary. If I am asked a question, I know what I think and try to answer the question in a way that is direct and truthful, but also understandable. Very often, though, I am concerned with redirecting the line of inquiry if it is not touching on important issues. I may have been asked, for example, whether black people were upset by the O. J. Simpson verdict, but that may not have been a line of inquiry that I find productive. I would rather have been asked how the level of distrust between the races might be reduced, or what should be done about the racism in the criminal justice system. So, in many instances, my task is figuring out not how to answer the questions asked but how to redirect a line of questioning that is already going off in a flawed direction. Usually a number of things just do not get talked about. We in the media who do have a chance to speak— and I feel very privileged in that regard—have to stop being sheep and start setting the agenda. I do not do that enough. I just don't.

I am not going to pretend; people have different comfort zones with regard to how real they are willing to be and how boldly they will get into these issues. I certainly try to be consistent. I am not going to say that I think that the media is racist here and then go on television or write a story that says the media is doing a good job on race. But some people do that, and you have to hold them accountable. I think more often, though, a subtle but firm pressure is exerted on black journalists, not so much to give up their own ideals, but simply not to do stories that they may feel are important. Editors will tell us that stories we are interested in working on are simply not news. It was their news judgment that the racist application of the death penalty, for example, was just not news that caused black people to be fried without adequate media scrutiny. That sort of thing happens quite often. Black journalists may appear not to care about such issues, but quite often we are simply not allowed to do the stories we find compelling.

I threw down in my office on the issue of race and the death penalty; I walked down the hall, literally helling with my editor, and people came out of their offices in disbelief that I was raising such a stink. You can do that only so many times before your butt is on the street. Sometimes it is better for a black journalist or a journalist, regardless of race, who cares about racially equal coverage (and some white journalists are fighting very hard to get good stories out there) to hold her or his tongue but to keep pressing, rather than to be out on the street, a nobody to the process. When I felt that I was not being effective, when I felt burned out and thought that I could do nothing further, I left that organization and went someplace else where the problems were the same, but where I was starting with a fresh slate.

There are really four kinds of journalistic fighters. Some struggle so loud and so strong that they get fired. Others pick their battles, fighting when they can and seething with anger the rest of the time. Those in a third category constantly find themselves banging up against a brick wall or a glass ceiling; they voluntarily decide to move on in order to stay engaged. The fourth kind of fighter becomes physically sick or clinically insane. That is the worst option. Fighting all the time is not always the solution. Fighting as hard as you can *when* you can may be.

I will give you an example of something I once did. Perhaps it was a little devious. My employer, like much of the media, had practically no black reporters and therefore had a problem scheduling stories on issues of importance to the black community. I fought as hard as I could, and when I was ready to leave wrote a long memo about all of the problems I saw. Protocol suggested that I send it to my boss, but since he was part of the problem, I sent it to the top guy and to everyone else. When asked how

I could circulate the memo so widely, I replied that I just didn't know the protocol. "I had no idea that I was suppose to send it to you, Mr. Racist Boss."

Every form of black identity and black consciousness should be represented among the black voices in the media. At this point, conservatives are overrepresented, given their minority status among blacks. There are television shows that book only black conservatives. There are several reasons for this. White people sometimes confuse speaking of justice with anger. A black person who "tells it like it is" is accused of being angry, when she or he is merely being realistic. Many people have no stomach for dealing with the realities of race. Only a few designated folks are allowed to serve as the voice of black America. This has worked in my favor, and I do not like it. Mine is one of the acceptable black voices now. There's a list. I do not know who keeps it, but there must be a list of people who can get on television. I support other young black women being put into the position of being a voice. There should be many more young black women on television. I am supportive of there being a huge variety of black voices on television because then I can say what I want to say with the knowledge that others will say what they want to say. If there are too few black voices, I have to represent everybody, and that is impossible. The result is a homogenized voice, which is not really what is needed.

Blacks in television news can have a huge influence. The most mainstream of the mainstream news media is television news— local news first and network news second. Many more people watch the news on television than read the newspapers. However, many local stations have a black person in the team of two or three anchors or reporters who bring you the nightly news. Just because there is a black person sitting there reading the news does not mean that the news was written by a black person, approved by a black person, thought about or even underlined and spell-checked by a black person. The more important positions tend to be in the producers' offices, particularly the executive producers' offices. The cosmetic use of blackness is generally not accompanied by blacks in those thinking roles occupied by people who get the final say over the stories. Most black journalists on television do as much as they can, but the reality is that most of the decisions are made completely aside from the anchors, completely aside. Television news is absolutely collaborative. There are no one-person stories as there are in print journalism. In television, you have the producer, the executive producer, the cameraman, the soundman, the assignment editor, the anchor, and the reporter. In a whole cast of thousands, it is easy for your voice to get lost. African Americans can have an influence in television, but they need to think more about going into the jobs where one is on the track to become an executive producer. Not enough black people work behind the scenes, on the track to make it up to the top of the ladder in decision making.

In sum, then, we need to control the media because the news judgment of the people at the top is tied up with the pervasive norms of American society. In some senses that is good. There is an inquisitiveness reflected in the U.S. media. America is a land of people with questions. We all want to know what is going on. But there are also other norms of American society that are less praiseworthy: the assumptions that blacks and Latinos are inferior, that women are inferior; that people in the inner city deserve their fate, that they are somehow almost genetically, or according to Charles Murray definitely genetically, preordained to live lives of degradation. These assumptions are brought into America's newsrooms every day because reporters are people. If we grow up in this society, we absorb some of these assumptions and bring them into the newsroom with us. It is only by constant vigilance on the part of the U.S. public that we can hope to change this.

Flexing Our Power as Media Consumers

Now, a lot of people tell me that the news media will not listen, that if they write a letter, no one will care. One of my first jobs at *Newsweek* was as a researcher/reporter. The magazine received error letters, which we called Barbies (not because of the doll, but because of the last name of the woman who handled them). The researcher/reporters were judged by how well they cleared up the Barbies—assessing them, sometimes getting the magazine to admit an error and print an apology. From my firsthand experience, I can say that interacting with the media in this way does make a difference.

You are all consumers of the media in the sense that you take in the images and absorb them whether or not you think you do. You are consumers in the sense that even when you are watching free television you are taking in the advertising and deciding whether or not to buy Tide detergent or Jell-O pudding pops. You can use that as leverage when you interact with the media. Simply by being someone who consumes products that are advertised in newspapers and magazines and on television, you are someone whom they have a vested interest in keeping happy. And if you are not happy, you need to speak out about that. Write that letter. The more specific you are, the better. Address the letter to the reporter of the story and send copies to the general manager of the television station or the managing editor of the newspaper and, if the story is particularly egregious, some of the advertisers.

There is so much economic power in the black community that we do not tap, because we do not believe we are an economic force. Yes, white Americans, individually in terms of relative statistics, and collectively because they are a larger group, have more influence than we do, but there would not be so many black sitcoms on television if the networks were not making money off them. The question, then, is why this same audience cannot support black drama or better coverage of blacks in the news programs. In serious, egregious instances, we need to rely on our power as an economic force and write the advertisers. I am not advocating that we do this in every case; the panic button can be pushed too quickly. There was a Christian group that did not like the show *Married with Children*. It organized a huge boycott against the advertisers, and it worked. Certain advertisers pulled their support. I have mixed feelings about this because important issues of free speech are involved. Nonetheless, we should think about asserting our economic muscle, as a group of 35 million individuals, more often.

We need to leverage the power of black organizations that should be benefiting us by impacting on the media. One of the things the media does is give us black leaders. There is no such thing as a white leader, but there are black leaders. They change from time to time. It can be Farrakhan today and Mfume tomorrow, but if there are black leaders, we should leverage their media power, their identification in our favor. We should not only write the media organizations; we should write our own organizations and ask them to stand up on our behalf.

Shareholder control of media corporations might also be relevant, though not significantly so. Randall Robinson of Trans-Africa, whose essay is included in this volume, was instrumental in the South African divestment movement which leveraged the political and economic power of black Americans and of Americans of all races in forcing public and private institutions to divest themselves of stock in companies that did business in South Africa. I would love to see that sort of leverage applied to media entities, but realistically speaking I do not think that it is going to happen. Some of us may be stockholders, but nearly all of us are consumers of the media in some form. Almost everyone has some exposure to the media. In my opinion, it is probably more effective in the long run to join together as consumers and say that we will just stop (a) buying your product or (b) supporting the advertisers that pay you to put out your product—than it is to go into the boardrooms and threaten a revolt from the inside.

There is a story I often tell when I talk about the media. This woman stood up in a church basement in the Bronx and said to me, "I'm so sick of my son, my fifteen-year-old son, reading that black men are nothing, reading only about crime, that I just canceled my newspaper subscription." I asked her if she told the newspaper why she had canceled her subscription. She said no. And I replied, "Well, then you're just another black person who doesn't read, because if they don't know why you're upset, they don't care." Indeed, they think that we do not care. Of course, we care, but feel powerless to do anything about the media.

People are supposed to feel somewhat, but not totally, powerless when they watch the news or read the newspaper. If they feel too powerless, they may cancel their subscriptions or not watch. If they feel too empowered, they ask questions, they challenge the media, and they require the reporters to do more work. The reason that writing letters, for example, works is that so few people write letters, so few people even feel empowered to do something as simple as sending in a letter. So when a news organization gets one letter from a reader or a viewer, it is absolutely shocked. Suppose it got hundreds or thousands of letters every day? Each viewer's individual strength might be diminished, but their collective strength would be increased. Until that day, though, as long as people do not feel empowered, the lone individual should feel powerful enough to stand up for her or his own views, confident that her or his letter will get through to them.

Something is accomplished when we write to magazines or newspapers, even if they do not print the letters. It broadens their constituency. If the media perceives that its constituency is limited to white readers or viewers, it will not feel particularly compelled to address the lives of nonwhite readers or viewers realistically. It is quite similar to the focus of the automotive section being directed entirely at males. If the newspapers thought that a hefty chunk, not the majority, but a hefty chunk of the readers of the automotive section were female, they would not always think only about what guys want. Because of the realities of American demographics, blacks will never constitute the majority of consumers of national news coverage, but that does not mean that our voices should not be heard. Putting ourselves out there with letters, E-mail, and phone comments can help correct that.

If we have any hopes of changing the stereotypical portrayals and perceptions of African Americans and many other groups in this society through the media, then we have to interact. To interact requires that we assume a level of responsibility and a level of risk. It is very easy to say that the media is racist and then continue with our lives and never try to do anything about it. It is something very different to take the chance, write a letter, track down who should receive that letter, and find out if anybody in the community is working on the same issue. (At San Francisco State, a group newly formed by Professor Yvonne Raman monitors the media on behalf of people of color in particular.) There are ways that we can join together and change these perceptions. The first one is simply to talk and write about it.

You might wonder how the black community can exercise collective control over the media, given the community's rich diversity, a diversity that encompasses a host of political perspectives represented by various folks, ranging from Angela Davis to Louis Farrakhan to Shelby Steele to Charles Johnson and finally to Sista Souljah. We must join together along lines of common interest. There are countless white Americans who are angry about the racism of the media, just as there are some black Americans who do not perceive any racism in the media. We must band together along lines of alliance and draw support from people who see the same issues and problems that we do. There have been, at different times, very strong protests against the media by various groups of African Americans. I wish there was more concerted action of this kind. Any group can become a media lobbying group. Your church can. Your book club can. The people who end up at a poetry reading in Fort Greene, Brooklyn, can. So can any group of people who you believe might have an interest in something that you have read that strikes you as being particularly deplorable.

For example, *60 Minutes* did a segment on Afrocentricism which prominently featured Professor Mary Lefkowitz, who wrote *Not Out of Africa: How Afrocentrism Became an Excuse to Teach Myth as History,* which basically asserts that Afrocentrism is bunk. Focusing on her would have been fine if the program had given equal time, weight, or respect to people advocating opposing views. Lefkowitz was accorded more than her due, however, in that she was allowed to utter a very incendiary sound bite without follow-up; she stated that Afrocentrism inspired hate, and no one asked her what she meant by that statement. She was not asked what kind of hate she was referring to, nor was she asked whether Afrocentrism had ever, to her knowledge, resulted in an incidence of violence. This was one way in which structuring a piece journalistically and, I believe, sensationally was detrimental. I think I probably should have gotten together with people I know and done something about it. When my roommate, who is South Asian, saw a piece in *Elle* magazine that was a completely scatological view of the Indian continent, she decided that it merited a letter. Not only did she write her letter; she presented it to several of her friends, including myself, and we all signed it. Her letter was the first one published in the magazine. I am not South Asian, but I cared that the image was completely pejorative and simple-minded, and so I joined with my room-mate along lines of common interest.

Supporting Alternatives to the Mainstream

Not only do we need to demand accountability from the main-stream press, but I feel very strongly that we need to support the black press, as well as other ethnic presses, women's presses, gay and lesbian presses, and the alternative media. In truth, most black Americans and nearly everyone else get most of their news from mainstream organizations, from *Time* magazine to *Newsweek*, from the *New York Times* and the *Washington Post* to whatever the local daily paper is. We have passed, for better or worse, the era where the black press is the be-all and end-all of news for black people. At best, the black press is a supplement to the mainstream press. We also need the black press as a reality check because there are times when the black press tells us things straight, things that other media will not. Despite this, sales are low. As with everything else, there is a level of racism within the black community in terms of how we consume our own media. Even if we have a perfectly good black newspaper, we may think that the white-owned newspaper is better. True, some of the black newspapers are not as tight or as focused as they could be, but there are times when we have access to a very good black media product and it folds because we do not believe in it.

There has been a real shakeout of black publications, such that the only thriving ones are those that have really put some thought into what their market is and what African Americans need. There is little dead wood among black publications, because they just fold. It would be preferable if some of these newspapers and magazines redefined their mission and, like *Emerge*, directed their focus toward providing hard news from a black perspective to black Americans. Black publishers really need to think about what black America needs. I think blacks need to find out what issues are affecting the black community and how to respond to them. In general, the black press could play more of a role in delineating possible courses of action. That is one thing I also fault the mainstream press for. This happened, this happened, this happened, and this happened. Isn't that sad? We are a nation of people who very often have the ability to influence the course of events. There are ways of contacting people in power. The press should provide information on routes of access to decision makers, the names of persons to contact, E-mail addresses, and telephone numbers. The black press should not necessarily issue a call to arms to which all must respond or not be considered good black people, but it should provide those who want to affect what is going on with information on what they can do.

In order for us to be able to make critical judgments about our society and about the way the media portrays it, we need sound, balanced information. That is why I advocate reading the black press *and* the mainstream press, reading books *and* watching television shows, listening to Pacifica Radio *and* National Public Radio. Statistics are slippery, and they are often abused. Get some basic knowledge about where you live and who you live with, and use that as a reference point for understanding the news stories you read. If you do not have independent information, you cannot evaluate whether the media is lying or telling the truth. You do not have to consult five different sources of information every day, but during the course of a week you should really try to familiarize yourself with the contents of two or three. Don't just watch the nightly news every night. Listen to WBAI and then one day read *Emerge*. Try to get a sense of what different organizations are trying to tell you; every organization has an agenda. Most mainstream news organizations are big corporations which favor the interests of big corporations over the interests of the people who work for them. Moreover, their readership is composed of people who are at the top of the hierarchy as opposed to working people who are in the middle or below. This affects how mainstream newspapers discuss a labor dispute or union organizing. They may not even cover issues that are of interest to people who are workers. Turning to different sources of information, however, may give you more of what you need.

Conclusion

I am not going to pretend that we can change the media over night. But I think what we have going in our favor as a nation is our growing awareness of our own diversity. Right now, Americans who are baby boomers and older are about 20 percent nonwhite, while Americans who are between the ages of fifteen and twenty-five are one-third nonwhite. By the year 2050, this nation will have no racial majority. Whites will constitute slightly under 50 percent of the population; the remainder will be a mix of blacks, Latinos, Asian Americans, and Native Americans. The sheer force of the demographics favors transforming the media into a more racially equitable media.

I would like to encourage more African Americans to enter the media. It is a great career, a tough career. I love it. We in the news media set the pace of public opinion. When I do commentaries on issues that I really think would benefit from public participation, I try to say so. I attempt to give people the opportunity to weigh in. Take campaign finance, for example. I said that if there was more of a public outcry, reform legislation would get passed. It is time for people to stand up and be heard. Writing a single letter is not going to produce campaign finance reform, but writing your letter and getting other people around you to do the same could very well make a difference. Many laws have been passed because a congressperson got a letter, an E-mail, or a fax from a couple of hundred people who weighed in so that the congressperson knew that her or his job was on the line unless she or he took care of business. The one thing that we can all do as journalists to heal the divide between the people in the newsrooms and the people we are addressing is to encourage participation. I hope that those of you who have read this essay will come away with a sense that we are on the same team, at least most of us, trying to make the media more representative and responsive.

Stanley Crouch

We underestimate Stanley Crouch. To our peril. Amid the smoke and fire of his public reputation, the keynote of his persona is "controversialist." And that reputation is one he has worked at and well earned. By the title of his best-known essay collection, Notes of a Hanging Judge, *Crouch served notice that he does not mind going unloved. In these and other essays, he has bared his sword against some of the most highly respected or feared personalities of his times. It is almost as if the assault on the politically correct was created to form a background for his fusillades directed toward any opinion whose credit outran its provability.*

As a controversialist, Crouch brings to mind the macho gun brawlers of the rugged West, always on the ready to throw down against any opponent. His self-styled emulation of Judge Roy Bean, "the meanest judge west of the Pecos," and the original "hangin' judge," places him in this rough-and-ready mythography. But this reputation and his high-profile appearances on the Oprah Winfrey Show, Nightline, *and the* Charlie Rose Show *merely establish his easily vouched credentials as a personality with passionate opinions always on the ready.*

The image of controversialist may serve Crouch's needs to get his points across to a wide audience. He has used it well as a journalist who now writes a twice-weekly column for the New York Daily News *and whose work has appeared regularly in the* New Republic *and the* Village Voice, *and frequently in publications such as* Harper's, *the* New York Times, Down Beat, *and* Vogue. *But the term "controversialist" characterizes a range of exhibitionists from sensation mongers like Howard Stern to any soapbox orator in Times Square. One doubts that Crouch won a MacArthur "genius" award in 1993 for his capacity to set a fire.*

When the smoke clears, Stanley Crouch deserves respect he has not yet gathered for his artistry as a writer. The sting of his opinions may obscure the poise and verve of his pen for some readers of his essays. But catch him in an arena where social policy and ideology are less at stake, and you may notice the quality of his prose. Some people may have written equally well on jazz, but nobody has written better. He has established a new, graphic vocabulary for descriptions of individual jazz performers and performances. His knowledge of jazz is reflected in the programming of Jazz at Lincoln Center, where he is an artistic consultant. Stanley Crouch the artist will be even more apparent when his long-awaited novel, First Snow in Kokomo, *is published, and when his also highly anticipated biography of Charlie Parker becomes available.*

Until the force of Crouch's creative personality is recognized for both his artistry and his gift for spiky debate, we could do worse than appreciate the bracing note he brings to considerations of black life in America. Crouch has a critical nose for untested abstractions and generalizations. In response, he quickly runs to the aid of the commonsense perception, and to the defense of black people who might become the victims of loosely stitched policy assumptions. Speak regretfully of the legions of young black men warehoused in national prisons, and Crouch will remind you of the terror some of these inmates can evoke when running rampant on inner-city streets. As a moralist, he will not accept any removal of responsibility from an individual for his actions, no matter what the social apologist might diagnose as cause. This function of Crouch's—to always add another, ground-level angle on the issues facing black people—is put to good use in his recent collection of essays, Always in Pursuit: Fresh American Perspectives, *1995–1997. It is a function that, curiously, fits very comfortably among other representers in the Black Genius series, and their common search for solutions that might actually, concretely work to improve black life.*

CLYDE TAYLOR

STRAIGHTEN UP AND FLY RIGHT

An Improvisation on the Podium

My title comes from a song by Nat King Cole about a monkey who is flying on the back of a buzzard. The monkey thinks that everything is on the square, but when he gets wise to what the buzzard is really up to, he offers the buzzard the sage advice "Straighten up and fly right." Therein lies a metaphor for a problem we all have to address in American life today. That is, our culinary/cultural standards are being set by buzzards, those creatures that ingest rotten and putrefying flesh, and they have convinced many of us that we should like the same fare they do.

None of this is to say that there are not ongoing victories across race, across sex, and across class that are quite observable in American life. If we look at what has happened in America over the last forty years, say since 1957, it is very, very clear how many victories have been won in this society. I was born in 1945, so I remember 1957 rather clearly. In 1957, it seemed as though things of importance other than political agitation, entertainment, and athletics were done only by white guys in gray or black suits, white shirts, and dark ties. Now, of course, if you turn on television you see people of every hue and of both sexes who are mayors of cities, scientists, police chiefs, and commentators on the action on Wall Street. Everyone you might want to see is there. To those professional whiners who say, "Well, they ain't gonna never let us in," I say that is a bunch of garbage. It is so obvious that the world has changed very, very drastically through the efforts of a good number of people.

Indeed, the problems with the black buzzards I want to address are ones that afflict *all* Americans. In addition, we cannot avoid them by sinking to excuses based on race, class, or sex. The problems are illustrated by the stark, extreme contrasts that exist between certain contemporary black figures in the worlds of sports, entertainment, and economic celebrity. In sports, we have, say, a Tiger Woods and what he represents on the one hand and we have a Dennis Rodman on the other. In music, on the one hand we have Wynton Marsalis writing *Blood on the Fields*. On the other hand we had Biggie Smalls and Tupac Shakur. On the one hand we have a black guy named Cedric Johnson, a technological genius who is probably going to become the first black Bill Gates. He's likely to amass billions when his innovations get out. But on the other side of the business aisle we have Shug Knight.

Let's look at Dennis Rodman of the Chicago Bulls. Dennis Rodman represents the way in which the society has changed. I remember when I met Oscar Robertson, the great basketball player, in 1988 while I was on the road covering the presidential campaign of Jesse Jackson. We went to this little coffee shop, and Oscar Robertson said to me, Man, let me ask you something. Do they have a factory where they make these crazy Negroes or what? I asked him what he meant. This is the gist of what he told me: The way that these guys conduct themselves in sports today! I can't even believe the things that they do. Not only are so many of them bad sportsmen; they make so many dumb decisions. The way they get sucked into these different tricks; the way they get addicted to this and to that! I don't understand what this is, because when we were coming up, we just knew, we had been informed up front, that this sort of behavior wasn't what you do. I feel too embarrassed sometimes when I look at these guys to even tell anybody that I was an athlete.

The behavior Robertson observed is something that was widely discussed in connection with the fiftieth anniversary of Jackie Robinson's suiting up in major league baseball. The level of discipline athletes used to have has to some extent left sports because the society has accepted a certain level of bitchery from people. I am not talking about bitchery in terms of sex. I am talking about *being* a bitch. I am talking about the player who gets bumped on the basketball court and wants to start a fight; or the player who runs over a cameraman and kicks him; or the player who does not like a referee's call and spits on the referee. Those kinds of things are sheer bitchery. It is based on the worst interpretation of irresponsible aristocratic behavior. It has nothing to do with being on the bottom; it has to do with thinking that you have the freedom that comes with having power. You see, we find out who people really are, not when they think they are weak, but when they think they are strong. When they think you really cannot do any-thing to them, that is when you find out who they are. For instance, in sports today the fines are inadequate, given the kind of money that these athletes make. If a player making $2 million a year does something very nasty on the court or the field and is fined only $5,000, he'll go out there and do the same thing again.

Like everything else American, all of these bad sportsmen are connected. If you ever watched John McEnroe play tennis, you know that he wasn't a sportsman at all. He was an upper-class white guy who engaged in the same kind of unsportsmanlike conduct exhibited by people from whatever other racial groups, from whatever other classes.

The behavior I have described, it seems to me, falls into our society from the world of popular entertainment. We have become accustomed in America to seeing all kinds of meaningless violence executed by purported heroes whose only engagement lies in the idea that he or she should be able to do it. Moreover, in a pattern that started with the James Bond movies or that was popularized with them, the hero does something very violent to somebody and then finishes it off with a quip at the end. For instance, he crushes somebody's body under something; when they ask what happened to Bob, the hero says, "Oh, he's getting his suit pressed." So somebody gets beheaded or somebody gets dragged to death, and we're all reduced to laughter. What began with the Bond movies and got picked up by people like Arnold Schwarzenegger, Bruce Willis, and Mel Gibson of *Lethal Weapon* has ended up a standard feature of the endless string of slice-and-dice, hang-them-up, drape-them-up, murder-them-up, shoot-them-up movies that we see on cable TV.

The flip side of this is gangster rap, the American Negro audio version of the slice-and-dice movie with the unfortunate addition of the idea that the performers are the *real* black people. I am not referring to all rap, only to the rap that is misogynistic, flaunts and celebrates the most ruthless forms of materialism, and exhibits absolute barbaric tendencies without context. I was on a show with Patrick Buchanan's sister, Bay, and she asked me why I thought gangster rap was so popular in the white suburbs. I was reminded of this guy from Britain who commenced to tell me that he thought that this stuff was valuable. I told him, as I told Buchanan's sister, that I knew why he felt as he did: when you hear this rhymed doggerel and see images of these illiterates, there is one thing that you're convinced of, and that is that *you're* superior to *them*.

The dumber, more obnoxious, and more ridiculous a Negro is, the more varieties of popularity he or she has in certain areas of America. The gangster rapper is just an update of the "Stepin Fetchit" character, except now we have Stepin Fetchit with a handgun and a crack pipe. So instead of Stepin Fetchit going, "I don't know what I was doing," he's going, "Well, I'm trying to get my pipe; you know what I'm saying. . . ." They are the same person. Further, as Armond White points out, there is a group of people in or in *with* the media who support the likes of Snoop Doggy Dogg, Tupac Shakur, Biggie Smalls, Ice-T, Ice Cube, and other visions of Negro imbecility. It has become an intellectual version of "tomming." White says that it is another way of saying, "Yes boss, that's the way we are; we still up under you." There is one thing we can be sure of, though—if we look at American culture and books like *Blacking Up: The Minstrel Show in Nineteenth Century America,* by Robert C. Toll—the "Tupac Shakur" character was popular 150 years ago. Back then it was called either "zip coon" or "Jasper Jack." The character was a razor-toting, ignorant, obnoxious person whom people liked to see. Back then it was white guys made up to look like what they thought black Americans looked like. Today it is black Americans tomming themselves up and pretending that they are what *real* Afro-Americans are like.

Biggie Smalls and these people also have a lot in common with the movie characters of the 1930s. The only difference is that the pay scale has changed dramatically. The gangster rappers and such represent an opportunity for suburban white kids to go on what I call an audio safari. A hundred years ago, they would have had to don a pith helmet, get mosquito netting, take a boat to Africa, India, or some such place, hire gun bearers, and run the risk of being bitten by malarial insects in order to get a real feel of the jungle in the center of the wild. All they have to do now is go to Tower Records, and they can be transported straight to the black American jungle, or what they think that is, and be absolutely safe. They can sit up in Scarsdale or wherever, turn their caps backward, untie their shoes, take their belts off, let their pants almost fall off, and "become" urban savages for a day, if that is what they want to do.

I have a large problem with this projection. I was recently at a school in the Bed-Stuy section of Brooklyn for the "Principal for a Day" program. While there, I asked these kids, who are right in the middle of things, what they thought about the gangster rap phenomenon. They said that they liked to listen to it. What is it that they like about it? "We like the beat," they replied. Then I asked them how they felt about the kinds of people who are represented in this stuff, and they answered, "Oh, we don't like *them*. We don't like those kinds of people, because those are the kinds of people who make our lives *horrible*. They are the ones who turn out the parties. They are the ones who attack people for staring at them. They're the ones who want to fight because someone bumps into them on the subway or steps on their feet at a party."

Of course, this means that there has been a new development, Truth in Advertising. As a friend of mine pointed out when Sid Vicious, this monstrous rock-and-roll fellow from England, murdered his girlfriend in a New York hotel, that was surely truth in advertising. He did, after all, call himself Sid Vicious. Some gangster rappers and such *are* what they depict themselves to be. Shug Knight, the president and CEO of Death Row Records, is at present serving a nine-year sentence in the penitentiary after being caught on video tape, with Tupac Shakur, chasing, beating, and stomping a guy in the lobby of a hotel an hour or two before Shakur was shot. Edward G. Robinson was an actor, James Cagney was an actor, Humphrey Bogart was an actor, and Marlon Brando was an actor. Al Pacino and Arnold Schwarzenegger say words in front of a camera, as do Bruce Willis and Mel Gibson. Never in the history of American popular entertainment has a person who got roles as a gangster chased anybody down the lobby of a hotel. Never has the president of a record company stomped some guy in the hallway. This has never happened before. Nor to my knowledge was James Cagney or any of these other guys ever shot at, except with blanks. What we have here is a real problem because these people today are not acting.

Take Tupac Shakur and Shug Knight. If they *were* acting, they didn't know the consequences. What would make two black guys, one of whom is the president of a company that is worth $300 million, chase somebody down the hall of a hotel and beat up two security guards on the way. "Thug Life," a title that Tupac Shakur used, is very accurate because he was no gangster. Even John Gotti would not have done what he did. John Gotti was a gangster; he wasn't a thug. He may have felt thug feelings but he exhibited gangster actions. If Shug Knight had been like John Gotti, when he and Tupac saw the guy they wanted to get, he would have stopped Tupac from running after the guy and told one of these bozos, one of these two-legged pit bulls that hang around them, that he, Shug, wanted that guy right there in the hospital or dead within twenty-four hours. That's how a gangster would have done it. Shug would have been sitting in his expensive car when his orders were carried out, just like when Paul Castellano was killed on Gotti's orders. Gotti was in the neighborhood to make sure everything went the way he wanted it to go, but he was not in front of the place where Castellano got shot. That is narcissism of the sort that real gangsters learned about a long time ago. Meyer Lansky told Charles (Lucky) Luciano about it before Lucky Luciano found out how right Lansky was. Lansky told Luciano, "Charlie"—he called him Charlie—"I pick up the newspaper. I see you in the Stork Club. You got two show girls sitting with you eating lobster; you're eating steak; you're pouring champagne. I see you getting out of a chauffeured car. I see you at another place; you got a whole table full of people; you're picking up the tab; you're buying everybody champagne. Charlie, you *don't have* a *job*. People will soon notice

this." You know what happened to Luciano; people noticed it
and he went to jail.

Many of these developments can be attributed to the phenomenon Chris Rock talks about, of "keeping it real." In a very
important stand-up routine, the comedian and actor Chris Rock
noted that there is a lot of racism out here and he asked, "Who
do you think is more racist, black people or white people?" He
answered, "Black people because we hate niggers too. There's a
civil war going on, and that war is between black people and niggers and the niggers got to go." Rock goes on to explain what he
meant: "Niggers love to *not* know. Niggers are proud of not
knowing. If you say what is the capital of Zaire [now the Republic of Congo], the answer from a nigger will be 'I don't know any
of that shit. I'm trying to keep it real.'" The less you know, the
realer a black person you are. The more removed from civilized
behavior you are, the realer you are. The more inarticulate you
are, the realer you are. Rock was essentially saying that black people do not celebrate ignorance, criminality, and lack of initiative,
any more than any other community. Rock, with scathing but
hilarious contempt, was attacking the notion that ignorance is a
form of vitality.

The people I have cited here are part of the celebration of rednecks that is going on in American culture at large. This is not
something that we are doing by ourselves; nobody is doing anything by themselves. If there had not been a Madonna, we would
not have a Dennis Rodman. Dennis Rodman got like he got after
he got with her. He got with her and he said, "Oh, that's how you
do that." Then he probably looked at his birth certificate and
concluded that he was only going to be playing basketball for a

couple of more years. He figured that if he put all of these rings in his nose, ears, lips, and belly button, dyed his hair a different color every day, covered his body with all these strange tattoos, and put on a dress and some lipstick, people would notice him just as they did Madonna. If you remember Madonna's career, she did all of that. She did every kind of strange, bizarre thing she could do until she became a mother. As they say in show business, "That was me then; this is me now." Dennis Rodman, right now, is still in the *early* Madonna phase. If he becomes sufficiently popular doing that, then when he becomes forty or forty-five years old, he'll probably put on a business suit, take all the rings out of his nose and ears, and say, "That was me *then*; this is me *now*."

All of this is related to the fact that we live in a time when the flight plans of the buzzards are omnidirectional. That allows them to set the culinary/cultural standards all over the place. Whenever elected members of either or both political parties are caught flapping the wind in their buzzard suits, the politicians tell us that we are not seeing what we are seeing, we are not hearing what we are hearing, and we should not say what we are saying about them. For instance, Bill Clinton—I mean, gee whiz, Bill—now that's a country boy, and the kind of corruption he is dealing with is some country-style corruption. We have a Charlie Tree who comes into a place with a couple of bags full of checks and money orders that are sequentially numbered so that check no. 101 is from Little Rock, Arkansas, no. 102 is from Portland, Oregon, no. 103 is from Houston, Texas, and no. 104 is from Miami; leaves over $300,000 on the desk; and walks out. That is probably the way they do business in Little Rock, but you cannot do that in Washington, D.C. Then there is Newt Gingrich. This guy has a $300,000 fine dropped on him for flagrant abuse of House ethical rules, and he gets up on the new session's opening day and acts like he got a traffic ticket on the way there.

What I am saying, then, is that there is *some*times no difference between the vision of the public that we get from the people in Hollywood, or at Death Row Records, and in Washington, D.C. Yet, I am by no means suggesting that we should just give up. The history of the country is based upon engaging these various forms of abuses of power, whether they are in the private sector, in politics, or in educational structures. That is our history. We must recognize that, at this particular point, everybody is suffering from the imposition of these decadent and ruthless attitudes on public communication, public imagery, and politics.

That is why black Americans cannot attempt to step back and say that this has nothing to do with us, just because we don't look like those people. There used to be a routine on *Saturday Night Live* which definitely reflected a truth about Afro-American culture. The segment was called "Black Crime/White Crime." A guy goes to work, shoots eighteen people, and kills himself: white crime. A guy runs out of a liquor store with two six-packs in his hands and a bottle of whiskey in his back pocket. The whiskey falls out, so he goes back to pick it up and is arrested: black crime, or so many black people seem to think. Moreover, there was a period when nobody I know could have imagined Colin Ferguson. When I first heard the announcement of the 1993 shooting on the Long Island Railroad train that left six people dead and nineteen people injured, I *knew* that the perpetrator was a white guy. When I saw Colin Ferguson in handcuffs, I said,

"Well, I guess we *have* gotten there." The same thing is true of those cases in which parents torture and murder their children. There was a period when black people would say, "You know, we don't do that to our kids." Turn on the news tonight and hear the stories involving brutal black parents. The time of smug dismissal has passed. *We* are there, *too*.

Our society also suffers from the actions of a number of people across races and classes who have lost a sense of anything other than what it is they want to do. That is, what Christopher Lasch called the culture of narcissism is fully in place, and one of the things that narcissism begets is a totally uncivilized way of dealing with other people, not to mention total delusion. For example, consider a man who was not an American but who was as deluded as an American or a certain *kind* of American—Mobutu Sese Seko of the former Zaire. This guy stole, conservatively, five billion dollars. Do you know that he did not pay the army that was defending him for over a year. That is total narcissism and delusion. Only a jerk would think that way.

So Americans at large have before us an extraordinary challenge, but one that has been met in the past. The rise of American nationalism that followed the War of 1812 was accompanied by a very visceral rejection of sophisticated types whom common Americans associated with what was considered European decadence. In fact, people would get angry if they heard that an actor or actress rode a horse English-style. The contemporary obsession with or the embracing of rednecks, thugs, ne'er-do-wells, nihilists, and the like is a polluted extension of a difficulty we have had in the United States for a long time. It is related to the difficulty of maintaining vitality in an upwardly mobile society.

There is the clichéd idea that, as we become more sophisticated, we lose vitality and that the vital is somewhere down there.
For instance, people have told me that what is of value comes out
of the streets and that if I listen to these rap records I'll learn what
is going on. Learn what? That people with guns who are vicious
shoot other people. Is that *news*? Or that when armed members
of one drug-dealing gang encounter armed members of another
drug-dealing gang, they will get into a fight. This is news? Or
that people with terrible taste will buy huge gold jewelry and diamonds. I once had a dream in which I imagined that people who
had paralytic problems with their hands would buy some of these
rings that these rappers wear and use them like weights to build
up the strength in their fingers. I saw one of these kids on the
train and realized that the contraption that covered four of his
fingers was an update of something hustlers used to do when I
was a kid. They would grow very long nails and put nail polish
on them in order to prove that they did not do manual labor.
When you saw that hand, it meant "I'm not a day laborer." You
cannot do very much with the things that kid had on his hand,
two things that looked like miniature aircraft carriers and had his
name or something spelled on them. I guess that was his way of
saying to the world, "I don't work."

We have always had those types in America. We have always
had the gaudiness which can beget a certain kind of vitality in a
narrow space. We have also always had people who are outside
the norm, who have invented things that are of great value. Our
big problem is figuring out whether we are looking at a Louis
Armstrong or a Biggie Smalls and how to make sure that we do
not confuse the two. We have to learn again how to distinguish

between what I call "heroic individuality" and "anarchic individuality." Heroic individuality is exemplified by the person whose individual expression actually intensifies general freedom, like an Abraham Lincoln or a Martin Luther King. Their efforts lead to greater freedom rather than less. On the other hand, anarchic individuality, which I've written about before, is symbolized by a figure like Billy the Kid whose individuality comes at the expense of everybody else. The anarchic individual is the kind of person who is going to do what he wants to do regardless of what it costs others for him to be happy.

We need as well a reinvention of the intelligent and engaged person as a symbol of vitality. When I was a kid, television stations presented a weekly Million Dollar Movie, which was repeated every night Monday through Friday, and then twice on Saturday and Sunday. If you looked at them over and over again, you learned about camera position, lighting, and all that; you could actually learn about film. You didn't know that that was what you were learning, but you actually learned it because you saw the films so many times. One of the things that you realized when you watched these films, many of which were made in the 1930s, was that the very same people who made gangster films made very obvious musicals, maudlin love stories, simple pro-proletariat movies, and conversely equally simple-minded movies about the joys of having a lot of money. Those very same studios could make movies in which an actor like Spencer Tracy played Thomas Edison and made the intellectual job of discovering how to produce electric light as exciting as a film in which there was a series of gunfights, storms at sea, et cetera. Or they could turn around, take Don Ameche and make him Alexander Graham

Bell, and create excitement as he tried to perfect the telephone.

I say this because we have a very serious problem in this country in that there are a number of black kids who believe that participation in certain forms of intellectual engagement will make them white. Like going to the library, or being able to use the English language well. I recently read a book about a substitute teacher who went to a school in Detroit and suddenly heard the beginning of a chant. The chant was "Stop trying to eat white," and it got louder and louder. The teacher looked around and saw a kid eating chicken with a knife and fork, instead of with his hands. All of these people had declared that this kid was trying to be white because the kid was not eating with his hands.

Now, I must say as a person who is fifty-two years old, that whatever confusions Negroes had when I was growing up, they did not have *these*. They might have been confused about a number of things because they were Americans and Americans always have a repository of confusion, but nobody ever told me, whatever his or her station was, that being a dummy made one a real black person. I never heard anybody say that, not even the thugs. When I was growing up, thugs would cut you off at a certain point. If you wanted to be a "play thug" and run around with them, at a certain point they'd say, "Man, you'd better go home and study. If you stick with us you're gonna get shot or stabbed, or you're gonna go to the penitentiary. If you lucky, you won't, but most people aren't that lucky." The thugs would just cut you out of the gang or not let you in. You had something else to do and it was not being with them, because they knew they were jerks. They had decided what path they were going down, and that was that. They did not have any black intellectuals on col-

lege campuses describing them as being real or informing us
about their supposed importance.

I remember when this phenomenon began. It began in the
1960s with the Black Panthers. They were the first ones to run
that hustle because they had these naive groupie-like followers.
All these guys had to do was pull out a rap sheet, and these girls
got excited. A guy would say that he'd been arrested so many
times, and the girl would say, "Oh, this is a real black guy. He's
not like the sons of the pharmacists, doctors, and lawyers that I
grew up around. He doesn't know anything about Jack 'n' Jill.
This guy is a *real* goon and I *like* that." In actuality, the only people who think criminals are interesting are people who do not
know criminals, because criminals are boring. Once the bloody
or suspenseful anecdotes have run out, the sheer dullness, however loudly expressed, becomes readily apparent.

The problems of confusing heroic individuality with anarchic
individuality are not black problems. They are, as I have been
saying all along, all-American. The grandest irony of it all is that
while these mush-mouthed Negroes, and their nappy-headed
academic supporters, go on and on about some kind of black culture that decidedly disavows white middle-class standards, they
are only proving how much they have been influenced by the
white ideas that followed the War of 1812. The Negroes of the
nineteenth century never elevated ignorance and vulgarity as
aspects of liberation. Stubbornly ignorant black people were as
much the enemy as the white races to whom they provided flesh
and blood excuses for their ruthless refusal to allow the Constitu-
tion its rightful place below the Mason-Dixon line.

There is a competing mythology that we have to regenerate.

Again, we need to figure out, as a society, how to portray the work of an intellectual or an inventor like Thomas Edison as really exciting. It is very important for people who have intellectual gifts to see their endeavors depicted with the excitement and suspense that exists in everything else. Every now and then, in one of these science fiction films, there is a problem or something breaks down and the guy who is the computer nerd, who is always eating candy bars or always has some stuff stuck in his hair, is called. He just seems like this jerk, but in the last twenty minutes of the movie they go get him, and he helps them figure out how to get rid of the beast or whatever. We need to do better than that, and I think we can.

I will conclude this improvisation on the podium with a short address I gave in October of 1996 at the Century Club in New York City, where R. W. B. Lewis and Skip Gates brought together a number of writers and friends to recall and celebrate Ralph Ellison, who died in the spring of 1994. As included in my most recent book of essays, *Always in Pursuit*, I call this piece "The Reach of the Oklahoma Kid."

Discussing the influence of Ralph Ellison is much like describing the impact of strong wind on high grass and natural gardens: the things it touches are bent by its direction while remaining exactly what they are. Ellison had that kind of impact because his ideas weren't the sort that required imitation of his style. One could draw from them and maintain individuality because they were big enough for broad interpretation. His ideas about American democracy, the arts, the far-from-simple meanings of race, class, and culture, and his sense of the hilarious interweaving itself with the tragic, the charismatic with the repulsive, and the courageous engagement that our American moment demands of us all, have—*very, very slowly*—had an informing influence on thinking about this nation and, at least as important in the summoning of the present and the war against time that is art, those ideas have also had an informing influence on the making of things designed to aesthetically capture the strutting, belly-rubbing, signifying, high-signing, profiling, conning, crooning, seducing, aristocratically moaning, tap-dancing, back-paddling, forward-thrusting, Fosberry-flopping, Cassius Marcellus Clay-to-Muhammad Ali butterfly-floating and bee-stinging, and the whole kit and caboodle always-breaking-out epic of collective Americana.

Ellison's impact has come into our national intellectual consciousness very slowly because it had to drill through the rock of pieties and reductions on both the right and the left. He was not easily drafted into movements and his work was resented by those who had decided that the country was finished, down for the count, and a done and dirty deal. Ellison wasn't one to be taken in by special-interest groups. As patient and as much a tinkerer as the Oklahoma oilmen of his home state, he kept drilling away, recognizing the difference between the liquid black gold that fueled modern life and the dirty salt water of propaganda. Given his understanding of both sides of a question, Ellison would also have been in pursuit of what we now call "clean fuel," the kind that has the lowest level of pollutants. His love and sense of the blues encompassed our battle with the spiritual pollutants that recur in our consciousness, moving us rapidly along while destroying our clarity of purpose, our impulse to civilize ourselves and our world. But civilization in an American context has to rise above what is usually meant because it has to incorporate so many things from so many places.

Ellison knew that improvisation is essential to what we make of ourselves as Americans and he recognized that we are constantly integrating the things that we find attractive in others, whether the integration is conscious or unconscious. Ellison knew well that the American wears a top hat with an Indian feather sticking out of it, carries a banjo and a harmonica, knows how to summon the voice of the blues by applying a bathroom plunger to the bell of a trumpet or a trombone, will argue about the best Chinese restaurants, eat sushi with you one on one, turn the corner and explain the differences between the dishes on the menu at an Indian restaurant, drink plenty of Tequila, get down with the martial arts, sip some vodka, recite favorite passages from the Koran, have some scotch on the rocks, show you the yarmulke worn at a friend's wedding, savor some French and Italian wine made from grapes grown in the Napa Valley, charm a snake, roll some ham and cheese up in a heated flour tortilla, tell you what it was like learning to square dance or ballroom or get the pelvic twists of rhythm and blues right, or how it felt in one of those sweltering Latin dance halls when the mambo got as hot as gumbo on a high boil.

Given his perspective, Ellison would well have enjoyed how this last summer's blockbusting thriller, *Twister*, pivoted on the protagonists improvising a way to fix their machine intended to measure the speed and power of cyclones. When they find that the homemade machine is not heavy enough to resist being knocked over by the winds and that the measuring bulbs programmed into their computer aren't automatically pulled up into the storm funnel as they had assumed, the estranged husband and wife—who fall in love again as they make it from one situation in harm's way to another—must face the challenge of the moment with improvisation. This American Mars and Diana, far more than a century ago, became the pioneer man and woman on our frontier and have now been remade yet again to speak for the rallying point of the sexes in the face of our shifting redefinitions of each other and of the frontier that is now at least partially about how we shall use our technology to better human life. This middle-1990s whirlwind-chasing couple improvises wings for their measuring bulbs, wings made from beer and soda cans, and lashes the machine that carries them to a truck for the weight necessary to hold everything in place until the tornado funnel pulls their Christmas tree decoration–looking technology into the air and the big winds reveal their secrets to the computers, lighting the screens with multicolored patterns. The combination of trucks, computers, electronic metal bulbs, beer cans, and mother wit would have gotten to Ellison because he made note of such Americanness in his introduction to the latest publication of John A. Kouwenhoven's *Beer Can by the Highway*, writing of when his wife, Fanny, brought home a Shasta lemon-lime soda can that had been transformed into an object of art by a spieling Negro guy in the street. It was now a goblet with open strips cut into its sides which would have made holding liquid impossible—the image of a banquet chalice appropriated for an aesthetic moment in tin, which Ellison describes sitting on the "glass topped, stainless steel table in our living room."

In the huge cycles of our sorrow and our celebration we now and again find ourselves thinking about Americans like Ralph

Ellison, knowing that each of them has in common with all the others the unpredictable magnetism that comes of an illuminated and illuminating individuality. All that Ellison contributed he worked for, seeking out the ways in which he would improvise the wings for the measuring bulbs that he stuck into the funnel of Americana, knowing that there had to be some way of understanding the dimensions of a culture that whirled by so rapidly, sucking up into its center all that it crossed, remaking at the same time that it destroyed, ever realigning and creating new relationships. Unlike the tornado or the cyclone, the huge funnel of Americana can be saddled and ridden by those like Ellison, whose aesthetic and intellectual powers can function like spurs, a bridle, and a saddle, turning the random power of the other into a focused part of the self, fusing one's personality with the force of nature that is the sweep of this society. Perhaps more than anything else, Ralph Ellison was telling us, over and over and over, that our passage on this land need be neither in vain nor narcissistic. If we learn to look closely enough at each other, we will see far beyond the barriers of race, class, religion, and sex. We will recognize the human heart pumping its blood to a syncopated beat, a jazz time in which the double consciousness created by sadness moving at a dance pulsation becomes the occasion to blow the blues away, not forever but just long enough to build up the sober but celebratory strength necessary to face them goddam blues when they make their inevitable return.

Anna Deavere Smith

Anna Deavere Smith has been described in the national media as the most exciting individual in American theater, and they are not wrong in that perception. With her roots in drama teaching at Stanford University, Anna Deavere Smith is best known for two theatrical works: Fires in the Mirror: Crown Heights, Brooklyn, and Other Identities *and* Twilight: Los Angeles 1992.

Now, if you have not seen one of her performances, you may need a description. Take a rather standard description of the press release variety: "These plays project multiple social personages and their feelings about public issues based on interviews." That is phenomenally inadequate. It just does not begin to capture her work.

Let me tell you more. In Twilight, *Anna Deavere Smith presents fifty-six characters in a presentation that lasts three hours or more. She gets into the personalities of real people. Everything she says onstage is what people have said to her in interviews. Since I can-*

not adequately describe what goes on in these works, let me con-
sider some of the skills that are involved. First of all, Anna must be
a major monkey-oil salesperson because she talks these people into
letting her interview them in the first place. During these inter-
views, they come out with amazing, unguarded revelations of
themselves and the society that we live in. With all due respect to
ABC's Barbara Walters, if Anna Deavere Smith wanted another
career, she would be one of the greatest interviewers on the scene
today. Anna's performances also include a great deal of acting and
miming. The sets and the lighting are done according to her needs
and instructions. Finally, she writes these works. You must under-
stand that these works must be written, must be shaped, must be
edited, must be given as a presentation. She does the theorizing
behind them.

All of these elements together, then, make for a performance that
has some of the impact of a play, but it is not a play. Fires in the
Mirror *and* Twilight *are one-person theater pieces, but they are not*
one-person theater pieces either. They convey information rather like
a documentary film, but differently. They resemble perhaps a jour-
nalistic collage, but they are not quite that either. They approach
political analysis, but then they do something else. In both of these
presentations, a fascination with storytelling is part of the mix; there
is poetry; and there is a love of language, all of which makes me
think that Mark Twain would have loved to see one of these perfor-
mances, though I think that Anna would invoke, not Mark Twain,
but Studs Terkel.

Anna Deavere Smith's works seem particularly timely in the way
that each asks the question "Why is it so difficult to be a human
being in America?" I know that she has a new work coming. I look

forward to whatever she does because she is not only the most exciting person in American theater today; she is without doubt one of the most interesting, artistic, creative, intellectual people working in the world anywhere at all.

CLYDE TAYLOR

PUBLIC LIVES, PRIVATE SELVES

Toward an Open Conversation

When Manthia Diawara asked me to participate in this series, I was less than enthusiastic. I tried to get out of it by arguing that I did not want to be forced out of my position as an artist, which is actually where I am most comfortable, into that of an academic, although I am an academic as well. I just did not want to be in the position of explaining. At the time, I was feeling very confined by what public conversations can be and certainly very intimidated by this idea of the black genius. There are, after all, so many limits in the public conversation, so many limits in rhetoric, so many possibilities for being misquoted, so many opportunities for misunderstanding. I told Manthia that what concerned me most was the impossibility of having an open conversation in public. Manthia immediately latched onto that and said that it sounded like a very interesting subject for me to discuss.

I was thinking about those limitations at that very moment because I was trying to put together a conversation between the African American playwright August Wilson (whose plays include *Ma Rainey's Black Bottom, The Piano Lesson* and *Fences*) and Robert Brustein, drama critic and artistic director of the American Repertory Theater in Cambridge, Massachusetts. They were then in the midst of a so-called "public debate" on color-blind casting and the mounting of black plays by white theater production companies. The word "debate," of course, referred only to their monologues, since the two of them had never met in public. On the day that Manthia and I spoke, I was trying to work out the logistics, trying in particular to find a neutral place for them to hold their conversation. The couple of places that had been suggested to me did not seem neutral enough. I did not even have a producer at that time. I was looking for a location where the cards were not stacked on either side, a space where members of the audience could come with their minds not yet made up.

In the end, the conversation between the two men was likened to a prizefight. I have to admit to you now openly that bringing the episode further into the public spotlight only made the lines of division more apparent. Much as I wanted them to have an open conversation, perhaps I would have accomplished more by not bringing the dialogue between Mr. Wilson and Mr. Brustein before the public. I probably should have gone with them behind closed doors for about seven hours, re-creating the circumstances of the conversation between Margaret Mead and James Baldwin—the one found in *A Rap on Race*—that had inspired me.

Should we take our conversations to the public only after they

have been rehearsed, like plays? What does it mean if society ultimately wants only plays? What does it mean to call an event "a
conversation" when my audience may only really be coming to
see me? Much as I love my art and would like to bring it closer to
the center of civic discourse, what would happen—indeed, what
has happened—to spontaneity and fluidity if every time we speak
the public anticipates witnessing a public play? What would such
rehearsed presentations do to the possibility of strangers and
unlikely advocates joining in the conversation and, more important, in the action? What does neatness do to public discourse?
What does conforming it to sound bites do? What does consent-
ing to binary structures do?

Some say that public space is dominated by the media and
that looking for space that the media has not already occupied is
useless; looking for a place where conversations can occur pub-
licly, without being defined in advance, is difficult; looking for a
place to have that dialogue where content will be as important as
form is difficult; looking for a place where the message is not
deafened by the messenger is difficult.

I received an honorary degree at a large university on the West
Coast the year before last. The commencement ceremony was
held in a large stadium-like hall. At a certain point during the
ceremony, the students stood up in groups according to their academic disciplines. For every discipline, there were comparatively
modest-sized groups of students. When the Department of Communications was called, more than half the crowd stood. The
entire hall literally rattled from the sound of their chairs as they
rose. I whispered to the faculty member sitting next to me, "Are
there jobs for all these people?" What are these people going to

do? What are they going to communicate? What is going to be the text, the body of their communications, and for what purpose? I was reminded of something that Studs Turkel, who has around fifty years or more of interviewing and chronicling America under his belt, said to me: "We're more and more into communica/shun and less and less into communica*tions*."

I am actually so seriously concerned about the open conversation that I dreamt about it. I dreamt I was visiting a school, probably a high school, though maybe an undergraduate college. The students were very young. It had the feel of a public, perhaps an urban or inner-city school. The class was diverse and predominantly working class. I entered the classroom from the back. I was expected there as a guest speaker, but no one made very much of my entrance. I stood quietly, and at a certain point the teacher told the class that I had come to visit them and she called me by name. They were not engaged and talked among themselves and so forth even as I was being introduced. I still had not moved to the front of the room. Just as I was about to go forward, the teacher added to her description of me: "She's an actress." At this point, everybody in the class turned around with cameras and started to take pictures. The students did not know who I was, but they acted as if the pictures had value. No questions. No discussion. Just pictures. Since they had all turned to the back of the room, I started to talk to them from there. I tried to explain that I was doing a project about democracy and was hoping that they would join in with me. The more I talked, however, the more my voice was drowned out by their talking among themselves, their eagerness to get a picture, and the snapping of their snapshots.

I recently interviewed the university professors Hayden White and Judith Butler. Both study rhetoric, and they emphasized to me that we are living in the time of a visual, rather than an oral, rhetoric. In some ways my dream was an attempt to come to grips with that. The students were young and educated in a very modest way with just the essentials, but they were the future. The dream felt like a nightmare, and I awoke from it with an anxiety similar to what I have experienced in my classic actor's nightmare, which is, of course, the nightmare about forgetting my lines. There I was, speaking my lines which were a call, really, for the students to join me in what I was calling democracy. It was a call for an open conversation, a civic conversation. I needed their help and they were distracted. They were distracted because of their instinct to get something, to capture something fast, that they could take with them, like a snapshot. What was horrifying to me then was not that I had forgotten my lines, but that my lines were irrelevant. I could not speak them; my voice was mute; no sound was coming out. All that was really needed was for me to pose. And yet I became an actress because I was interested in shifting identities and moving out of a pose.

Los Angeles, California. I went to Los Angeles at the request of Gordon Davidson, artistic director of the Mark Taper Forum, to join in a panel discussion as part of the celebration of the thirty-fifth anniversary of that theater. Also on the panel were the playwrights Tony Kushner (*Angels in America: A Gay Fantasia on National Themes*) and Athol Fugard of South Africa (*The Blood Knot, Master Harold . . . and the Boys, Boesman and Lena*); the moderator was John Sullivan, current director of the Theater Communications Group, an organization which supports and convenes regional theaters in this country. I was very proud to be included. Tony, Athol, and I talked about a wide variety of issues. At one point, Tony made a remark about multiculturalism; he indicated that one of the consequences that we would suffer with the demise of the NEA (National Endowment for the Arts) was a loss in terms of multiculturalism. He credited the birth of multiculturalism to the funding that supported it. I sort of mumbled, not really realizing that I was mumbling and not really realizing that I was heard, "It's not just money that challenged the existence of multiculturalism." I had on a mike, so it was picked up. Tony countered, "It's not just money, but money helps." I felt very strongly that money was in fact not the only problem with the attempt to include more people in the theater, but I did not go any further. I knew that the real conversation I needed to have I *really* needed to have, and I did not want my position to be misunderstood before I had had the opportunity to have it. I really needed to have that conversation with Tony, and not in front of an audience, for two reasons: (1) It would be boring because there would be no big phrases, no big sound bites for folks to take away; I hadn't thought up any. And (2) it would be misunderstood, because the phrases, the terms of discourse had not been constructed in advance and did not have adequate resonance. So I just let it slide.

The three of us went on and talked about a number of things, including our work, how we worked, and so forth. Now mind you, this was to be a celebration of thirty-five years of vibrant, important, and frequently successful theater in, of all cities, Los Angeles, which is completely dominated by the movies. A gala mood would have been appropriate. In fact, Tony looked rather dapper in a three-piece suit and bow tie. Athol was strong and confident; he came exactly as he was and stated it in what he had on. This is me, he said. When he made his initial remarks, he made them from his heart, rather than off the page. He was himself in a truly expert way for the occasion. As for myself, I had arrived in Los Angeles after a cross-country flight with a stop in Chicago and went immediately to a beauty parlor to become as coiffed as the celebration demanded.

When the lights were brought up, the first cry was not one of celebration. It came from a voice, first of all a voice in the dark, from a person we could not see, did not know, or did not know if we knew—a voice that yielded a very sharp and accusatory tone: "What's multiculturalism!" I glanced over to Tony to see how he was reacting. John Sullivan, thank God, put the question first of all to Athol: "Athol, let's start with you." I was hoping that whatever Athol said would be so fantastic and so provocative that we could go on to other things. Athol said, "I never use the word." Someone from the audience screamed, "Bravo!" Tony winced, visibly. For the rest of the evening, we struggled through points and counterpoints that ranged from "Well, I'm seventy years old, and I think we've come a long way" to speculation about the Internet as a place where people are curious about identity and willing to cross boundaries. I pointed out that identities on the Internet and wandering on the Internet are very different from identity in reality. In reality, we still have to tackle breath and flesh, and some people are very uncomfortable with that. A well-known actress, who probably would not mind if I used her name but I will not just in case, took me to task with a great heroic voice because she assumed that I had indicated that we should all give up on multiculturalism. Wearily I then dared to flirt with the dangerous territory of identity politics by saying that I had meant to suggest only that perhaps multiculturalism had never been sufficiently in our hearts in the first place. Most of my colleagues in the theater are white. Although some of us were schooled together, we did not work together. I ended by saying that I thought multiculturalism had become identity politics.

There is, in fact, a way to look at multiculturalism as a system of classification that may or may not have been helpful. Any artist of color is seen as part of the multicultural movement. An artist's potential is therefore politicized in a way that may or may not have been constructive. Most of us who went to major academies learned techniques which to date would have to be considered, to some extent, in that dangerous, dangerous way, universalist. I know the trap of that word. Yet, the fact is, in the theater at least, the art of speaking still is grounded in the European aesthetic. It is almost as if the only way the field could absorb artists of color was to assign them multicultural identities, in order to justify their cultural existence. From there, we all became a part of a football game. Some do not mind, while others do. Any other kind of conversation that the artist may have hoped to have is very nearly impossible.

I knew I had best not get into the benefits and shortcomings of identity politics with that LA audience, if multiculturalism had gotten us to the point of contention where we then stood. Tony, who believes in identity politics, quickly defended identity politics as a guard against oppression. I was very happy to give him the last word and to just keep my conversation closed off, because again I believe that that conversation about identity politics would be better served by being held behind closed doors. The spaces that we have for public conversation are so few. I so deeply believe that to have an open conversation, to have an exchange where identity does not already claim an apparent priority to the space, we must move out of the houses identity politics erects. In this movement from a house of identity to another, there is an ironic lack of space which I think in the end could encourage open conversation. I am interested in shifting identities as a strategy toward a more open conversation.

Athol Fugard said very little that night, which I found actually quite elegant. After all, he was the real lion among us. His plays, to some extent, contributed to the downfall of apartheid by helping teach the world about South Africa and apartheid long before some of us knew anything about the politics or history of apartheid. I saw the *Blood Knot* before I knew very much about South Africa, and it went right to my heart. Indeed, Athol had worked in a theater in Johannesburg that was considered illegal because multicultural groups were not allowed to convene. A lawyer in a stroke of luck learned that that theater happened to be situated in a market; markets were places in which persons of mixed races could be together and have an open conversation. Hence, the first interracial audiences could convene in the space of the Market Theater. If anyone knew about multiculturalism, even if he never used the word, it was Athol Fugard. His silence seemed to me to be the grace of a lion sitting with the lambs. Perhaps he was entertained by our American rhetorical exercise.

We spend so much time bantering about the words when the real open conversations might very well be our actions. I worry about our rhetoric. I worry about it because it is very easy to grab a conversation and disrupt it or to disrupt any action that may be going on by getting the participants so wrapped up in the activity of talking. When I refer to an "open conversation" I am thinking of a conversation that can cause change because of its power, because of the vigor with which words flow back and forth and bump up against each other. I am thinking of an open conversation as being one which allows us to create new alliances. Indeed, cynicism is bred because the public knows very well the gap between words and action. We can talk about diversity until we are blue in the face, but it may not significantly change the demographics of where we work or who has power there.

I had begun my remarks in Los Angeles with excerpts from a speech called "Metaphor's Funeral." I had given versions of that speech before. It was originally written at the request of Jane Alexander, who asked me to address the NEA on the occasion of her having to dismiss eighty some people from the agency because of budgetary cutbacks. I left the theater in Los Angeles thinking, "What I am really witnessing is not metaphor's funeral; the metaphor will live for as long as we can speak." Rather, I left thinking that I was watching multiculturalism's funeral.

Don't worry; you didn't miss it! I do not anticipate that multiculturalism's funeral will be one event. I think it will be more like Lincoln's funeral. When Abraham Lincoln was killed, his body was taken to the White House, where it remained from April 15 to April 18, 1865. It then went to the Rotunda of the Capitol, where it was displayed from April 19 to April 20. On April 21, it was taken to a railway station for transport to Springfield, Illinois. The funeral procession took twelve days. There were stops along the way at Baltimore, Harrisburg, Philadelphia, New York

City, Buffalo, Cleveland, Columbus, Indianapolis, and Chicago; at each people paid their respects. Lincoln was buried, finally, nearly three weeks later on May 4, 1865. His body was moved seventeen times from the night of April 14, 1865, when he was shot at Ford's Theater, until it was finally laid to rest in a solid block of concrete in the Lincoln Tomb at Springfield in 1901.

Some say that multiculturalism will not die. The numbers tell us and the demographics warn us of a more multicultural society in the twenty-first century. Of course, numbers do not mean sharing power. Numbers do not mean cultural equity. Numbers do not mean a varied identity. Numbers do not mean that all identities will be recognized. Numbers do not mean that all will have the right to speak. Numbers do not tell us who can speak for whom and about what. Numbers do not ensure an open conversation. Numbers do not tell us anything about power, as Athol Fugard would certainly know. Rhetoric possibly does. Even if the spirit behind multiculturalism does not die, the word loses its meaning even as I write. When it is replaced by yet another word, that does not mean that the reality that is multiculturalism will be killed. Its promise and fulfillment may be delayed and threatened. I do believe that the word itself is really in the throes of death. The birth and death of the words we use to effect our conversation affect the degree to which our conversation is open or closed. We can inadvertently contribute to the death of a word by using it loosely, saying it without meaning, saying it without understanding, saying it without connecting it to action.

Columbus, Ohio; another story. We need a language of caring. We need a language that allows caring to be something other than warm and fuzzy. We need a tough vocabulary of caring. We need a discourse that allows "I care" to mean "I do" or "I will" or "I promise." We need a conversation in which "What can I do?" is a response to what is cared about.

I was in Columbus, Ohio, just before the 1996 presidential elections and decided to visit some junior high schools in order to talk to the students about the political campaigns and to see whether they cared about it or were thinking about it at all. If they did not care about the political campaigns, I wanted to know what they did care about. I went to two public schools. One was an arts magnet school. Both schools had students from working-class households. The first school I visited was not the arts magnet school. I sat in a classroom and talked with some students; when I asked them what they cared about, nobody had anything to say. After a while, a few of them told me they cared about God. One girl aroused the group by saying she cared about abortion. It was hard to get their few mumblings to develop into a conversation. Searching for something that might be on their minds, I asked them what they thought about the death of the rapper Tupac Shakur, who had recently died. One black girl shrugged her shoulders and said, "Ain't got nothing to do with me. He don't care 'bout me, why should I care 'bout him?"

I left there and went to the arts magnet school. The principal was extremely excited about my visit and told me that ninety students were waiting for me. I told her that I had not expected such a large group and hoped that it was possible to organize something smaller, a group of eighteen or nineteen students, a number more conducive to a real conversation. In the end, I had to compromise. I took forty students or so into a large classroom. "I'd like to talk to you all about the current presidential campaign," I said. "I'd like to know what you care about. You don't have to care about the campaign, but you have to care about something." Hands went up like a flock of birds at dusk. One by one, they each got up to passionately share with the group what they cared about. At a certain point in each person's monologue, I loudly blurted out from the back of the room, "What can we do?" At the moment I said that, the person's ability to communicate became visibly more apparent. She or he became more articulate. One girl told us about her brother, who was twelve and had no father. She cared about him. She cared that he was getting into trouble and did not have any male role models. She cared about the kind of man he would become. When I called from the back of the room, "What can we do?" she said, "Well, the boys can help me out by telling me what I should tell him about being a man." At this point, the girls protested, "We can help. We have brothers. We have fathers." At the end, a group crowded around her to give her suggestions. It seemed to me that that little tale was the beginning of a healthy democracy in which people care and want to do something and their talking is linked to that. That was an open conversation.

Part of what an open conversation does is to invite a person to feel empowered by her or his own voice, and to learn how to use it, as well as how to be an active participant rather than a passive observer. The most exaggerated passive observers I have encountered are in jail. I spent some time in prisons last year. What the incarcerated told me was that they knew so much about the guards: they knew if a guard had had a fight at home, or was on her period, or had just gotten into trouble with a supervisor. Why is that? Because all they could do was watch. Just watching with no intent to contribute anything of your own is very dangerous. It leads to cynicism and unfortunate ways of judging the world and those around you.

People often ask me, "How did you get the people you portray in your plays to trust you, how did you create a safe space in which you could talk?" Let me say two things about that, two things which are about my field, about my aesthetic, what I understand about acting and how I try to take that into society. When I was getting classical training in theater, I learned that every actor has to have a very strong will to communicate. I also understood that putting what is in life on the stage is pedestrian, but what makes it not pedestrian is an accelerated will to communicate. I have gone to places where people had an accelerated will to communicate because intense things have happened to them. Usually some structure in their society has been turned upside down. Without a traditional identity, they are all grasping to put themselves in language. I believe that if I were a flea, they would tell me their stories.

The honest truth is that I listen to people with all the skills that I learned while studying acting and while teaching acting. If you teach acting, you have to listen and watch, very intently, no matter who is in front of you. I learned this from Mamaco, one of my mime teachers. At the conservatory I attended, we were taught two kinds of mime. I consider one form of mime to be more male; the teachers were these fast-talking, very funny guys who taught us how to walk through imaginary doors and pretend that we had just smelled a fart in an elevator. Mamaco was exactly the opposite. First of all, she spoke very little English, so she could not begin to be quick-witted. She did not dominate the room, commanding the center of the room; rather, she sat on the floor. She had a reputation for doing things like going out for drinks with students and crying in despair over her art. I was very intimidated by her, but I really thought she was pretty fantastic. I was afraid of her because I did not have any physical talent; my strengths were all verbal. One day she gave us an exercise to do. Whereas the man's directive would have been something like pretend you smelled a fart in the elevator, hers were very abstract, like be a cloud or—I don't know—something like that. Whatever her directive was that day, it was to do something that was supposed to be funny. I got up to do this exercise with great trepidation because I did not think I could communicate funny stuff with just my body. The minute I walked into the performance space, Mamaco, who again said very little, began to howl with laughter. I did not know what I was doing, but I knew that whatever it was was making her laugh. So I did more, and soon not only was she howling with laughter but people were literally rolling on the floor. This event taught me that I was funny, organically funny. It all came from Mamaco's having the ability to see something about me before I saw it myself. That was her expertise. She had a very sophisticated eye. She was the opposite of the passive audience which, like the jail inmates, has a sophisticated eye from watching because it can do nothing else. Mamaco was watching with a purpose.

The ideal conversants are people who can hear what might happen before it happens. Rather than listening to tell you that you have gotten it wrong ("Gotcha!"), they listen to say, "Come on, brother; you got it right. Can I get a witness! Teach! Right." This is what I think you need to create a safe space, a place which

says, "I'm here to watch; I'm here to watch you be fabulous." I
have heard people talk to me about black schools before integration. One of their benefits was that when the roll was called, the
teacher read the class list as if everyone was great. Recently, I was
working at the Rockefeller Foundation's estate in Bellagio, Italy.
As I was leaving to go, the person who was sort of the grande
dame of the place said to me, "Stay exactly as you are. You are
wonderful at this moment." I cried because I thought, How
many of us hear anybody tell us that, ever in our lives? We need a
great deal more of that.

Those kids in Columbus, Ohio, had a certain amount of confidence. We have to discover what gave them that kind of confidence, as well as their willingness to show how fabulous they
were and their belief that what they cared about, we should all
care about. Encouraging that kind of audacity and getting people
to be proud of what they have to say is probably what we have
to do.

An open conversation is most likely in an atmosphere where
everyone who has a part comes prepared to act. Perhaps an open
conversation is by nature activist. Communion comes from having a common goal that needs, at some point, to be spoken.
Then structure does not matter as much. I am thinking about a
black church in Tuscaloosa, Alabama, that I visited in the wake of
the recent wave of black church burnings in the South. With me
was a Latino student of mine, a Catholic who had never been in a
black church before. At a certain point during the service, these
two little kids got up from their seats and walked right up to
where the preacher was. My student was taken aback because that
would not have happened in a Catholic church. And when the

preacher said certain things, people hollered out. Even though the preacher seemed not to be finished with the sermon, somebody got up and started singing this song: "I'm glad. I'm so glad about it. It's another day's journey and I'm so glad, so glad about it." They all started singing and when they finished, the preacher preached again. The congregation had this common goal that everyone understood, which was that they were there, not for each of their own performances, but to bring Jesus into the room. This was a goal that was outside of them. Maybe we have to resort to those old techniques of remembering that we need a goal that is outside of our individual selves and our particular individual smartness or talents. That our individual smartness, our individual black genius, is nothing compared with our collective group genius.

Perhaps an open conversation can happen only in a special space. Is there a fraction of public space that is not occupied by the media? Is there a part of public space where the media and conversants can talk in nontraditional ways? Are there protected spaces where even dangerous things can happen in terms of new configurations, with new collaborations between unlikely conversants? In the arts, for example, will we always be subject to the political mood? Is there a space where all artists can brag of different political allegiances? The artist seems to me to be a possible conversant in the open conversation because her or his technique has already separated form from content. Why is it that one political agenda must always prevail in public space? The open conversationalist, it seems to me, is not afraid of affecting others and not afraid of being affected in turn.

I hope that my work suggests to people that there is a possibility of living in somebody else's point of view because they see me making the effort to do that. The audience that watches me carefully in fact sees that frequently I fail to get to the person that I'm supposedly embodying. By watching my effort, however, they themselves can begin to translate what they have seen into techniques and approaches by which they can use the same ideology where it will be most effective. If an actor of really traditional training in psychological realism takes from my work something new about specificity and the psychological gesture, then I am happier than if my work were generically touted: "You should do this because it worked for her." My work comes from my very private self. Going back to the title of this piece, I took something that is essentially extremely private to my identity and personality and made it into art by bringing it into the public space, but it is highly specific to me and my biography. I am happy if others want to do it, but I do not think that it is some kind of gospel beyond what I was able to figure out about it, in theater language.

Here is my last story: David Henry Hwang, the Asian American playwright, was telling me that when he first came into identity politics, while he was a student at Stanford University, he was very afraid that an overwhelming white culture would take over his Asian identity, and so he began to work very hard to assert his Asianness. Now he understands that the white culture is affecting him, but, for his part, he is affecting it. It seems to me that the open conversation is one that understands this fluidity and is not afraid of change.

Having an open conversation involves coming out of the house, whether it is a house of identity politics in a big way or the house of you, and being willing to walk toward something else without knowing what is going to happen. It goes back to the old-fashioned principles of improvisation which require that you suspend what you know. To bring it within the politics of the classroom, it entails people being willing to come to class ready to say what they do not know, but also to admit what they do know when they know it.

Randall Robinson

An internationally respected advocate for human rights and democracy, Randall Robinson has spent his adult life in the effort to secure a place for black Americans at the table of U.S. foreign policy decision making. In the face of a black leadership class that was, and to some extent still is, indifferent to, if not wholly ignorant of, the economic and political impact of American policies on the global black world, he has worked to inform, focus, and mobilize ordinary black American citizens to use their considerable political will and clout to harness and redirect the oppressive power of America's political, economic, and military might so as to lighten its weight on the backs of the peoples of Africa and the African diaspora.

Randall Robinson understood long ago that the advancement of blacks in America is inextricably tied to the advancement of blacks in other parts of the globe. This insight has ignited and guided his life's work, eloquently described in his book, Defending the Spirit: A

Black Life in America *(1998). As a student at Harvard Law School, Robinson and others organized the Pan African Liberation Committee, which campaigned to force Harvard University to divest itself of its stock in the Gulf Oil Company, which supported Portuguese colonialism in Angola, Mozambique, and Guinea-Bissau. After graduation, he spent a year as a Ford Foundation Fellow in Dar es Salaam, Tanzania, where he conducted research on the Africanization of European law and its social impact. He went on to work on Capitol Hill as an assistant first to Congressman Charles Diggs and then to Congressman William Clay. In 1978, he became the executive director of TransAfrica, the African American foreign policy advocacy organization, of which he was a founder. He is currently president of TransAfrica and the TransAfrica Forum.*

Using the techniques of civil disobedience and nonviolent protest that were staples of the black civil rights movement, TransAfrica, under Robinson's leadership, has brought attention to the complicity of the U.S. government in the oppression of the nations of Africa and the Caribbean. Robinson and TransAfrica achieved their most notable successes in changing America's policies toward South Africa and Haiti. In 1984, the government of apartheid South Africa was reorganized and blacks, unlike coloreds and Indians, were totally excluded from any form of representative democratic participation. On November 21, 1984, the day before Thanksgiving, Robinson, Mary Frances Berry of the U.S. Commission on Civil Rights, and District of Columbia Representative Walter Fauntroy were arrested for refusing to leave the office of the South African ambassador to the United States in Washington, D.C. Daily demonstrations at the South African embassy and arrests continued for more than a year. Over three thousand people were arrested. The protests led to the enactment in 1986, over President

Reagan's veto, of legislation mandating the imposition of economic sanctions against South Africa. The sanctions ultimately resulted in the collapse of the apartheid government and the release from prison of Nelson Mandela and his eventual election as president of South Africa.

As for Haiti, despite campaign promises to the contrary, the Clinton administration continued the policy adopted under President Bush of automatically returning Haitians who had fled their country's brutal military regime by boat, without according them asylum hearings to determine whether their lives were in danger. Not only did the practice violate international law; it was also much harsher than the treatment accorded Cubans picked up by the Coast Guard at sea. Robinson went on a twenty-seven-day hunger strike to protest the automatic repatriation of Haitian refugees. The Clinton administration relented. The sheer number of detained Haitian refugees put pressure on the United States to intervene militarily in Haiti. The military junta gave in just as the U.S. intervention force was on the verge of landing. Jean-Bertrand Aristide, the duly elected president of the country, was able to return from exile in America.

Randall Robinson understands the American democratic system, believes in the ideals for which it stands, and knows how to mine its better elements for the benefit of African and Caribbean countries. He has devoted his integrity and his ingenuity to the emancipation of the black world from the ravages of American imperialism and neo-colonialism. Politically perceptive and pragmatic, he has succeeded in engendering the belief that African Americans must face the international problems of the peoples of Africa and the African diaspora and that we have the wherewithal to address them on our own terms and with our own resources.

MANTHIA DIAWARA AND REGINA AUSTIN

PERFECTING OUR DEMOCRACY FOR THE BENEFIT OF THE BLACK WORLD

I want to talk a bit about our democracy here in America—its health, how it works, and how it does not work. Democracy is not a static notion. Most people mistakenly think the business of democracy is entirely described in some plan for elections. I think democracy has less to do with elections and more to do with the existence of a culture of tolerance, civility, and forbearance. Our democracy, specifically, has to be rooted in an enlightened citizenry because, in the last analysis, that citizenry has to cause those who govern to account to us for what they do. In many respects, totalitarianism is more painful, but easier to operate; you simply do what you are told to do. Democracy, on the other hand, requires of all of us participation, vigorous participation beyond elections and involvement in policy making from A to Z.

Caribbean Bananas and American Trade Policy

Let me describe a few examples that illustrate the failure of our democracy and its impact on the black world. I begin with a bit of history about the United Fruit Company, which later came to be known as Chiquita Brands International. Back in the 1950s, Allen Dulles was the director of the Central Intelligence Agency (CIA), and his brother John Foster Dulles was the secretary of state. Both Dulles brothers were associated with the law firm that represented the United Fruit Company. A man named Jacobo Arbenz Guzman came to power democratically in Guatemala in 1951, and in 1954 he was overthrown, almost directly at the instigation of United Fruit because he had run afoul of the company. Arbenz thought that the people of Guatemala ought to run their country, not United Fruit. The coup was engineered by the CIA, which was run by one Dulles, and promoted and supported by the State Department, run by the other Dulles.

Fast-forward to 1996. The African, Caribbean, and Pacific nations that were former colonies of European countries have enjoyed something of a special, concessional trade relationship with those countries under an agreement called the Lome Convention. Under its provisions, these former colonies have the opportunity to sell certain products to the European Union countries at special tariff rates. Thus, the English-speaking Caribbean democracies were able to sell their bananas nearly duty-free. If countries like Dominica and St. Lucia cannot sell bananas, they risk going under. Sixty percent of St. Lucia's income is generated by the sale of bananas and 70 percent of

Dominica's. If they cannot sell bananas, their governments and their economies might implode. If they cannot sell bananas, drugs are potentially all they have left to sell. Remember that the nations of the literate, English-speaking stable democracies of the Caribbean have been steadfast friends of the United States for the longest time. Recall that Eugenia Charles, when prime minister of Dominica, stood with Ronald Reagan to endorse the invasion of Grenada.

Now, Caribbean farmers grow their bananas on rocky hillsides (these islands are largely volcanic, after all). Because they do not grow their bananas on flat acreage, like the banana growers of Latin America, it costs more to grow a banana in the Caribbean than in Latin America. The Caribbeans cannot compete in an open market, because the playing field is forever uneven for them—geography, economies of scale, and such being what they are.

Chiquita Brands, or Chiquita Bananas, is run by a fellow in Cincinnati named Carl Lindner. Lindner, a former "guest" occupant of the Lincoln Bedroom of the White House, routinely gives the Democratic and Republican parties at least a quarter million dollars a year. Chiquita employs next to nobody in the United States and grows not a single banana in this country. All of its bananas are grown in Mexico, Guatemala, and other countries of Latin America. Lindner was bothered that Chiquita did not have the whole of the European market, and he wanted the special concession that the Europeans negotiated with the Caribbean countries invalidated. He wanted the matter taken up by the World Trade Organization (WTO).

California Congresswoman Maxine Waters and I sallied forth

to defend the banana-producing Caribbean countries. We organized a meeting in Washington with Mickey Kantor, then the U.S. trade representative. We brought to the meeting the Caribbean ambassadors, a representative from the NAACP, a representative from labor, and Donald Payne, who was then the chairman of the Congressional Black Caucus. Now, American officials are sometimes very deceptive to foreigners because Americans, unlike the Brits, have this facility for affability. I mean, they are immediately on a first-name basis. "How are you, Chuck? So good to see you." Kantor is armed with this kind of charm. We talked and we talked, and he told us across the table, "Look, why don't we have informal discussions with all of the parties. We will have the Latin American countries in the room; we will have the Caribbean countries in the room; and we will be there as well. Of course, Chiquita won't be in the room, because, Randall, you know that Chiquita's gift of a quarter of a million dollars to the Democratic Party has nothing to do with the formulation of American policy. Nothing whatsoever. And as long as these informal discussions are going on, there will be no application to the WTO to strike down this special banana regime that benefits these countries with regard to the only crop on which they can earn an income and keep their people employed." So the Caribbean countries, Maxine, and I, now battle hardened from many years of doing these kinds of things, left the meeting thinking that we had won something of a victory.

The first informal meeting was scheduled for Miami, about a month and a half later. The Caribbean countries brought people from all over the world, including some ambassadors from Brussels. They went to great expense, spending money that they could not afford to spend, preparing for the meeting and trying to come up with ideas that would satisfy the United States so that they would be able to sell their crops. During the afternoon session of the meeting, however, the Guatemalans confessed to the Caribbeans across the table that, before the meeting had begun, the United States and the Latin American countries had already gone to the WTO. Mickey Kantor had looked us straight in the eye and told us a bald-faced lie. The next morning in the hotel, U.S. trade representative officials were seen having breakfast with officers of Chiquita Bananas. American policy had been bought. The WTO ultimately ruled in Chiquita's favor.

General Jack Sheehan, who ran the Atlantic command, had told the administration that, if we destroy the Caribbean economies, we weaken their capacity to interdict the drug traffic that moves from Latin America through this chain of islands into the United States. If we do that, we will have wrecked these countries and disserved our own interests. But we did it anyhow, because a private interest in the United States had bought American foreign policy.

That is a weakness of our democracy. It goes far and away beyond the Lincoln Bedroom. If the other side has enough money and your side cannot muster the public outrage necessary to counter that kind of influence, you can lose the battle.

Rwanda

Perhaps a more dramatic example of my point can be found in Rwanda. Rwanda illustrates the consequences of the ignorance in

American society regarding the making of American foreign policy. Because Americans are so little armed to bring information to
the table, and so little armed to cause their politicians to account
to us for what they do, awful things sometimes get done in our
name. When Howard Wolpe was chairman of the House Sub-
committee on Africa, he once told me he didn't think there were
twenty members of Congress who could name five African countries. When a survey was done to measure Americans' global
sophistication against that of the citizens of the other industrialized nations of the world, the United States finished at the
absolute bottom. During his first term as president, Ronald Reagan visited a Latin American country and managed to toast the
people of the wrong country. When he was told he was not in
that country, he said that was where he was going next, even
though he was not going there at all.

In the spring of 1994, I was invited to lunch at the White
House by a friend, whom I should not name, who later became
an ambassador but who was then a member of the National
Security Agency. He said to me that something terrible was brew-
ing in Rwanda.

I should say something by way of background here because
Americans, in addition to their staggering ignorance, also seem to
think that everything happened yesterday. Their attitude reminds
me of how my brother Max and I used to go to the movies back
in the 1950s. In those days, we never checked the schedule to see
when the movie was going to start. We just went to the theater,
paid our nine cents, and went on in. Sometimes we would catch
the beginning of the film; sometimes we would hit the middle;
and sometimes we would walk in, sit down, and see on the screen

"The End." It did not make any difference to us, because we were going to see the damn thing six times anyhow. This was before they started the terribly capitalist practice of emptying the movie theater after each showing.

Even if one can go to the movies like that, one really cannot come to foreign policy like that—but Americans do. We tend to confuse news coverage with history and education. As a result, we have no context in which to understand anything. So we look at Rwanda and Burundi and ask, What is this conflict between the Hutus and Tutsis, what is this enmity about? In fact, it is centuries old; it began when the Tutsis migrated from the vicinity of Ethiopia to what is now Rwanda and Burundi. The Tutsis tended to be tall with keener features, while the Hutus were thought to be shorter with broader features. When the Europeans divided up Africa in 1885, Germany got those two pieces of territory. As there were no Aryans among the people of Burundi and Rwanda, the Germans practiced the racism of relativity. They chose the next-best thing and decided to favor the Tutsis. They even had a height requirement; if one did not measure up, as none of the Hutus did, one could not go to college. At independence, virtually everything that needed to be run, every privilege that could have been had, and every advantage that could have been gained was enjoyed by the Tutsis, and the Hutus had virtually nothing in the way of power and opportunity, although they composed the majority in both societies.

There was a great deal of anger and enmity in both Rwanda and Burundi. Such a situation required the kind of leadership that we have seen in South Africa. Real leadership depends on the willingness of a leader to tell his people often what they do not want to hear, to lead people away from the abyss, and to bring about reconciliation, but not at the expense of principle. That did not exist in Rwanda. A Hutu president took office, negotiated a deal to share power with the Tutsis and with moderate Hutus in his country, and then did not want to carry through with the deal. His name was Juvenal Habyarimana. Broadcasting on the radio from Kigali, the capital—when Americans were not watching and did not know Rwanda from a hubcap—he exhorted people to carry out genocide against the Tutsis, and our government knew about it. He trained militias to carry out the genocide, and our government knew about it. Egypt had given him arms, the old South Africa had given him arms, and George Bush had given him a few as well, and our government knew what he was going to do.

So my friend, who sat me down for lunch that day in the White House, said that if we didn't do something to get between the two sides, something awful was going to happen in Rwanda. Could I help him? Could I do some of what I did on South Africa? Could I stir up some kind of public protest? His office was fifty feet from the president's. He was asking me to initiate a campaign from the outside to get the White House to do what it should have done in the first place. He said that we were negotiating with the UN, which wanted to lease armored personnel carriers to supply to Ghanaian peacekeepers who were trained and ready to go to Rwanda to get between the two sides. The negotiations were dragging on because we were haggling over the lease price of nine million dollars, and there was a disagreement about the color that the personnel carriers would be painted, whether they would be UN white or American olive drab. My friend said that if we didn't do something, all hell was going to break loose.

I, unfortunately, could not figure any way to make Americans care about a place of which they had never in their lives heard. Then the plane carrying the presidents of both Burundi and Rwanda was shot down, and all hell did break loose. Five hundred thousand to one million people were slaughtered. The United States, which had haggled with the UN about a few million dollars, ended up spending more than a billion, and it was all so terribly avoidable.

My point is that we should never believe that we make policy as a nation because it is the sensible thing to do or the sensible way to act. American foreign policy issues largely from a domestic mill of competing forces. If the forces are not there competing to cause us to do the right thing, invariably nothing right happens.

Somalia

I would suggest that Americans look at Somalia. When Somalia had its disastrous civil war beginning in the early 1990s, we would ask what in the world is wrong with Somalia. Somalia has existed as a coherent, proud society for virtually thousands of years. Mogadishu was established in the 1100s. The Somalis are proudest, above all, of their poetry. What happened to Somalia? When I was a child growing up in Richmond, Virginia, Haile Selassie, then the emperor of Ethiopia, was on American television more than Howdy Doody. I thought he was an American because he belonged to us. We armed him; we sponsored him. He was our guy. After colonialism ended, a chap by the name of Muhammad Siyad Barre, a member of the Italian police force in Somalia, knew that America was sponsoring Somalia's enemy in Ethiopia right across the border. He needed arms because his aspiration in life was to be a dictator, and to be a dictator one just has to have guns. So he applied to the Soviet Union, and it gave him some guns. During this period in the United States all one had to do to get American support was to say that one was anti-Communist. We did not care what you did either for or to the people in your country. If you served our interests in containing communism, you would get help from us. The Soviet Union did virtually the reverse of that.

A few years later, Haile Selassie was overthrown and replaced by Haile Mariam Mengistu, a godless Communist who had not smiled since 1943. The United States said that we could not support this fellow. It was almost as if the Soviets and the Americans had sat down at the UN, winked at each other, and switched sides. Soviet assistance started to go to Mengistu, the dictator in Ethiopia, while between 1977 and 1989—beginning, ironically enough, under the presidency of Jimmy Carter—we supplied the dictator in Somalia $887 million in American aid, including $200 million in weapons. Tanks, surface-to-air missiles, mortars, training—you name it, we gave it to him, and with it he destroyed his country. But when Somalia fell apart, Americans woke up and asked what happened, without any insight, without a sense of history, largely because we came to the issue late, like at the end of a movie. We cannot hope to understand anything about foreign policy in that way.

American Responsibility for Troubles
in the Black World

When Haiti was coming apart and refugees were fleeing into the
waters, Americans must have wondered (or you would have
thought they should have wondered) what in the world is wrong
with Haiti. Why is Haiti so different from the rest of the stable
English-speaking Caribbean? Haitians have a proud history.
These people as slaves in the late 1700s took on the 60,000-man
army of Napoleon Bonaparte and, over the course of twelve or so
years, won and put in place the world's first black republic. They
had accomplished a monumental victory. Because they had so
weakened Napoleon, the Haitians thought that his vision of an
empire in the Americas had ended. And because Henri
Christophe had fought with George Washington at Savannah in
the American Revolution, they thought that this great democracy
would favor them and be supportive. But Thomas Jefferson had a
different idea; if these people in Haiti could accomplish so much
against the army of Napoleon Bonaparte, then people in Mississippi, Louisiana, South Carolina, and Georgia, who looked like
them, might get ideas. Mightn't the blacks he was looking at
through his window at Monticello be emboldened by this success
too? So the new nation of Haiti, thinking it would be embraced
by the West, was met by seventy-five years of sanctions from the
United States and the rest of the Western community. This was
before Woodrow Wilson occupied Haiti early in this century
because he thought Germany had designs on it and before the
Cold War, when the United States at the School for the Americas

trained the armies of Papa and Baby Doc Duvalier, who set them loose on their people—armies that killed 5,000 people, chased 50,000 into the sea, and drove another 350,000 into internal exile. Much of the responsibility for what has happened to Haiti is ours, but we Americans did not understand that because we came in late, like at the end of a movie.

During the last thirty years, the United States gave the lion's share of its foreign assistance to Africa to just six countries. Not really six countries. Rather, we gave the money to six leaders, only one of whom, Daniel arap Moi of Kenya, was elected. The leaders of Somalia, Ethiopia, Sudan, Zaire, and Liberia were the other recipients. Liberia, settled by returned American slaves, had a fractious democracy that was overthrown in the early 1980s by Samuel K. Doe, a sergeant with a grade school education, who executed members of the previous government on the beach, without trials and due process of law. Ronald Reagan immediately sent American troops to Liberia to train Sergeant Doe's troops, and the United States provided this murderous dictator with $500 million in American aid. Liberia is a basket case now, largely because of the role of the United States.

In the media's coverage of Zaire's recent troubles, it was hard to find any discussion of the source of those problems. Zaire, now the Republic of Congo, might have had an entirely different history, not unlike Botswana's, or Tanzania's, not unlike that of a number of stable nations in Africa, had the CIA thirty years ago not installed and maintained in power Mobutu Sese Seko. He may have been one of the richest men in the world. He was the only leader I know of who had crystal chandeliers hanging on the outside of his house. He looted the state treasury, he robbed his country blind, and three times he was saved by the U.S. Army, the last two times (in 1977 and 1978) by President Jimmy Carter. Zaire would have been rid of Mobutu long ago had it had not been for the United States. So one might ask, Why isn't Zaire democratic? Don't blame the people of Zaire. We ought to look at ourselves.

Finally, Kenya offers an example of a tyrannical leader who was elected once and has stolen every election since. The countries we have aided in Africa have uniformly done worse in terms of economic performance, human rights, democratic stability, or any pretense at them than any of the other countries on the African continent. It is no stretch to suggest that the United States during the Cold War never wanted democracy in Africa. We simply wanted people who would do our bidding. Herein lies our responsibility.

South Africa and Haiti

When we went to work on South Africa almost twenty years ago, when I was still in law school, nobody knew who Nelson Mandela was. I have learned much since then. When I was a young man, I used to think that good would win out over evil and that good things would happen because good people could not suffer forever and things would change. Now that I am older, I know that one has to chart a course, relentlessly stick to it, and do the job until one has won. I remember when I was at Harvard in the 1960s. I really loved the sixties. I miss the sixties. I used to promise myself I would never talk like my daddy—you know, when old people start talking about what they miss. Daddy would tell me how he walked four hundred miles to school, came home for lunch, and then walked back again. Every time he walked it, it got farther and farther away. I said I would never do that, but I do miss the sixties, because they had a kind of froth. Everybody was political, and we all wore field jackets. I had an Afro big enough to camp a snowstorm on, and we all read Frantz Fanon. I did not understand any of it, but it was mandatory that we read Fanon.

I remember once in a law school corporations class we started to discuss corporate support for South Africa, and I rose before my class, struck a revolutionary pose, and launched into a soliloquy, the brilliance of which has never been equaled. I went on and on. The thing was pyramidal: it started up here at a point, and then it began to develop. It was cogent, it was seamless, it was irresistible, and at some point I lost control of it. It became disembodied, and so I threw it down like a gauntlet, looked at my professor, and said so there! The man looked at me like a patient, older person dealing with a naïve child and said, "Mr. Robinson, that is all very well and good, but the divinity school is one block down and two blocks over." I learned on that day that things do not happen just because they are right. Things happen because people armed with the facts relentlessly pursue a result until that result is won.

In the last analysis, the United States was responsible for South Africa. I went there in 1976, with a congressional delegation. When you travel to a place you have never been to before, you see similarities between it and the place from which you came. I was in Johannesburg and I looked around. Their white people looked like our white people; their black people looked like our black people. I looked up at the billboards and saw B. F. Goodrich, General Motors, and Colgate-Palmolive. Their cars were our cars. Then I began for the first time to understand something about the seamlessness of the world. It is one place, operated by small groups of people from small rooms, who make no distinction at borders. They run the world. They seek to keep the rest of us ignorant about its operations and sought to persuade us that American corporate investment in a society that was 99 percent owned and 100 percent run by the white minority, against the interest of the black majority, was to the blacks' advantage. This situation would have gone on because the people who believed that and benefited from it wrote articles and made speeches with so much impressive sophistry, and nothing would ever change. CIA Director William Casey went down to South Africa and negotiated a cordon sanitaire, in order to throw a fence around it, to protect it from its enemies from without.

Yet we believed, when we went to the South African embassy in 1984, on the day before Thanksgiving, and refused to leave, that we would do anything to shake up the situation in South Africa. Following our arrests that day, five thousand Americans were arrested in this country. Every day at that embassy, somebody was arrested. I flew to New York City to give the speech on which this essay is based with former Connecticut Governor Lowell Weicker, who was a Republican member of the Senate and who became the only member of the U.S. Senate ever to be arrested for an act of civil disobedience. We overrode the veto of Ronald Reagan, and to the shock of South Africa, in 1986 we imposed comprehensive American sanctions, which triggered sanctions in Europe, which triggered sanctions in Japan, which triggered the closing of the money windows, which triggered the release of Mandela, which triggered the negotiation between De Klerk and Mandela, which led to the democracy that we had never expected to see in our lifetimes.

Similarly, not so long ago, Jean-Bertrand Aristide was parked in an office six blocks from mine; he was thinking that he might never go home again. This little Catholic priest, who registered for the election in 1990, just a day before the deadline, who ran in a field of eleven candidates without a penny of campaign money to spend, who was opposed by the United States and its chosen candidate Marc Bazin, a former World Bank official, and who won 70 percent of the vote before he was overthrown—this little Catholic priest was now living in exile. At about the same time, I was on a program with a Haitian woman who had supported democracy when, for simply having a picture of Aristide, one could be killed by the army or the paramilitary thugs. This woman did not get out the back window in front of her husband, and the thugs caught her, chopped off her arm, hacked into her face, and left her for dead. She was one of many victims; she was lucky to survive. The people who attacked her were armed and trained by the United States.

We forced President Clinton to honor his campaign promise to screen the Haitian refugees and provide them safe haven. We knew all the time that the Clinton administration did not want them in Florida. The federal government had a rule that if we stopped a boat in the ocean and it had Cubans aboard, the Cubans were immediately to be brought to Florida and would within one year become eligible for American citizenship. The

Haitians, on the other hand, were automatically taken back to Haiti, where they might be plucked out of a Red Cross line by thugs and killed. We knew that hundreds of people had been killed just like that. So we told the administration that it had to come back into compliance with international law. Haitians were fleeing out of a well-founded fear of persecution. The United States had an obligation as a member of the family of nations to provide them safe haven. In any case, we could not treat black Haitians differently from white Cubans. It was simply intolerable. We focused on this, knowing that Clinton would want to put these black refugees anywhere but in the state of Florida, which did not want them. He accordingly put thousands of Haitians in Jamaica and thousands on Guantánamo. Panama decided not to accept any more, and he ran out of room in which to put these people. We knew the administration would have no choice but to remove the Haitian military and restoire democracy.

Our Responsibility as Citizens and African Americans

All of this serves to prove what citizen power can do when we apply ourselves. America has over the last thirty years done the black world an enormous injustice with its foreign policies, and in part we are accomplices in its crimes if we have done little or nothing to stop it. First comes information and then comes action on it. Years ago, Eldridge Cleaver said something that still makes sense: you're either part of the solution, or you're part of the problem.

The Caribbean is fighting for its survival. Nigerians are fighting for theirs, Kenyans are fighting for theirs, people in southern Sudan are fighting for theirs. Across the black world, the current administration has demonstrated little concern and little compassion. It will continue along the same lines unless we make it account to us. This is our job. It is our job as human beings because we care about the world in which we live. It is our job as Americans because we want to perfect the quality of our own democracy. African Americans, however, have a special responsibility, for we are the sons and daughters of Africa. We are indissolubly bound up with it, and we must always understand that, from Los Angeles to Ouagadougou, from Kingston, Jamaica, to Johannesburg, South Africa, for the sons and daughters of Africa, the blood that unites us is always thicker than the waters that divide us.

ACKNOWLEDGMENTS

A s *Black Genius* gained momentum from an idea to a small crusade, the project picked up many friends and collaborators. Thanks must be given to all of them, and notably to those named here. The "reverberators" or respondents who widened discussions and extended the range of perceptions include:

Malaika Adero, Amir Al-Islam, Kathy Bowser, Herb Boyd, Joe Brewster, Shirley Campbell, Mary Schmidt Campbell, W. Paul Coates, Kinshasha H. Conwill, Thulani Davis, David Dent, Howard Dotson, Joseph Edward, Siffiyah Elijah, Joy Elliot, Gerry Howard, Warrington Hudlin, Robin D. G. Kelley, Woodie King, Jr., Janick Rice Lamb, Daa'iya Lomax, Louis Massiah, Mora McLean, Kobena Mercer, Peter Noel, Robert O'Meally,

Max Rodriguez, Tricia Rose, Eve Sandler, Tanya Selvaratnam, Pablo Tejada, Beth Turner, and Joe Wood.

Appreciation is also due to those who saw the project through by providing crucial editorial or administrative support:

Glenda Noel Doyle, Donette A. Francis, Fatima S. Legrand, and Gloria Loomis.